Crooks Kill, Cops Lie

The True Story of the St. Louis Mobster Wars

Timothy C. Richards

ISBN: 978-0-9859778-6-3

$19.95

Printed in the United States of America

Bluebird Publishing Co.
St. Louis, MO
www.BluebirdBookPub.com

1

The Mississippi River City of St. Louis, Missouri, is almost an entity within itself. It doesn't belong to the political boundary of affluent St. Louis County. It has no County government, just the City politicians to rule it. It is tucked away from the rest of the state of Missouri, down at the eastern edge, more identifiable with the state of Illinois than with outstate Missouri.

Metropolitan St. Louis has the largest population of any other state area but there hasn't been a governor elected from St. Louis since Henry Caulfield, who was elected in 1933. Out state folks control Missouri government and they don't trust any politician from St. Louis.

The St. Louis residents scorn the Illinois side of the Mississippi. It is where East St. Louis, Illinois is situated. St. Louis folks are superior to Eastside folks. At least that's the myth they wish to believe. The economy and the crime rate on the Eastside is equivalent to Port au Prince, Haiti and the populace mirrors that island nation. Not that there aren't good folks there. There are. I was born in East St. Louis and raised in the Metro-East.

The west side, (St. Louis) has a fairly strong economy for a Midwest river town, and the Federal Government dotes on it. The Feds built the Gateway Arch for the City residents to ogle and brag about. And there is a new and impressive federal court house in the downtown section of the City. It is near the new and impressive baseball stadium, the new hockey venue, and the new football stadium.

Downtown St. Louis has lofts, department stores, parks and young inhabitants. It is far superior to downtown East St. Louis, but the west side neighborhoods north and west of downtown are the same as the neighborhoods on the east side. Both are havens for crime, with murder being the product of most verbal confrontations. The citizens on the west side are more likely to be murdered sitting on their front porch or walking their dog to the neighborhood park than the beaten down citizens of the Eastside, because many of the Eastside folks don't have front porches to sit on, or dogs to walk. That's how poor they are.

St. Louis is always ranked in the top five cities, per capita for murder, and is usually number one. It has been deemed "murder City" for decades, ahead of Detroit, Miami, Los Angeles, Chicago, and New York. But we have good tap water. The confluence of the Missouri and Mississippi Rivers is within the City limits of St. Louis, and the Illinois River joins the Mississippi just twenty miles north at Grafton, Illinois, giving us an ample supply of treatable water. It's been voted the best tasting and best smelling tap water in the country.

The mayor and chief of police act offended when the crime statistics are tabulated and the news comes out on television and in the Post-Dispatch. They counter with the argument the stats are wrong and that the City is safe. The FBI stats don't just pertain to murder. Rape, robbery, burglary and assault are added into the affray, and in St. Louis we're the champions in those categories, too, but murder seems to be the number one crime.

The ruling class in St. Louis, the upper middle class folks, black and white, rationalize the FBI statistics by privately stating these are unstoppable, unavoidable crimes committed by criminals with the victims being criminals, and no amount of police patrol could keep these crimes from occurring. It is a sociological mindset and a criminologist point of view and it may be correct. Poor folks don't rationalize. They kill.

Education seems to be the antidote for crime within the lower classes. At least that's what educators say. But in St. Louis and in East St. Louis the schools are blackboard jungles, unsafe for caring students and on the job training for the future criminals of the world. The State of Missouri took control of the St. Louis Public School System. The City couldn't control the snowballing failure of the public schools.

No amount of cash thrown at the problem would solve it. It has been the same in every past society. The cream eventually rises to the top. The cottage cheese and the sour milk find their own way. The citizens living in the metropolitan area shrug their shoulders and scrape to make a living and to try and keep their families safe. Parents warn their children; "Don't go to the Eastside. Don't go to north St. Louis."

In October of 1977, Joseph Paul Franklin, a member of the American Nazi Party, the Ku Klux Klan and the National States Rights Party, arrived in St. Louis with murder on his mind. God had told him to start a race war, he told investigators when he was eventually captured. His victims of choice were mixed race couples and Jews. He started his killing spree slowly, as if he was testing the water to see how it felt. His first venture into the race war business was spraying a mixed race couple with mace. He then fire bombed the Beth Shalom Synagogue in Chattanooga, Tennessee.

On August 7, 1977; leaving a bank robbery he had committed in Madison, Wisconsin, he became angry that the car in front of his wasn't going fast enough. It had a black driver and a white woman as a passenger. The black man eventually pulled over and walked back to Franklin's car. Franklin dressed in cowboy regalia shot and killed the black driver, then walked to the car and shot and killed the white woman passenger. Then he came to St. Louis.

He had purchased a Remington seven-hundred hunting rifle, a bicycle, a guitar case and some ten inch nails, parked his car at a safe distance away from the synagogue and rode his bicycle to some tall weeds about one hundred feet away from the target area.

He hammered the nails into a telephone pole to serve as a gun rest and waited for his victims to arrive. For him to be a sniper was highly unlikely. He was partially blind in one eye and completely blind in the other.

Franklin shot and killed Gerald Gordon of Chesterfield, Missouri. The victim had lived in an affluent safe west St. Louis County town. His synagogue was in safe Richmond Heights. It wasn't the City and it wasn't the Eastside. Franklin then shot and wounded two other men, Steven Goldman and William Ash, wiped the rifle clean of fingerprints climbed onto his bicycle and rode to his car. He had gotten away with the crime.

Before he was eventually captured he had shot or killed over twenty people. Some of them prominent; Vernon Jordan, President Bill Clinton's friend, shot because he allegedly had a white girlfriend, and Hustler Magazine publisher Larry Flynt and Flynt's attorney.

These were random crimes, not the ethnic murders the police in the St. Louis area were familiar with. Folks going to worship in the County aren't supposed to end up as murder victims. It didn't fit and it terrorized the cops, the Jewish community and the B'nai B'rith society.

But this memoir isn't about the serial murderer John Paul Franklin and it isn't about the death of an innocent man going to temple in benign Richmond Heights, Missouri. It's about cops and crooks. Both are organization men. They survive by conspiring with each other, making pacts with outsiders and planning the demise of their co-conspirators and friends. In the cop/crook business you are in competition with your colleagues and every cop and every crook knows there can only be one winner. Crooks are the same everywhere. So are the cops.

There are groups of people who study their local police departments. B'nai B'rith is interested in the information the police gather regarding anti-Semitism, but they don't have access to the secret cop information. Their goal is to overcome the forces of hate. A lofty goal, maybe an impossible one, but they plod their way toward it.

It is generally denied by local law enforcement that subversive groups like the Ku Klux Klan, or the American Nazi Party are continuously investigated and monitored. Americans aren't supposed to be spied upon by the government for their political beliefs, but they are.

A unit in the St. Louis Police Department, the Intelligence Unit, has the responsibility to actively investigate all hate groups, as well as any organized criminal group operating within the boundaries of the City of St. Louis.

There are rooms of file cabinets containing active dossiers on most criminals in the United States. If they ever come through St. Louis and are seen or documented by informant information, a memorandum is made and entered into a file, cross referenced with associates, photographs, fingerprint cards, rap sheets, and hidden in some obscure file cabinet protected with a number instead of a name.

The unit is affiliated with other intelligence gathering organizations throughout the country. One is the Law Enforcement Intelligence Unit, (LEIU) in Sacramento, California. The detectives in the St. Louis unit exchange information with the Sacramento unit on a daily basis. It's all about information and the tracking of career criminals and subversive groups travelling throughout the United States.

The folks at B'nai B'rith know about the intelligence sharing and they know there are files in the intelligence unit. The unit in St. Louis is a national intelligence clearing house for information pertaining to subversive groups. The cops in Richmond Heights didn't have an intelligence unit. They relied on any information they could get from the City of St. Louis, and that information wasn't forthcoming.

Intelligence information on subversives and criminal groups was and still is power. He who controls the information controls the situation. It is the intelligence unit creed. Every cop assigned to the unit realizes this fact. It is an ego builder and makes ordinary cops very important people.

The consensus by the cops and the Jewish community was that the unknown person who sniped Steven Goldman and William Ash, and murdered Gerald Gordon outside of their synagogue on a crisp sunny October morning had a dossier in the files of the St. Louis Metropolitan Police Department Intelligence Unit. Needless to say, they deeply desired access to those files.

There are certain people in the business world who are familiar with and friendly with local cops; jewelers and pawn brokers, to name a few. The rank and file detectives of the intelligence unit get discounts on jewelry, or tools, televisions, computers and guns from the local pawn brokers and diamond rings for their wives and girlfriends from the jewelers. A uniform cop could go into a pawn shop just before deer or turkey season and try to get a deal on a rifle or shotgun, but there would be no deal.

An intelligence unit detective would get a good deal on anything in the shop at any time; a deal worth bragging about. The deputy commander of the intelligence unit would get anything he wanted for free. It would cost him friendship, but it is what deputy commanders of secret investigative units desire. They are constantly seeking friends outside of the department. Outside friends who are wealthy are also influential. Influential friends equate to clout within the state legislature. The state controls the police department. Promotions are made by state legislators. Politics make strange bedfellows. It's akin to the settlers exchanging trinkets for gold nuggets from the Native Americans, or the purchase of the Island of Manhattan.

A year had passed since Joseph Paul Franklin had done his dastardly deed in Richmond Heights, Missouri, and the crime was still unsolved. I was an undercover detective in another secret but federally funded unit within the Bureau of Investigation. We used government funds to pay street people who had larceny on their minds. We would cruise the streets and stop folks who were loitering, then ask them to help us unload some alleged stolen items in the trunk of the car. We had a Caddy and a cooler of beer and a pocket full of federal cash.

We would drive to a store front, operated by us, and fence the items in the presence of the street creature. The theory was the street person would return with merchandise he stole, or convey the message to his friends that an active fence was willing to pay cash for stolen merchandise; an interesting job, but not one with longevity. I had spent eight years in a north St. Louis neighborhood and I wasn't relishing the fact of going back there.

I had witnessed the carnage. north St. Louis was a third world country. The law of the gun prevailed there. The Black Liberators, a street gang, cruised by the ninth district station and shot it up with a machine gun. Every night was fight night, and I had outgrown it. I was looking for a new home and the intelligence unit was where I wished to go.

I had the appearance of a German SS officer, blonde and blue, and a detective in the intelligence unit allegedly was in need of someone to go undercover to penetrate the St. Louis Chapter of the American Nazi Party. The department designation of the unit was and still is, INTEL 210.

I was asked if I was interested. I accepted. I knew about the intelligence unit. It was the personal unit of the Chief of Police. Detectives assigned there are usually related to someone of importance. High ranking cops' kids, relatives of a state legislator, or personal friends of the Chief. I didn't know anyone influential, and I had no important relatives.

The lieutenant I was currently working for had sent my personnel jacket to intelligence. I overheard him ordering his secretary to perform the task. I knew what that act meant. It meant every detective would read it before I knocked on the door for the first time. They would know I was born on the Eastside, I had a bachelor's degree from the University of Missouri, I had been in the Marine Corps, and I was married with one child and another one on the way, and I had never been suspended.

A couple of hours passed when I was summoned to go to intelligence. I strolled over. The unit offices are situated on the fourth floor of headquarters, just at the opposite corner of the huge building where the bureau of investigation offices are situated.

The Bureau of Investigation is controlled by the chief of detectives. At that time it was Colonel John Doherty. He was a man's man; a Marine, war hero, killer of the bad guy on the streets of St. Louis, a legend. I respected him and revered him, but almost everyone did. The Chief of Police hated him and the feeling was mutual. The chief's office, (intelligence unit) and the chief of detectives, (bureau) were in competition for glory.

I was seen as a traitor by the lieutenant I had worked for in the bureau of investigation. I was jumping ship as far as he was concerned, going to the dark side. At least that's what he told me. I figured he told me that to warn me and to manipulate me. Police commanders desire to be your big brother and father rolled into one package. "Intelligence is the chief's office guys, snitches and politicians," he said. "Remember, you're wanted in the bureau don't get mesmerized by intelligence." I was just going to be there for a short undercover assignment. I would probably be back, I rationalized.

I knocked on the closed and locked door. There was an alarm and two locks protecting the interior of the office. A young guy in jeans and a T answered. I told him who I was and he slammed the door in my face. I heard him shouting for some other detective while I waited at the locked door. A young detective came out and introduced himself. Then we went inside.

The young detective was chubby but tall with a beard and he chain smoked. The office was dreary with the walls lined with file cabinets, just about what I had imagined. We sat at his desk, him behind it and me beside it like a kid meeting with his school counselor. Detectives were walking past staring at us. I had been a cop for eight years and I had never seen any of them before.

Some of the detectives made disparaging comments disguised as a joke to the young kid I was going to be working for. Through the comments I figured he only had about a year on the police department, and he had been on the job for six months when he got transferred to intelligence. His dad was a high ranking guy within the department, and I had never heard of him either.

The young cop had a nickname, apparently all of the detectives did. His was the Irish Prince. He told me the deputy commander, a lieutenant had to be referred to as Lieutenant, or Deputy Commander. Most of the guys in the office smoked cigars or cigarettes. It was like being in a bar with pool tables.

The detectives kept filing by, making comments and prodding the Irish Prince. Someone said something about Boob, and I picked up on it. "It's the Deputy Commander's nickname," he advised. "He's not a Boob, he's actually a smart guy, but he had a Cuban informant who called the office on a regular basis and asked for Boob, and it stuck."

Lieutenant Boob came out of his office and eyeballed me, then walked back inside. There were three big offices connected, and three offices which were private, with doors. One of them was Boob's. The building was old and I was amazed that in this new era of law enforcement the old building continued to be functional. The foresight of the architect was brilliant. He somehow knew that cops and crooks would always be the same no matter what technology brought into the game.

The Irish Prince explained to me he had an informant who belonged to the American Nazi Party and the informant had access to another Nazi who was looking for someone to sell guns to. The plan, if I chose to accept it, was to be introduced to the Nazi with the guns to sell by the Nazi informant, and to buy a gun from him. It was a machine gun.

The Irish Prince went on to say, the catch in the gun buying plan was that three guns had to be purchased at three different transactions. The Nazi gun dealer case had to be taken federal, and for that to happen three transactions had to be made, and the buys had to be documented, which meant I had to wear a wire, and that a surveillance van had to videotape me going into the store front and coming out with the purchased firearm.

I had worked undercover and I knew the criminal game. I didn't see any problem with the operation, so I told the Irish Prince that I would do it. We shook hands and he told me to follow him. We left the offices and took the elevator down to the lobby and then to the courtyard where the detective's undercover car was parked. We were headed to a City park on the south side to meet with the informant Nazi.

The undercover car was a perk for important cops, or relatives of important cops. The detective had total access to it, taking it home and using the City's gas to do his errands. The perks for downtown detectives are carefully laid out like mine fields in a country club golf course. The guys in the know are advised where the mines are. The cop with the untrained eye clambers about the beautiful lush landscape until he steps on one.

The key to being a cop with longevity is to stay away from emotional baggage. It's what brings cops down. The average cop thinks about God, family and career. To do this job you must stay focused on those three things. The take home funny car is a tool to manipulate the detectives. It distorts your focus. You begin to believe you are important.

All of the other detectives want a funny car, if they don't already have one. They will politic for their detective associates to get them a funny car. It makes investigating, surveillance, and running errands much easier. The down side is that if you have one you are in the cross hairs of any cop in your unit who doesn't have one. There might as well be a neon flashing sign on the funny cars in a small unit like intelligence. "I have a funny car, I am more important than you are and my relatives are more important than yours."

There are certain things I had noticed and documented from the cops I had worked with in the police department. There is a certain amount of desperation. It is what it takes to do the cop job. The insight of the hierarchy of the City fathers is impeccable. They know what type of person they want to police their streets. If the applicant didn't have a detectable degree of desperation, then why would he take this desperate job?

They feed off of this inner desperation when they train you in the police academy. Then they give you a badge and a gun. That experience is unforgettable and difficult to describe. It means you are somebody in the world. Holding the gun and the badge gives you warmth and completeness. It is why it is so easy to feel important when you go to an elite unit investigating hate and organized criminals.

The establishment has your undivided attention and more emotional baggage gets loaded onto your psyche. You will do anything to satisfy the controlling members of the establishment, for you are always looking for an experience like the gun and badge gift.

For some cops the emotional baggage becomes too heavy and they end their lives. It is a fact that cops and federal agents shoot themselves for imagined failure. Booze and troubled romance stoke the fire of suicide and every cop knows if you live by the gun you will die by it. I have had cop friends who have ended their own lives. They all had access to weaponry of all sorts. Exotic handguns, rifles and shotguns, but when they do the deed to themselves they always use the gun that was presented to them by the City or government.

They turn their demise into a symbolic death. It is because of emotional baggage. I didn't detect desperation in the Irish Prince. But the detectives in intelligence were a different breed. Most of them were starting at the top of the heap. They were at the top of the corporate ladder when most of us were working in the warehouse or mailroom. And they will always be at the top for they all have been coached by their relatives and/or friends to strive for promotion. It is the only way to leave the unit. And if they would fail there is always another job the influential relative can get for them. They'll start at the top somewhere else.

We stopped in the park off of South Broadway and sat at a picnic table. I had been scruffy when I worked undercover in the bureau of investigation. I had been a military man for most of my young adult life and I didn't like being scruffy. I didn't have any idea what an American Nazi looked like, but I knew what the Nazis were depicted as during World War Two.

I was mentally prepared to give the Nazi salute, shout Heil Hitler and goose step on command to some obscure German recording. I had a haircut, was clean shaven, wore denim jeans, a collared shirt and an expensive black leather jacket. I wore my expensive gold chronograph and had a gold coin ring where my wedding ring usually was. We sat and waited while the young detective smoked. There wasn't much conversation. We had nothing in common, except for being cops.

"Here he comes," the Irish Prince said. He was driving an old Chevy, rusted and dirty with the tail pipe dragging on the pavement. He parked, got out and walked to us. He was young, maybe in his early twenties and as dirty as his car. He wore old clothing, a jacket that came from one of the marts, and he was unshaven. He shook hands with the young detective, and then I was introduced.

He was studying me as we conversed about nothing. He was the type of guy I worked on when I was undercover in the bureau. The kind we would see loitering on the street. The type of guy who would climb into the backseat of our Caddy, drink beer with us and help us unload stolen merchandise into the back door of a storefront.

This is an American Nazi? I said to myself. This is the type of guy who lives on hatred? The type of person who murders people because of their choice of religion? I instantly disliked the worm of a man. I didn't wish to be introduced by him as a fellow Nazi who wanted to buy machine guns to shoot Jews and black folks. But I was in, and I knew there was no backing out.

"What do you think?" The Irish prince asked the Nazi.

The scummy Nazi paused and said, "He's too clean. He needs to get rid of that watch and ring and he needs some scruff on his face. Stop shaving. Other than that he might make it." The Nazi wanted to talk to the Irish Prince in private so they both walked to the Nazi's junky car while I sat on the picnic bench watching the traffic go by.

The Irish Prince came back. "It's set up for a week from today. Can you get scruffy in a week?"

"Yeah," I replied. We drove back to the office. We sat in the office like bumps on a log. The Irish Prince typed up a memorandum which would eventually be read by Boob and everyone else in the office then placed in a Nazi folder and filed away.

I eyeballed the rows and rows of filing cabinets. I was eager to read about the gangsters who had been terrorizing the metropolitan area for decades. When I was a kid on the Eastside the gangsters were everywhere.

It seemed they had free reign to go back and forth between Missouri and Illinois, doing whatever they desired. Robbing and killing and controlling labor unions.

I was a guest in the unit, but I was still a cop detective. I wondered if I could view some of the files, so I asked. The Irish Prince told me he would ask Boob and eventually I was shown how to access the files and given the time to read and ponder. The reading was spellbinding to me and I was instantly hooked. I couldn't get enough of the conspiracies which unraveled before me.

I wanted to be permanently assigned to intelligence. It seemed to be my calling in life. As the days passed, and my beard grew, I had gotten a clear understanding of the criminal factions working in St. Louis and the Eastside.

I stayed late one evening intrigued by the American Nazi Party dossier. There were about fifty of them in the St. Louis area, documented. They were all big time losers, petty criminals, people who probably should be detained in mental hospitals. "Which one of you rejects was the synagogue sniper?" I asked myself.

There was a large envelope with colored pictures taken at demonstrations and rallies. One was recent, taken by members of the intelligence unit, obviously from a surveillance van. The rally was in central Illinois. The Nazi rejects were dressed in their hate regalia, goose stepping and raising their right hands in the hate salute. Each Nazi face was clear in the photographs.

A group of blacks converged on them. The fighting began. The blacks beat the Nazis badly. The blacks were big and in shape, and they knew how to fight. The photographer caught almost every punch. It was like a championship prize fight where every punch is photographed landing on the combatants jaw.

The local cops eventually broke up the fight, but the Nazis had been punished by the in-shape black guys. They continued their shouts of hatred, their goose stepping and their stupid salute with blood spewing from their noses and mouths. Someone in these pictures killed Gerald Gordon at his synagogue, I surmised. The scene in Illinois was close enough in proximity to Richmond Heights, Missouri for there to be a connection.

Captain Bud strolled in. He was the commander of the unit. He was rarely seen, leaving the day to day operations to Lieutenant Boob. There were two people with him. One I recognized. His name was Paul, at one time a pawn broker in my North City district. He'd made a fiscal killing when the price of gold plummeted in the mid-seventies.

He had capital, so he invested in gold; purchased gold all over the country. He had cop friends and he paid them to fly around the country picking up gold he'd purchased over the telephone. Gold went up drastically and he was super wealthy. He sold his pawn shop and was now a jeweler.

There was another wealthy man with them. They observed me and introduced themselves. The guy's name was David. They were nice guys, educated and refined. David owned property. I couldn't figure why they pursued a friendship with the Captain.

I figured they were made aware that I, the German looking cop, was making headway in penetrating the American Nazi Party in St. Louis. I could see and feel their enthusiasm. I wanted to be known as the cop who had infiltrated the Nazis. It sounded good to me

2

I had the weekend off, which is rare in the cop business but not in the intelligence business. I enjoyed spending quality time with my pregnant wife and my young son. It seemed normal to be relaxed on a weekend, like a regular guy instead of a Wednesday or Thursday, my normal days off.

I reported back to intelligence on Monday morning with the rest of the detectives. I grabbed an empty desk and resumed my studying of the files. I was informed by the unit secretary the lieutenant in the bureau of investigation had called and wanted me to come to his office. I strolled the forty yards, taking my time and conversing with detective friends as I walked.

I tapped on his cubicle door jam and he smiled and motioned for me to enter. It was a small little office, temporary and inappropriate. Big decisions were made there. The lieutenant was the purveyor of federal grant funds used for undercover police operations. He had the power because he controlled the money, but his power was waning because he didn't control the information.

He smoked, and I wondered why an intelligent person would allow such a habit to control him. There were potted plants behind him, and a large window with a view of Gothic City Hall. All of this leadership, City, federal and state were in about a square mile of downtown real estate. It's where most of the decisions concerning government in ethnic little St. Louis were made. Federal money flowed in and out in the form of grants, and the lieutenant took his fiscal responsibility seriously.

"What's going on over there? When is this machine gun buy supposed to go down?"

"This week, sir," I replied. "I've met with the informant and he's going to introduce me sometime this week."

"I gave that young kid five hundred dollars of federal grant money. I want to make certain those funds are accountable. You keep your eyes on him, you understand?"

"Yes, sir."

"What's the informant like?"

"Country bumpkin," I replied.

"What's the deal look like to you?"

"Iffy," I mumbled.

"Don't fall in love with it over there. The chief wants you back here in the bureau. You know why you're there, don't you? Why you were the one chosen?"

By Chief, he meant the Chief of Detectives, Colonel John Doherty. That is the only chief he recognized.

"Because I look the part," I said.

"No, I chose you because I knew you wouldn't be swayed by those assholes over in intelligence. I've been around this building for over thirty years and I've never witnessed a good case that came out of intelligence. There's a good possibility you're being used as a pawn. The commander and the deputy commander desire to impress their influential buddies. This Nazi thing is probably a farce. Don't be smitten by those files. I'm the purveyor of federal funds for any and all undercover operations within this department. I'll stop dolling out the cash if I have to."

"What do you want me to do?" I asked.

"Go back over there and play it by ear," he ordered. "Keep in touch with me. Keep me apprised of what's going on with the alleged case."

"Yes, sir," I muttered and walked out of the office. I strolled to intelligence and tapped on the door. The Irish Prince opened it. "Where were you?" He asked.

"Restroom," I replied.

"We've got our own private restrooms in these offices. Use them from now on." I didn't respond to him. "The introduction is this morning. Are you ready to make a buy?"

"Yeah, I'm ready." I followed him into the electronics room of the offices. A cop who I had seen before but whose name I didn't know wired me for sound. He fitted me with a wife beater type contraption with a battery pack, a tape recorder and a transmitter under my shirt. I would be transmitting and recording. "Overkill," I thought. They told me to go out into the hallway and speak normally. I did and they received my transmission.

"We're going to be in a surveillance van monitoring your activities," the Irish Prince said. "We're meeting the confidential informant near the target area and you'll hop in with him. Any questions?"

"No," I muttered. We took the elevator down to the lobby then entered the Irish Prince's funny car and drove to the secret location where the surveillance van was stored near the cop garage. We parked the funny car and left it on the street then walked into the garage and entered the surveillance van. They wanted me to view it.

It was state of the art. It had a cushioned bucket seat on a pedestal with a periscope where the surveillance man could watch three-hundred and sixty-degrees and take thirty-five millimeter pictures or video tape. I was impressed. The Feds purchased it for us," the electronics cop told me. "We've also got enough money in our budget to have it painted every six months for five years so it doesn't get burned."

I clambered out with the Irish Prince and re-entered the funny car. We headed south to the same park where we had met him before. He was there, parked at the curb, smoking and sulking as if the pressure was getting to him. I exited the funny car and entered the stinking dirty Chevy.

We didn't drive far, just about three blocks to a storefront on Meramec Street. It was a shop that housed second hand furniture and clothing. I read the sign on the side of the building and I figured it was where the confidential informant had purchased his clothing. I was disgusted at the circumstances.

We exited the dirty Chevy and strolled in the side door of the storefront. A country looking guy, heavy, unkempt and crafty acting eyeballed me. There were several neighborhood creeps hanging around inside of the place. "Burglars and stick-up men," I figured. They all watched me as if I was a possible victim. They knew why I was there, to buy a gun, preferably a machine gun, so they all knew I was carrying a wad of cash.

"This is the guy I was telling you about, Jim," the informant began. I shook hands with him then stood my ground. He didn't look like anything perceivable as far as being a Nazi was concerned; just a normal looking criminal, fronting a fencing operation in a storefront.

"What's your name," the criminal gun dealer asked.

I gave him a cold stare. “I don’t have a name.” He smiled, and the other criminal associates loitering in the cramped quarters smiled along with him. It was a standoff and there was a lull in the conversation.

“Are you from around here?” He asked.

“No,” I countered. “I’m here to purchase an automatic weapon. I was told you had one for sale. Do you? If you do break it out and let’s get on with it.”

“You got cash with you?” he asked.

“Do you have the weapon?” I countered.

It was bait and switch time for the alleged Nazi. “I don’t have it right now, but I’ve got a twenty-five automatic, a Beretta. He took it out of his pocket and showed it to me. It was beat up and didn’t look as if it would fire.

“Let me look at it,” I said with my hand out. He handed it to me and I examined it. It was junk, not worth twenty-bucks, and it was fully loaded. I handed it back to him, “I doubt that gun would fire, it’s so old.”

“It’ll fire,” he replied and he shot it three times into the wooden floor of the rag-tag shop. I expected the troops to come storming in the door. This was an undercover assignment where shots were fired, but no one came. I had to play the game. I was there to purchase a firearm, but more importantly I was there to gain the confidence of the seller so I could eventually purchase a better weapon from him.

“When can you get me an automatic weapon?” I asked.

“I get them from time to time, but they don’t last long,” he replied. “I’ll give you a deal on the twenty-five auto, though.”

“How much?”

“Hundred and fifty,” he replied.

“No way,” I said. “I’ll give you seventy-five bucks, no more.”

“Sold,” the crook said. “Give me the cash.”

I rolled off the cash from my government wad, handed it to him and took possession of the junky gun. “When will I know about the automatic weapon?” I asked.

“I’ll tell your Nazi buddy when I get it.”

“Okay,” I replied. We walked out the same door we walked in and climbed into the nasty Chevy. We met up with the Irish Prince. I hopped out of the Nazi car and hopped in with the Prince. We headed back to headquarters.

We made our way into the intelligence offices. I plopped down at a vacant desk, placed the junky automatic in front of me and unloaded it. The Irish Prince made a bee-line for Lieutenant Boob's office. They strolled out together and stood in front of the desk I was using. Cigar smoke was being blown my way. Lieutenant Boob was studying and measuring me.

He picked up the gun. "It's junk," he said. "But it's a gun purchased from a Nazi with an informant who is a Nazi, so that makes it good junk," he continued with a laugh.

The unit secretary walked to the desk and advised me that I was being summoned to the bureau of investigation. I thanked her, stood, tucked the junk gun in my pocket and headed for the door.

"Do not divulge any information from this office to the bureau," Boob said. I looked at him and nodded, then walked out of the offices. It took about twenty-five seconds to get the lieutenant's office. I didn't have to tap, he was waiting for me.

"What did you buy?" He asked.

"Twenty-five automatic," I replied as I placed it on his desk.

He examined it then looked up at me. "It's junk," he muttered. "How much did you pay for it?"

"Seventy-five bucks," I replied.

"It isn't worth ten bucks," he mumbled. "I doubt it fires."

"It fires. When I purchased it the seller fired three shots into the floor as a demonstration." His dark eyes were burning a hole in my face.

"Who is the guy selling junk guns?" he wearily asked.

"All I know about him is that his name is Jim. He runs a second hand store on Meramec. The folks over in intelligence probably know his pedigree." He continued to stare. I figured he thought I was lying to him. He had been a cop for thirty years and had been lied to by the best. I was hoping he could read me well enough to know I wasn't stalling on him.

"Okay," He continued. "Here's how we're going to work this from now on out. If you wish to pursue this fiasco with intelligence you must first see the weapon and get me the serial number before I will give you federal funds to purchase it. If it's junk, like this piece of trash," he tossed it toward me on his desk, "I won't allow you to purchase it. If you went to court with this junky so called gun, there's a good possibility you wouldn't get a conviction. The jury knows junk."

We stared. "Yes, sir," I replied.

"Tell that big Irish kid that he owes me four-hundred and twenty-five dollars of federal undercover buy money. I expect it before the end of today's work day."

"Yes, sir," I muttered.

"You're getting in too deep over there. The door is still open for you to come back here. Every day that door starts to close a little at a time. It won't be long before the door will shut on you. You'll be trapped there with those damn snitches and politicians. You make the decision."

"Yes, sir," I mumbled.

He leaned back and continued to stare at me like a father studying his son. "You like it there?"

"Yes, sir," I admitted.

"Why?"

"They've got conspiracies. I'm attracted to them," I quietly said. But I was partially fooling myself. The unit was a brotherhood, something I had never experienced. The Marine Corps wasn't a brotherhood. It was a bunch of crazy guys with bad attitudes. The intelligence unit was a bunch of folks intent with destroying organized criminals. It was brotherhood versus brotherhood. I wanted to be a part of it.

"They do have conspiracies," he said. "But most of them are in-house. You can go now."

He looked down and resumed his paper shuffling. I picked up the junk gun, stuffed it into my jeans pocket, turned and walked out. I slowly made my way back to intelligence, knocked on the door and was admitted. I walked to my desk and plopped down. I was collecting emotional baggage.

The Irish Prince and I spent the morning in the office packaging the junk gun and writing a memorandum concerning the buy from the Nazis. I read the memorandum. The alleged Nazi gun seller was not identified, just referred to as Jim. Every other memorandum I had read had the police characters fully identified. Even in the American Nazi Party folder. I questioned the Irish Prince about it.

"It's the way Boob wants it for now," he explained. "It's got something to do with the sniping at the synagogue in Richmond Heights. This guy Jim allegedly knows something about it. Boob figures if we can get some gun buys on him we'll be able to squeeze him into telling us what we want to hear. He might even be the sniper. We aren't certain."

We went to lunch then came back to the office. I was told to transcribe the tape recording of the undercover deal. The Irish Prince told me the order came from Boob, so I did it. It was tedious, listening to the tape with ear-phones, stopping it and typing the mostly inaudible banter between an undercover cop and a crook. It took me days to finish it, but I wanted to get it out of the way. I wanted to get back into the unit gangster files.

I had been working late and the office was almost deserted. I had finished the transcribing of the undercover tape recording and was feeling a small sense of accomplishment. Captain Bud walked in with Paul and David, the pawn broker, and his wealthy friend. David had a large box with him and he made a big scene presenting it to Captain Bud in the presence of me and Boob, who had walked out of his office and joined us in the center office.

The box was filled with sterling silver goblets and flatware. Silver was way up in price per pound, and I tried to estimate the value of the gift. Way over a thousand dollars, I estimated. I continued to wonder why these educated and wealthy guys pursued friendship with the Captain and Boob. They all went back to the captain's office, which was private, but they left the door open and laughed and told stories and acted like fraternity brothers.

I submitted my transposed report by tossing it on Boob's desk then headed out the door. I was waiting at the elevator when I heard them coming, still laughing and speaking loudly. The door opened for me and I was able to get ahead of them. The other elevator was opening as I stepped onto the waiting elevator. I exited into the lobby and quickly walked to my GMC conversion van parked in the courtyard.

The Captain's funny car was parked a couple of rows away from my van. I observed the four of them pile into it. The Captain was driving, Boob was riding shotgun, and the two wealthy refined businessmen were trapped in the back seat of the two-door Chrysler.

Captain Bud and Lieutenant Boob were sucking on their cigars like they were in a contest to see who could make the most pollution. Paul and David looked like sheep heading to the slaughter house as they glanced at each other and tried to carry the conversation with the two cop commanders. It is what they had been trained to do in private grade school: keep the conversation moving. Always communicate.

I figured I would follow them for awhile. It was such an unusual association, and the sterling silver gift was perplexing me. It was rapidly getting dark. Late November in St. Louis is winter weather. The sun rarely peeks through the heavy sky.

The captain guided the big Chrysler out of the courtyard and gunned it, heading north toward the downtown business area. I kept a block behind them. They didn't go far. They stopped at an expensive Italian restaurant, climbed out, the captain gave the keys to the valet and they went inside.

I was intrigued but I didn't know why. So, the commanders have wealthy friends. Big deal! It wasn't a conspiracy. They weren't conspiring; at least I didn't know of any conspiracy, but the expensive gift was unusual. And the association was unusual. And the Nazi case which actually wasn't a Nazi case was unusual. I headed for home.

3

I parked my van in front of headquarters, climbed out and made my way into the building and up the elevator. The Irish Prince had called me at home and advised me our hours had been changed. It was cold and dark. The usually locked front door was standing open and I could smell coffee and cigarettes. The Irish Prince was smoking and drinking and reading a memorandum as I walked in.

He wasn't overly friendly. I figured he had been chastised by Lieutenant Boob for something relating to the Nazi case. Why else would our hours be changed at the spur of the moment? "Can you wire yourself?" He asked.

"Yeah," I replied. "What's up?"

"We're meeting the informant at the park. You're going to jump in with him and go to the store on Meramec, just like always. See if you can buy another gun from him. Boob wants us to get this thing going. He says we're wasting too much time on it."

"Did you give the federal cash back to the Lieutenant in the bureau?" I asked.

"No, not yet. We're going to use it tonight."

"He isn't going to be happy," I muttered. "He doesn't want me buying anymore junk guns. He wants me to view the weapon, then come to him and tell him what it looks like. He even wants the serial number of the gun. He wants to make the decision on the buy."

"I know all of that," the Irish Prince shot back. "It isn't his money. It's federal cash for making undercover cases. This is an undercover case. Boob says to use it."

I was caught in the middle of a dilemma. It was causing me more emotional baggage. Uniform guys in a district don't collect emotional baggage. They aren't faced with career decisions. They are faced with life or death decisions. I figured I would be closing the door to the bureau if I went along with the directives of Boob and the Irish Prince. I had to figure where my allegiance was. Intelligence unit? Or bureau of investigation?

I walked into the electronics room and slipped into the wire harness. I didn't bother to take the tape recorder. There was a tape on the listening end of the wire. I was glad the weather was cool. The harness was hot and uncomfortable.

We headed out, locked the door, set the alarm, took the elevator down and entered the funny car. We drove slowly through the City in the dark toward the park. The alleged Nazi was waiting for us. I climbed out without fanfare and slid into the stinking Chevy with the stupid Nazi.

It was the same routine. We parked on the side street and entered through the side door. The other alleged Nazi was there with the same neighborhood street creatures, burglars and stick-up men, eyeballing me and hanging on every word I spoke. Jim was standoffish, but I could see the greed in his eyes. He knew I had cash.

"He wants to buy that thirty-eight you told me about," the informant Nazi said to Jim. Jim gave me a long hard look. He was distrusting but greed was taking over.

"It isn't here," he stammered. "It's at my house, and I don't have a car right now. Maybe I can have it here tomorrow morning."

"I've got the cash now, Jim," I said. "I may not have it tomorrow morning."

"How much are you willing to pay for a Smith & Wesson thirty-eight special, bodyguard with a magnesium frame?" Jim asked.

"Depends on how good of shape it's in," I replied. I figured it was stolen in a burglary by one of the stooges hanging around the store and watching my every move. They just want as much money as it can pull. "I'll have to look at it," I sternly said.

"If I had a car I'd take you to my house. It's just a couple of blocks away. Do you have a car?"

"Use mine," the informant Nazi replied. He tossed the keys to Jim and we headed out the side door. Jim drove and I was feeling uncomfortable. It was dark and I didn't know where I was going, and I was with a criminal who might be a murderer. And he might be a Nazi.

We pulled up to a flat on Oregon Street, the kind of rental housing used by folks who are just trying their hands at scraping by in the big City, to see if they can make it. They usually head back to the Boot-Heel, the southern tip of the state with their tails between their legs. Nobody ever remembers them here in the nasty City.

We got out and walked inside. It stunk like tainted meat had been cooked in it and not aired out. The furniture was sparse and used, like the junk in Jim's shop. I stood in the living room while Jim went back to one of the other rooms. He came out pointing the thirty-eight at me. He was trying to get me to overreact. I had been in similar situations while I was acting like a crook instead of a cop. This is usually the time in the caper where the bad guy points the gun at your gut and says, "Okay, who the hell are you? You're a cop aren't you?" I was in no mood to go through this crook ritual.

"Let me see it," I said. I reached out and pried the weapon out of his hand. He acted like he didn't want to give it up. It all boils down to paranoia. I didn't give Jim time to question me. I now had possession of the loaded weapon and I acted like I was examining it, but my mind and eyes were on Jim.

Jim was surprised that I took it away from him. He didn't get to play his game with me. He walked out of the room as I tried to memorize the serial number. The gun was in good shape. I had made my decision. I wasn't going to buy it. I was anxious about handing Jim a loaded gun. Smith & Wesson's chambers rotate counter clockwise.

Colt handguns rotate clockwise. I removed two rounds from the chamber and adjusted the cylinder so it wouldn't fire on the first or second time. If Jim wanted to use it on me he would get two clicks instead of two bangs. That would give me enough time to draw my Smith & Wesson and get him before he figured out what happened. If I removed all of the rounds he would know it by the weight of the weapon.

Jim walked back into the living room. "What do you think?" He said in a used car dealer twang.

"How much are you asking?" I replied.

"Five hundred will get her," he twanged.

"I'll let you know tomorrow," I said as I handed him the partially loaded revolver. "Take me back to the store." We exited the flat, entered the stinking Chevy and drove back to the store. I didn't go inside. I could see Jim and the Nazi informant conversing through the open doorway.

The informant Nazi came out with the keys and we drove off.

"Why didn't you buy it?" the informant Nazi asked. I wondered what he was getting out of this. Was this a stepping stone to a life of a paid informant? If he was good, the Feds would pay him well. Of course he probably wouldn't be around long. He would be killed. The tail pipe that had apparently been haphazardly attached to the undercarriage of the stinking Chevy was dragging again.

We were driving up Meramec. The Nazi started driving in circles, in the dark with the tail pipe grinding away on the street surface. "Stop," I said. He pulled over and I jumped out and started walking. We were on Cherokee Street on the near south side. It's called that because it is close to the north side, which is the danger zone.

I walked down to Jefferson Street and started talking into the microphone at my chest. "I'm on Cherokee approaching Jefferson," I said with my face down and my chin touching my chest. "Pick me up."

South side folks aren't surprised when they see crazy folks walking on their streets. But I didn't look like a typical crazy. I looked like a dangerous man. I was big and in shape and I was disgusted and they could sense my demeanor. The Irish Prince didn't show so I stood on the corner periodically talking into my chest for about five minutes wondering what had happened.

I started walking again, spied a coin laundry and went inside. There were mostly women doing their laundry, and they were cautious. I wasn't carrying laundry, and there was a fight or flight look on all of their faces as I entered. I went to the coin phone and dialed nine-eleven and advised the dispatcher who I was, where I was and asked her to advise the Irish Prince. He showed up in about five minutes.

I jumped in and we drove off. "I thought you were with the informant," the Irish Prince began.

"I didn't feel like riding around with him,' I said. "I figured you were behind us. Did you get anything on the wire? Did you tape it?"

"No, you weren't coming through. I didn't get any of it."

I thought about his response. Was he lying to me? It was good for me if he didn't tape it. My allegiance was leaning toward the bureau of investigation. I was in possession of the four-hundred and twenty-five-dollars the Irish Prince had gotten from the lieutenant in the bureau. I had gotten it from the Irish Prince, but I would return it to the lieutenant and maybe get back into his good graces.

"The informant told me you didn't buy the gun he offered to you. Why was that?" The Irish Prince was ahead of me. He had met with and debriefed the informant prior to picking me up.

"He wanted five-hundred-dollars for it," I replied. "I didn't have five-hundred."

"He would've taken four-twenty-five," the Irish Prince sarcastically said. I didn't wish to get into a pissing contest with the Irish Prince. We drove around most of the night going by gangsters' houses and writing down license numbers. "We like to see who's visiting them," the Irish Prince said. "It shows association."

I wondered how it must have felt growing up in a cop family. It must have been like being in the police academy every day of the Irish Prince's life. He had been prepped like a rich kid going to prep school. He was like Paul and David, schooled in communication and the business world. They were out of their comfort zone, befriending two cop commanders.

But the Irish Prince wasn't out of his comfort zone. He was prepped on a daily basis by his cop commander dad and by Boob. Every step he made with me, the Nazi informant and the lieutenant in the bureau was well thought out and then executed. He was certain to be a star in the business. All of that power and he only had one year on the police department.

I had tried to remember the serial number on the Smith & Wesson. I wrote down what I thought it was but it didn't fly. We went into the office and telephoned the computer room. I read them the number and it wasn't a serial number for a gun. The Irish Prince laughed, and eventually I laughed. It was one of those stressful nights working in an undercover position. I had gotten stressed when Jim pointed the gun at me. I didn't perform to my expectations.

The next day we worked the day watch. I checked in to the intelligence unit and immediately left the offices and headed for the bureau of investigation. The federal buy money was burning a hole in my pocket. I wanted to give it back to the lieutenant in charge of it. It wasn't mine and I didn't know when Boob was going to order me to give it back to the Irish Prince.

I walked to the cubbyhole office and he wasn't there. I asked his secretary where he was and she told me he was on vacation. He would be gone for two weeks. I felt the door slam on me. I was never going back to the bureau. I gave her the government cash, got a receipt and trudged back to intelligence.

4

I had been sitting in the office reading files for a week. We would go out to lunch, the Irish Prince and me, then come back to the office and kill time. The Nazi case was all but dead. Jim told the Nazi informant that he wouldn't sell me any more guns. He thought I was an Alcohol Tobacco and Firearms Special Agent. "At the very least, he's a damn undercover cop," Jim said.

I wondered if he had noticed the missing two rounds of ammunition I had removed from the Smith & Wesson. That would be enough to spook him. But I couldn't take the chance of him turning the weapon on me again and going too far with his intimidation attempt. I was alone, undercover and I had to look out for myself.

There were rumblings within the office that promotions were coming out. The political cops were abuzz over it; each one thinking it was their time for the assault on becoming cop royalty. It was why they were there. It was their heritage. In their minds they deserved the honor and were owed it. Kind of like an inheritance.

The Irish Prince came to me as I studied the files. "If you've got anybody you can call now is the time to do it," he muttered. "There are going to be some openings in Intel 210. Some guys are going to be promoted and moved out. Do you know anybody?"

I thought for a couple of seconds. "No," I muttered. I was almost proud of the fact that I wasn't special. I figured I would be going back to a North City district, but at this point in time it didn't seem all that bad. The Irish Prince looked on me with pity then walked away. The promotions didn't come out on that day.

The week was almost over. It was Thursday and I was making headway with my reading. The promotions eventually came out. Only one person from the unit was on the list. This influential cop had an influential brother, a state representative, so he chose not to leave the plush assignment. He stayed and was made a supervisor.

There was a pall over the unit. The important cops moped around for several days then rationalized their way toward bigger and brighter days. They scratched for an investigation to hide in. Investigations were the key to being out of the office. They killed time and the cops would walk around with their heads up and brag about their surveillance skills. For that's what they were: surveillance. Nobody ever got arrested, just investigated, except for the stars. They arrested crooks on search warrants.

I had gotten a telephone call from a cop I had worked with in the CWE district, Mike Williams. He was attending law school during the day and working in the Chief's office answering telephones on the night watch. He was one of the super bright cops. Everyone recognized his potential and didn't mind helping him.

He had heard I was on temporary loan to the cushy job. "I'm friends with the Chief," he told me. By Chief, he meant the Chief of Police, not the Chief of Detectives. "Give me the word and I'll go in and speak up for you. Do you wish to stay there?"

"Yes," I replied. The transfers came out in about a week. My name was on the list, I was officially assigned to the unit. I was given a detective car, not a funny car. The influential cops in the unit were starting to warm to me. Nobody knew where I was coming from. They had made the assumption that I had influential relatives or friends.

Boob gave me a desk, a key to the front door and the alarm code. I came to work on time and drove around in my detective car, a four-door Chevy, little hub caps, black wall tires and an antenna on the back. All it needed was an insignia that said Metropolitan Police and some roof lights on it to be a full-fledged cop-car.

Since the transfers the office was packed with detectives, and mostly what they did was dignitary protection details, guarding politicians, friends of politicians, wealthy visitors from out of town, big-name entertainers and anybody else who someone with clout felt needed protection.

Presidential details were prevalent. We were assigned to the Secret Service, wore suits and had Secret Service pins identifying us as cops. The whole gig was an ego trip for cops. I felt important some of the time.

I was in the habit of arresting criminals. I asked Lieutenant Boob if I would be given a case to work on. He pointed to the file cabinets lining the walls, "Those contain information on every organized crook in the United States of America. Pick one out and start investigating him." It wasn't exactly what I wanted to hear.

I had time to myself. The Irish Prince distanced himself from me. I figured he blamed me for the Nazi case failure. I drove to the south side, to the second hand store on Meramec. I was going to arrest Jim the gun seller. It wasn't a good case. It was a case that probably wouldn't go to court, and if it did I would probably lose, but he deserved to be arrested. It was his turn at the cycle of incarceration for being a low life. At the very least I would get him identified through fingerprints.

The store had apparently been burglarized. The side door was standing open and there was junk lying around on the outside. I stopped the car and examined the door. It had been kicked off of the hinges. The inside of the store was in shambles like it had been ransacked. Neighborhood folks had pilfered and looted it.

I drove to the flat on Oregon where Jim said he lived. The door was standing open there, also. The interior of it was ransacked. I knocked on a door adjacent to Jims. A lady answered, smoking and coughing and nursing a beer. It was eleven A.M. and I figured the beer was breakfast.

"Where's Jim?" I asked.

"I don't know no Jim," she replied with a twang.

"The guy who lived here," I said motioning with my hand.

"Oh, was his name Jim? I didn't really know what his name was. He told me his name was Tom, or something. Nice fella. We'd drink a little in the evening. He always had cold beer. Why do you want to find him?"

I figured she had seen my detective car parked in front so I flashed the tin at her and said, "City Intelligence. You'd better start talking to me or I'm going to run a wanted on you and ruin your day."

"He didn't tell me he was leaving," she blurted out. "He left without paying his rent. His old busted and rusty truck is parked in the backyard. Maybe he's coming back to get it. I don't know where he is."

"Are you the landlord?" I asked.

"Yes, sir."

"Then you must have a lease agreement with Tom's full name on it, right?"

“No sir. He paid weekly, in cash, and I didn’t really know who he was. He was only here for a couple of months.”

“Is that his furniture?”

“No sir, it’s mine. I rent the flat furnished. Folks come and go quick around here.”

“Did he ever tell you anything about himself? You drank with him. That usually leads to conversation. What did he talk about?”

“He never got into his past life. I figured he was an ex-con or something. But the last time we got drunk together he was worried.”

“How long ago was that?”

She paused and looked down, then looked up. “About six weeks ago,” she mumbled.

“What was he worried about?” I asked.

“He said he was in some sort of danger. He said somebody might be coming for him, maybe to abduct him. He was scared. I could see it in his eyes.”

I had gotten everything I could have gotten out of the landlord. I thanked her and walked out to the yard, then walked to the backyard. The old rusted pickup truck was parked on a gravel pad adjacent to the alley. There weren’t any license plates on it so I copied the VIN, searched the inside of it and walked back to my Chevy.

I headed back to the office and ran the VIN in the computer for an issue. It was a salvage vehicle, registered to a salvage yard in the Boot Heel. Everything was a dead end. Jim or Tom or whoever he was, was gone. I headed back to the office.

The Irish Prince was acting busy reading and taking notes from a memorandum. I asked him about the Nazi informant. I never knew his name or anything about him. “He’s gone,” the Irish Prince advised me. “Chicago, maybe or some other big City.”

“What was his name?” I asked.

“His real name. Nobody knows for sure. He was just an informant with an alias. They come and they go up here. Get used to it.”

That aspect of the Nazi caper was closed but the sniping murder at the synagogue was still active in the mind of the Chief of Detectives in

Richmond Heights, Missouri. He was a high profile guy; had his own radio talk show a couple of nights a week. He was also an aware guy and he knew that if he could solve the synagogue murder he could write his own ticket in the business world in the St. Louis Metropolitan area. Being a cop was okay, but the American way is sponsorship to wealth.

When a cop is desperate to solve a high profile murder certain types of people recognize his desperation. Good citizens and bad, and a lot of crazies. Boob had the Richmond Heights cop's undivided attention. They talked together on the telephone, brain busting each other trying to identify a suspect who hated enough to commit this heinous crime.

The Richmond Heights cop had gotten a call, anonymously, from a guy who stated that he knew who the synagogue murderer was and that he would meet with the Chief of Detectives in Oak Knoll Park, a prestigious park in Richmond Heights. He telephoned Boob and asked him for surveillance assistance.

Winter had come and gone and it was now a hot spring, temperatures in the nineties. I was floundering in the office, reading and waiting for five o'clock to roll around. But it was just nearing noon and lunch was the next high point of the day.

Boob called me in. Little Pat, (Patty Rice) a female detective in the unit was sitting near his desk and had already been briefed by Boob. Little Pat had a funny car. "You and Little Pat are going to Richmond Heights," Boob said with enthusiasm.

An informant is going to meet with the chief of detectives out there and inform him who the synagogue sniper is. I've got our sound man out there right now. He's in an office overlooking Oak Knoll Park taking thirty-five millimeter pictures. The chief is wired and I'll be up in the office with the sound man monitoring the conversation. You two float around the park in the funny car and wait for me to give you instructions. Any questions?"

"No, sir, Lieutenant," we said in unison. We headed for the front door, took the elevator down and made our way to the court yard. Little Pat's funny car was a big Pontiac with an interceptor engine. It was comfortable and fast.

"You drive," Little Pat said as she tossed me the keys. I made a tour through a Steak and Shake drive through, and we were in Richmond Heights eating our lunch in the Pontiac in about twenty minutes. Oak Knoll Park is situated on Clayton Road, adjacent to an expensive girl's college and situated around the business area of the City. It's busy during the day, especially around lunch, and since the weather had finally turned hot, people were frequenting it on this investigative day.

I had binoculars and from our vantage point I could see the whole park. I observed the Richmond Heights detective chief sitting on a park bench by a giant elm tree. I kept watching. A person was walking toward him wearing a wool ski mask.

I wasn't the only one who had observed this strange sight. Park brown bagers were already paranoid since the sniping. Seeing a ski mask in the hot weather freaked them out. People were scrambling to get out of the way of a possible shooting.

"It's a nut in a ski mask," I advised Little Pat.

"Let me see," she said. I handed her the binoculars.

The conversation between the detective chief and the nut/informant lasted for about thirty minutes. Apparently the chief asked the nut to accompany him to the Richmond Heights detective bureau for a further conversation and the guy said he would, with a stipulation that he not be forced to remove his mask.

Little Pat and I didn't know about the stipulation. Boob got on the air, "Drive down into the park and pick up the informant. Convey him to the Richmond heights Detective Bureau."

"Yes, sir," I replied. I drove the gigantic Pontiac down the narrow bike path road, then drove on the grass to get to the informant and the detective chief. The Pontiac was a two-door, so Little Pat scrunched up toward the dash and raised the back of her seat so the informant could slide in. The chief of detectives walked away toward Clayton Avenue.

I drove east until I got on a hard road and then maneuvered the Pontiac toward a side street that would take me to Clayton Avenue. I felt unsafe looking in my rear view mirror and seeing a guy I didn't know, and one I hadn't searched, looking back at me with a mask on. For all I knew he was the synagogue sniper.

Apparently Little Pat wasn't comfortable with the scenario either. She turned around in her seat and stared at him. "What's your name, man?" she asked.

"I'm not telling you that," he curtly said.

"Pull into this alley," Little Pat said. I complied. "Now stop the car." I did. "Listen you asshole," Little Pat began. "You're not playing games with those pussy Richmond Heights cops. Were the real cops, downtown City Intelligence." She reached back and snatched the ski mask off of his head. "Now, I'll ask you again, what's your name?"

He shrieked like a little girl and tried to hide his face with his hands. I gunned the Pontiac and headed for the Richmond Heights Police Department. Pat threw the mask into his face and he quickly slid it back on.

We parked, got him out and escorted him into the bureau. Boob and the detective chief were waiting for us. They were patronizing him, treating him like a VIP. They escorted him into a private office and Boob was questioning him, lying to him telling him he could get paid a lot of cash if he comes up with the right guy. The nut/informant snitched on Little Pat for snatching his disguise.

Boob and the detective chief from Richmond Heights came out of the office. "Who removed his mask?" Neither of us fessed up, which meant we were both in trouble. Boob acted like he was embarrassed. The Richmond Heights cop walked around the office moaning with his face in his hands. I found humor in the chain of events and smirked. Little Pat smirked with me. It was a Keystone Kop moment.

Boob and the detective chief went back into the office and continued drilling the mask wearer. He didn't reveal anything to them. He didn't know anything. He was a nut, exercising his freedom of expression in America. Eventually he removed his mask and walked out with Boob and the other cop running after him like puppies. I smirked again. Little Pat laughed out loud. It was basically the end of the synagogue sniper caper for Richmond Heights and City Intelligence.

But Boob would tell Paul and David a different story. He would keep them on the line with some sort of intelligence information. They were his influential friends, more so than Captain Bud. Captain Bud was crude and rude to them. Boob patronized them. Paul and David kept hanging on.

I got into the swing of things and started protecting dignitaries. United States Congressman Dick Gephardt was a politician I continually guarded when he had visiting dignitaries in town. It wasn't a bad gig and I ate well. But the upper echelon of the police department didn't like Dick Gephardt. They prided themselves in their conservative political views. Dick was a liberal.

I guarded Bob Hope many times. Guarding Bob was fun, just because it was him. He needed walks, like a dog, and I walked him around St. Louis, usually in the Central West End, but sometimes downtown. I would give him the lead and follow him, just so he wouldn't get into any trouble.

When I wasn't guarding dignitaries I cruised the streets in my unmarked, four-door Chevy and pulled suspicious folks over. Most of them had guns on them and I would get an arrest and an arrest statistic.The high-profile cops always had nicknames. There were several detectives on the verge of stardom and they were the ones who had the neat assignments. Guido and Stretch were the undercover crew who followed the organized criminals around; the Mafia types mostly. It is what I longed to do but Boob told me I shouldn't because it might interfere with the other undercover crew, so I heeded his directive.

Guido and Stretch were smart guys. Stretch was tall, about six-foot-three, blonde hair and smooth. Guido was small in stature with Mediterranean features; a Pacino kind of guy.

There was a crew of guys who did narcotic search warrants, mostly in predominantly black north St. Louis, and north St. Louis County. They were referred to as the stars.

The lead detective of the stars sat at his desk all day long and into the night analyzing long distance telephone records of black St. Louis County dope dealers, chain smoking and drinking pot after pot of coffee. He dressed like a street person, and had long shaggy hair combed down over his forehead. He was a great cop but he was soured to humanity. He could have caused depression in the Pope. His dedication at catching the bad guy was all inspiring and unparalleled.

The lead star would predict when a load of dope would be coming into the area, then he would go to the jurisdiction where he suspected it would be hidden and obtain a search warrant. His predictions were usually outside of the City of St. Louis, but the dope would be destined for the City after it was broken up and distributed. He was a successful guy in his endeavors with a lot of arrests, a lot of seized cocaine and marijuana, and a lot of seized contraband.

Dope dealers take merchandise in trade for dope, most of it stolen. The stars did a search warrant on a house and came up with a whole room full of stolen items: televisions, artwork, guns, jewelry, stones, sterling flatware and decanters, rare bone China. It was a big haul, probably worth a couple-hundred-thousand-dollars.

Captain Bud told him to display it in the big office on a large twenty-person table and then to lock the room. It was where the stars' desks were located. I looked at the contraband; everybody in the unit did. I was impressed at the quality of the recovered loot. I was amazed at what lengths the dope user would go to obtain more dope. This neat stolen and recovered loot would probably go down to the property room and then be auctioned off at a fraction of its true market value.

The lead star had the responsibility to attempt to locate the owners of the seized contraband. There was a blog on the local television news stations, and folks thronged up to the fourth floor to the intelligence unit offices to try and retrieve their alleged belongings.

Folks were shopping more than retrieving. It was obvious. The lead star was courteous. He was an intelligent man. He recognized the fact that this contraband was most likely never going to go to its rightful owners. No telling where it had been stolen from. Maybe from another state.

The lead star would tell the interested parties that if they felt this merchandise was owned by them, then fill out a form, which was provided, and take said property. Some of the shoppers would balk due to fear, and their lying, and would retreat to the outside hallway and discuss the consequences of lying to the cops. Their fear was usually overridden by greed and they quickly returned, filled out the retrieval form and left with whatever piece of contraband they were smitten with.

A new guy came into the unit, a star in his own right from another unit, a friend of the lead detective of the stars. He had a reputation of being corrupt. I didn't believe the stories that preceded his entry into the unit. My theory was that if he was as corrupt as the gossip implied, then why had he been transferred to the elite Intelligence Unit? And if he actually did the deeds he was accused of, then why wasn't he in a federal penitentiary? Cops and crooks talk badly about hard charging detectives. I figured his reputation was the product of jealousy.

He and the lead star were to be partners at some point, but not immediately. They were both hard chargers, dedicated to a fault and Captain Bud didn't want them together. He would split them up, one strong guy with one weak guy. The lead star and his buddy were both famous cops, highly decorated and hard working. They didn't even take their vacations; they would schedule them and then show up at the office to do search warrants. They were desperate cops on a crusade for promotion; the Holy Grail.

The new star, who was small in stature and hyper, was a big talker and his reputation of having state political influence put him on the fast track with the bosses. He would talk to Boob and mesmerize him instantly.

Boob had no defense against the little star's personality, and the little star knew it.

The little star recognized Boob's vanity about his hair. He told him he'd had a partner in the district who had gotten a hair transplant. Boob picked up the ball immediately. He wanted to regain his youth and he was certain that if he had hair again he would be a young guy.

These hair conversations occurred on a daily basis, and Boob was getting more interested as the months went by. The little star even brought his old partner into the office and let Boob touch and admire his new hair, and I had to admit, the guy had movie-star hair.

Boob's wheels were turning, but that wasn't why the little star was courting Boob. He wanted the ear of the bosses, and he had it. He had the ability to recognize a weakness in the supervisor's aura, then work on him through the weakness. The little star had talent.

Captain Bud loved it when the stars played to him by not taking their vacations. He didn't want any of us to take ours. I always took mine. But Captain Bud wasn't in the office very much. Being the commander of an undercover unit was like a part-time job for him, and he had Boob to run the day-to-day operations for him.

The little star easily recognized the way to Captain Bud's heart. Captain Bud was a frustrated capitalist. He loved capital, but wasn't in the free enterprise part of the American dream. He was a fixed income capitalist, and upset about it.

The stars eventually started working together, although not officially. They just did whatever they wanted to do. It's the cop way. They did their search warrants and cash was seized on most of them. The rank and file guys in the unit didn't trust the little star; he knew it, but he didn't care. He was on a mission. For the average cop, not a super star, like me, there was a certain amount of evil in their police work. Their dedication and their quest to be promoted and to please the Captain was astounding to me and most of the unit detectives. We had been trained to detect evil. It's what cops do. So we just sat and watched as the little star would parade around the office with stacks of cash, fanning the bills for us, laughing and teasing, then he would walk into Captain Bud's office with the cash and come out empty handed. He would look at us, laugh, and slap his knee.

Every time the little star laughed and slapped his knee I couldn't help but think, "What kind of a dad made a guy like that?" And every time he made a point to let us see his ruthlessness, he would run into the big office where his buddy, the lead star was, and hide behind him. It was comedic and I couldn't help but laugh at the circumstances that mold cops into leaders of men. The stars would eventually be promoted many times and would lead all of us. It is what they desired more than anything else in the world.

The little star had the bosses eating out of his hand in no time. He had access to all of the department gossip, and the rank and file guys would ask him about certain rumors they had heard. He always had an answer. It was his personality to know the gossip, a tool for him. And if he didn't particularly care for the guy asking for information, he would say, "You don't know what I know," in a whiney voice, and walk away. It was raw comedy.

But, the lead star and the little star were in charge of the unit. If you had a conscience, you stayed away from the evilness of the event, did your job and went home to your family.

I soon figured out that this wasn't just a unit in a police department, it was a political action group for cops, the lowest rung on the political ladder where most of the cops had outside influence and that was why they were there, to get aligned for promotion.

The little star had state influence from being aligned with the Pipefitters Union, Local 562. It took state influence to get continual promotions. The state controlled the police department; a civil war leftover. The state legislature controlled our pay raises and benefits. If you desired a promotion, it was smart to have a state representative in your pocket, and promotions are what most of the detectives desired. But first they had to get by the Captain Bud and Lieutenant Boob show. They needed them to tell the chief, "He's okay."

So the lead-detective-star and his buddy worked like dogs, donating their vacations and their days off, talking down their work associates and talking themselves up. It worked for them.

The cop stars bragged and swaggered around the unit, something I had never witnessed before. I never knew a braggart. It was just something a person shouldn't do. It was boring and showed lack of character. The stars were lacking the basic principles of life; don't lie, don't speak badly about your neighbor or co-worker, don't take what doesn't belong to you.

Even folks from East St. Louis knew that. I figured they were acting from an impromptu script, not actually being themselves, but just trying to establish their roles with the captain in this absurd play.

They were mini-politicians telling their constituents how great they were; their constituents being their political aces and Captain Bud and Lieutenant Boob. They would write themselves glorious commendation recommendations, citing their bravery, dedication and intelligence, then take them into the captain, whenever he showed up, and have him sign them.

I had never known anybody who had ever gotten a commendation. They came from the chief of police, after the commander of the unit made his recommendation. The immediate supervisor was supposed to be the person writing the recommendation for the commander to sign. Then it was forwarded to the chief's office. The stars had their own set of rules. It was an educational experience for me.

I read the files on organized criminals during down time. I wanted to know everything about them on a national basis. I was semi-educated in about one year.

I felt alone in the unit and I complained aloud that I wanted to start investigating organized criminals. The City was full of them, and some of them were coming from the Eastside, my old home town. I was looking for a big-time criminal to investigate, someone deserving and interesting enough to keep me amused.

Most of the crooks in file were dead, incarcerated, or out of the organized crime business, and I could see the St. Louis gossip in the files about folks who might be criminals.

"Start doing search warrants," Boob said. "It's what the Captain wants."

I figured that suggestion was forthcoming. It wasn't something I desired. The stars were the search warrant crew. They didn't like me and the feeling was mutual. I knew the search-warrant drill. You lie to get one until you get informants, then with leverage, you continue to use the ill-gotten informants.

I wasn't a prude, but I resented my happiness and self-respect hinging on a lie on a search warrant affidavit. I didn't wish to do it, so I didn't. It was my personal preference as an American. I didn't wish to violate the Constitution of the United States of America.

The informant identification is secret information, a loophole in the law that benefits cops who don't mind fibbing, and then swearing to it. If a person is a professional in any endeavor, he or she has insight. In the judicial system, the pros knew at the outset that if there was a way to cheat, a cop would find and use it. So they make the cop swear that they are telling the truth. The swearing works in most instances. But desperation sometimes takes control. A defense lawyer can't make you reveal who your informant is.

But the prosecutor knows you've made him up. And the judge knows you've made him up. And the jury is almost certain you've made up an informant to get an arrest so you can get a pat on the head from your supervisor, and maybe if you meet the right politician, you might get promoted to sergeant. It is cheating; no different than an athlete taking performance enhancing, illegal substances. He can say he is doing it for the team. He's doing it for his ego.

It stunk, and I didn't want any part of it, and it was conforming, something I had trouble doing. My opinion on the affidavit lying was; it was the right of the person writing it to do what he or she wanted to do. If he or she wants to lie, then that's their business. I didn't want to. It was archaic. But in a cop's perception, I guess it all depends on what your dedication level is.

I had wandered into the stars territory. It was sacred ground within the unit offices. The lead star looked up from his research. He studied me. I figured he had been told by Boob that I was balking at being a search warrant cop. He hadn't been a made guy but he knew the system, somehow, and realized he had to be special to compete with the heritage guys. He worked like a machine.

"I can help you with an affidavit," he said. I had always respected him as a man's man. I didn't know why he was so quick to please the bosses. I figured it was still the impromptu script that he and the little star followed to the hilt. He knew he would need his buddy, the little star, to be continually promoted. Local 562 will be there forever and there will always be state representatives from that labor local. But I felt certain that he liked me in his blind dedication manner and that he felt he would help me, nurture me to the ways of cop stardom.

"I know how to do it," I said. "I just don't wish to swear to God that everything's true when in fact it's a bald-faced lie. How do you do it?"

"I don't believe in God, Detective. You see, I know the difference between the good guys and the bad guys."

My dream of becoming a brother in the unit of organized criminal destroyers was waning. I was mentally drifting toward the outside, something I had always done when absolute conformation is required. I stared and said to myself, “So much for God, family and career. Career is all that matters to these guys.”

I laughed like it was a joke, but we read each other loud and clear. He had a nickel-plated Colt-thirty-eight he would play with, fully loaded, bringing the hammer back and releasing it at the same time. I watched his nicotine stained fingers on the revolver, clicking, re-cocking and releasing as he had it pointed at my gut. I knew I had disgusted him.

His buddy, the little star, strolled in and stood beside me. He had been eavesdropping at the door to the office. “Somebody mention God?” He asked with a laugh. I didn’t respond. My nemesis continued to click his cocked, loaded Colt at my gut. His buddy stared at me, “You know who God is, Detective?”

It was a stupid question so I didn’t answer him. “God is the guy on the fifth floor with the corner office. He’s got eagles on his collar and he answers to the name of Chief.” He laughed like it was a joke and slapped his knee, but I knew where he was coming from. I was either in with him, and the lead star, or I was an outsider who couldn’t be trusted. As usual, I took the outsider role.

I figured I would probably have to go down fighting, but I realized something about myself. I had character and I wasn’t going to allow the carrot of politics to be dangled in my face so I could sell myself down the river for a damned promotion.

The lead star and the little star were desperate and unconscionable and capable of killing if a promotion was the reward. The lead star would have killed me if his union buddy told him to. Why? Because I didn’t conform to their idea of law enforcement. I was my own man now and the worst that could happen to me was to be put back in a district, a punishment for being honest and a non-follower.

5

I recognized my opportunity in the unit. I could make a difference. I was on my own, and I felt lucky for being so. I was going to work organized criminals, and hopefully lock some of them up. In my mind I wasn't a follower and I was proud of it.

I focused on one particular criminal, Jesse Stoneking, a henchman for Art Berne, the organized criminal who took the place of now deceased Buster Wortman on the east side. Stoneking was a true gangster, a killer who wouldn't back down. I read about his criminal past, in news clippings and memorandums. The guy had two complete families; wives, kids, dogs, houses and cars.

He had killed two other gangsters in a gun battle at the Kracker Box Tavern, on the Eastside, taking a bullet himself. Jesse was about my age, and I wondered how his childhood was, compared to mine. I wondered if he had a heavy handed dad. The only information about his parents was that his dad was a taxicab driver in St. Louis and the family had moved to the Eastside when he was nine.

The irony continued. We had flip-flopped. I grew up on the Eastside and moved to St. Louis. But I wasn't a crook or a killer, and I wasn't a gun guy. Jesse was. I read about the shooting at the Kracker Box Tavern: Jesse was at the bar when an associate entered, walked to him and told him that Jesse James Hollen and Wayne Harris were coming in to kill him. They walked into the tavern shortly thereafter.

But there was more to it than that. I read further. Jesse had been sent to the tavern by a St. Louis hoodlum to service some vending machines for him. It was a setup. Somebody on this side of the river wanted Jesse dead. Jesse Stoneking was Art Berne's hired warrior, proficient in the art of killing, and having him on the payroll gave Art Berne extra clout in the organized crime business. I wondered where the setup information came from. It had to be a hoodlum snitch, but which one?

Jesse testified at his trial that Jesse James Hollen made an insulting comment to him and went for his gun. Jesse Stoneking was quicker and he went for his. He took a slug in the chest, but managed to kill both men. The dead guys were small-time hoodlums. Stoneking was a big-time killer. The jury convicted Jesse of murder, but the sentence was eventually overturned and he was freed.

I learned that Joey (Doves) Aiuppa from the organized crime family they called The Outfit in Chicago ran everything on the Eastside, and some of the operations in St. Louis and St. Louis County.

The Chicago mob had control of Pipefitters Local 562, and Art Berne did whatever Joey Aiuppa told him to do. Berne was on the payroll of Local 562, and Jesse Stoneking, his second in command, would drive him to their compound in Spanish Lake to collect his weekly check.

I lived in Spanish Lake, and I was planning on setting up surveillance on the compound just to get a chance to see Art Berne and Jesse Stoneking. Boob couldn't get me for that. My plan was to follow them when they left the compound and to do a car stop on them when they slid into the St. Louis City limits. Jesse, the killer, would have a gun on him. I would get a chance to arrest both of them, even though it wouldn't stick in court, at least I could arrest them.

I learned about the three major crime families in and around St. Louis. The most dangerous seemed to be the Syrian faction headed by John Paul Leisure and his brother Anthony Leisure. Paul Leisure had been a hit man for the Italian faction on this side of the river, headed by Anthony Giordano and John Vitale.

Folklore had it that he had murdered over twenty people for Giordano and Vitale. Giordano and Vitale were some of the organized crime leaders in the United States who had a small stake in the Aladdin Hotel and Casino in Las Vegas, built by Teamster pension cash, and operated by Peter Webbe, a St. Louis politician (chief deputy St. Louis license collector), and brother of power broker, and attorney Sorkis Webbe Sr.

The Feds went after Sorkis Webbe Sr. They said he was tied to Vitale, Giordano and Paul Leisure, an underworld enforcer. He told the Feds that as a lawyer, he was occasionally in the presence of underworld figures.

He was targeted by an Organized Crime Task Force in St. Louis, and he had heat in Las Vegas. It was disclosed that couriers brought huge sums of money, millions of dollars, back to St. Louis, and that some of the money was given to Mafia co-leader, John Vitale.

The organized crime bosses in New York and Los Angeles held the brunt of the skimming rights to most of the casinos in Las Vegas, but Giordano and Vitale held onto a small share. If there was a problem with someone, the out-of-state gangster would contact Tony Giordano or John Vitale and one of them would dispatch Paul Leisure to eliminate the guy.

I did some surveillance on Paul Leisure and his brother Anthony. Paul was like a Neanderthal man, and he carried the same kind of look on his face; painful, annoyed, hungry and not to be tread upon. I had never seen a scarier guy. He was broad and thick with rippling muscles and a neck like a tree trunk. I got the feeling that I couldn't take him.

But I didn't feel that way about Anthony. He looked almost normal, tall and proportioned and a good dresser. He had a full head of hair, neatly trimmed and always in place, and he carried himself well. They had a cousin, David Leisure who was a doper, semi-retarded, fat and out of shape, and a stone cold killer of anyone, without remorse.

I followed him around some of the time hoping I could get to see him murdering someone, but it didn't happen. Mostly, he scored drugs and shot up in his pickup truck.

Anthony was the slickest. I tried to follow him once and I thought I got made. Of course my four-door Chevy with the black wall tires and the antenna on the trunk didn't help matters. But I backed off and eventually got on him again.

He drove a Caddy, a four-door with all of the trimmings. He was a pimp at heart. Anthony was an assistant business manager of Laborers Local 110, a position gotten for him through Anthony Giordano by Jimmy Michaels, the alleged leader of the Syrian faction in St. Louis. Like every pimp, Anthony had lots of women and he knew lots of people. He frequented bars on the south side when he wasn't working with his brother, Paul, at their tow lot on Chouteau.

I followed him to a south side bar, parked and walked in right after he did. The place was packed with working class guys and girls, and he went to the bar, stood and ordered a mixed drink. People were shouting his name, patting him on the back and acting like they liked him.

But that's always the case when a gangster goes into a bar. I had seen the same treatment when I was a kid when Buster Wortman's thugs walked into bars my old man and I were frequenting. It wasn't sincere. Working class folks live in constant fear of organized authority. They react to the fear with fake friendship. It's the way life has always been. The schoolyard bully is the leader, even off of the schoolyard.

I sat at the end of the bar and ordered a beer, watched and listened to the conversations around me. A guy was talking to a young lady, not too bad looking if you could get by the tattoos and the hair, but she looked clean, and she had a hard body.

The lady, who I guessed at about twenty-five, was telling the guy that Anthony's girlfriend was a switch hitter, and that she had plans on taking Anthony away from her. She sauntered up to Anthony, rubbed on him like a nymphomaniac in heat, and they started a conversation. He bought her a drink and things looked like they were going her way.

Without provocation, Anthony spit in her face with a mouth full of booze. The talking stopped and the bar patrons stared, but no one intervened. The tattooed lady was on her own. She stared at him, but she didn't overreact. She was apparently intelligent. She backed away and walked out of the bar wiping her face with a napkin.

The party atmosphere began again, as if nothing had happened. But everyone knew that this gal had gotten off easy. The pimp, home invader, murderer had spared her life for saying something to him that had infuriated him. If they had been in a car, Anthony would have probably killed her. It's what pimp gangsters do to wayward women.

I stayed on Anthony for the evening, hoping he would meet up with Ray Flynn, Labor Local 42 organizer, and they would do a home invasion. It was their specialty, and they were adept at it, but it never happened. He kept going to neighborhood bars, and I couldn't follow him into every bar he went into. Somewhere down the line he would figure me out, and he might even challenge me.

But that could have possibly been a good thing for me. I didn't like him and I wanted to beat him to a pulp. But, just like I wanted to beat the cop pukes in the intelligence unit offices, I could win the battle, but they would win the war. I would probably get fired for it, and Anthony and his brother and his cousins would laugh about it when they murdered some poor slob during a home invasion.

Local 42, the other labor local in the region, handled all of the work north of Chouteau. Tommy Harvill, an Art Berne guy, which meant the Chicago Outfit ran it too, was the head of the local.

Tony Giordano's nephew, Matthew "Mike" Trupiano was an officer in Local 110. He was allegedly being groomed to be the head of the Italian crime faction in St. Louis. John Vitale was old and not well, and Tony Giordano was allegedly dying of cancer. Mike Trupiano had the reputation of being a dud. He looked the part. Tall but pudgy, a cheap dresser, his body language was that of a bus driver, not a Mafia leader.

There was no question I couldn't answer about any of them. I knew them better than I knew my relatives in the Eastside. Paul Leisure hated Jimmy Michaels (the reputed head of the Syrian faction) and he would eventually murder him. Jimmy Michaels was preparing to have his grandson, Jimmy Michaels III, appointed to a business agent position within Local 110. Paul Leisure wanted his brother, Anthony Leisure to have the job. Apparently it was a job worth killing for.

I had been investigating organized criminals and Boob didn't know it. I felt good about it. I had read in a Guido memorandum to Captain Bud that Paul Leisure wanted to take over leadership of Laborers Locals 42 and 110. Geographically, Local 110 had labor jurisdiction on anything south of Chouteau Avenue.

Although most of these murdering mobsters hated each other, they got along well enough for all of them to make a decent living off of the union corruption provided to them by Aiuppa in Chicago, and Jimmy Michaels, John Vitale and Anthony Giordano in St. Louis.

They also got rich off of home invasions, burglaries, and murder for hire. St. Louis was a cesspool of organized crime, just like East St. Louis was when I lived there.

Guido introduced me to an FBI Agent named Sam Thompson. He was an expert on all of the organized criminals and he recognized my curiosity. He schooled me, along with Guido and Stretch, on the who's who of the underworld. I had read enough to understand what they were talking about.

There were some real talented and ambitious criminals here, but there were some real talented and ambitious cops and federal agents, also. I mentally compared some of the crooks to the cops and agents. They were close in character and ambition. It helped to be unconscionable on the cop and agent side. The criminals were like predatory animals.

I had to organize my attack plans on organized criminals. I made myself a cheat sheet and studied it. John Vitale and Anthony Giordano: heads of the Italian faction. They take orders from Joey Aiuppa in Chicago. Union corruption, casino skimming, and murder, burglaries and home invasions.

Jimmy Michaels: alleged head of the Syrian faction. Union corruption, burglaries and home invasions, murder for hire. Paul Leisure and his group are loosely followers of him. Not controlled by Chicago.

Eastside faction, controlled by Joey (Doves) Aiuppa in Chicago. Art Berne's group, Jesse Stoneking second in command. Murder, topless nightclubs, prostitution dope dealing, burglaries and home invasions, and the pearl of the region, Pipefitters Local 562 in St. Louis.

I thought I had it all down, but there were so many freelancers involved, coming from and going to St. Louis from all over the country, it was mind-boggling. I kept asking myself, why St. Louis? Why this mediocre City with these super crooks and super cops? It was an unusual phenomenon.

I asked FBI Agent Thompson over beers. "It's the unions," he replied. "Especially unions like 562, the Pipefitters, and local five-thirteen, the Hoisting Engineers; wealthy and headed by Chicago organized crime."

"But," I continued, "How did that come about?"

"The Poplar Street Bridge project in the mid-fifties," he replied. "When the federal government provided the funding for the bridge, the Chicago mob sent their crooked trade bosses to East St. Louis. Under the tutelage of Buster Wortman the trade unions' membership grew rapidly, but it was with gangsters, not tradesmen. Maybe one out of ten union members was an actual tradesman. They did the work, and most of the organized criminals just collected a paycheck without even showing up. As the bridge span came together, and the Illinois side and Missouri side started working together on it, the thugs from Chicago terrorized the local union leaders on the Missouri side and eventually took control of the trades."

"You mean they got elected as organizers and union representatives?"

"Yeah, the rank and file tradesman elected them, probably by being paid off."

"So it stuck?"

"Yeah, it stuck."

"What about the Teamsters?"

"Most of the locals are corrupt," he replied. "There's a made Mafia guy at Teamsters Local 682. Everybody knows it." Without fanfare he jotted the name on a piece of paper and handed it to me. "He's an officer at that local. He does nothing, but collects a fat check and drives a union Caddy."

I devised a plan about Teamsters Local 682, and the next morning I went to work and roamed into the electronics room looking for a wire to install on myself. I knew I couldn't trust the unit technician, he would snitch on me to Boob in a heartbeat. So I grabbed a small microphone to hook to my Pearl recorder and a tape, and walked out.

I drove to 300 South Grand, Teamsters Headquarters for the St. Louis area, parked my detective Chevy and walked into the complex. It was big and modern with an elevator to the second floor. I checked the directory and found his name: Local 682, business agent.

I took the elevator up and it opened right into the 682 offices. There was a classy looking blonde receptionist, who I was compelled to flirt with. She flirted back so I handed her my business card and told he who I wanted to see. She picked up the house phone and said, "A police detective to see you, sir." She hung up and said, "Go through those doors, first door on your left, sir." She held onto my business card.

I walked toward the office and activated the tape recorder right before I walked in. He (Nino Parrino) was sitting at a spacious cleared desk with a spectacular view of the Daniel Boone Parkway, the Arch, the Poplar Street Bridge, and an industrial area south of the Daniel Boone. I was taken aback by the view, but I focused my attention toward him.

He didn't stand, but sat back in his chair and played the gangster role. He sneered at me and checked me out from head to toe. I sneered back at him and checked him out, what I could see of him. He wasn't in shape. I noted that, and he was probably in his late forties. He was dressed casual, not business attire, and he wore an expensive wristwatch, maybe a Rolex, and sported large-karat diamond rings on each pinky.

I figured he had been watching too many Mafia movies and as much as he wanted to be scary, he wasn't. I figured he'd had guys killed in the past, and I knew for a fact that he had guys working for him, Teamster folks, who would kill me in a second if he gave the command, but I had lived with that my entire life and I wasn't frightened by him. Paul Leisure I would be afraid of, but not this out of shape guy.

There was a contrast in their thug philosophy. If this Teamster official wished to do me harm, he would have a meeting with the other made guys and they would discuss it. It would be civilized. If I waltzed into Paul Leisure's office and questioned him about being a gangster, he would leap across the desk and tear my throat out. It was blood lust with him.

I slid my business card onto his desk and sat down without being asked to. I crossed my legs and my left foot was partially resting on his spacious oak desk. He stared at my foot and then at me as if to say, "Get your damn foot off of my desk, cop," but he backed off when I smiled at him and kept my foot in place.

He had been around enough to know that I wasn't there for a friendly conversation so he read my card, tossed it on his desk and asked the typical gangster question; "What do you want from me?"

"I thought I'd pay you a courtesy call," I said in my most serious East St. Louis thug demeanor. I figured he was playing the thug game so I should play it back. "I hear you're a made guy, a Mafiosi. How could a Mafia guy like you hold such an office in the International Teamsters Union?"

It was as if I tossed dirty motor oil on him. His face turned different colors, then settled on bright red. "Who told you that? Where'd you hear that?"

"I read it in the St. Louis Globe-Democrat. How do you get by having this powerful job and being a Mafiosi at the same time? Who do you have in your pocket?"

"I ain't saying nothing to you," he said in a high-pitched tone. "Go see Bobby Sansone," he shouted as he pointed to an office off the hallway outside of his office. He was trying to restrain, himself. He turned his back to me and stared at the view. I stood and walked out. The classy blonde receptionist was staring at me like I had committed a crime against nature, and I wondered how she knew what our conversation was.

A man came out of an office, stood with his hands on his hips and stared at me as I walked toward the receptionist. It was Bobby Sansone, the president of the local. I figured there was a listening device in there and when the cops came calling, people listened to the conversation. I didn't feel like I was in any danger, but I could have been. Paul Leisure wasn't around and he was my only concern. He would kill me and eat my flesh if he was paid to.

I walked to my car and figured I would be followed by some union thug, but I wasn't. I cranked it and pulled out of the union complex with a smile on my face. I had just started my campaign to screw with the Mafia.

Later on in my cop career, after I had left the intelligence unit, I would take a brutal beating from a Teamster union thug, which I attributed to the Teamster escapade. Lone-wolf thugs, and lone-wolf cops are out there alone, vulnerable to revenge, if we let our guard down. We tend to forget who we tread upon, but the criminals, they don't forget. They want to get even for disrespect, and sometimes they do.

I drove to the office with my tape recording. Guido and Stretch were in the office, which was rare. They were intelligent guys and being in the office with the stars and Boob wasn't a pleasant experience, especially if Captain Bud strolled in.

I had listened to the recording before I walked into the office. I didn't know what to do with it; it wasn't relative to anything, it was just a recording done by a cop fishing for information, but I got Guido and Tim to listen to it. They had a laugh about it, but that's about it.

I figured somebody called Boob on his office phone and told him what I had done, because he flew into the center office where my desk was located. Stretch was playing it over again trying to find something incriminating when Boob slid in. Boob stopped and listened as he blew cigar smoke in my face. I moved away and he continued to blow it toward me.

"What good is that, Detective?" Boob asked me.

"Probably nothing," I replied. "But at least some Teamster gangsters know there's a local cop who knows about them and doesn't like their involvement in the labor movement in St. Louis. He's a damn Mafiosi for God's sake. Who gives a damn what he thinks in this office? He's in a powerful position. What the hell does that tell you? He's scum."

"Hum," Boob said as walked out in a cloud of smoke leaving a trail behind him. I figured I had placed myself on the chopping block, but I rationalized the situation. At least I could say I once was a big City detective working organized crime in a City where organized crime is an Olympic sport.

I was going to be transferred sometime and I wanted to delay it for as long as possible, but I could go back to a district and wear a uniform again, if I had to.

The Feds eventually forced the mafia guy out of the International Teamsters Union, but they didn't harm him. An informant told me he got a job with the Pipefitters, local 562, but I couldn't substantiate the information. If he did, he probably got a pay raise, and he didn't have to show up on any job site. You have to be skilled to be a fitter. Who is the victim? The hard working fitters and teamsters doing their jobs.

6

I wasn't ashamed or afraid to ask questions about the organized criminals running rampant on the St. Louis streets. The more information I gathered about these crooks, the more I realized they were a socially accepted entity in St. Louis, and throughout America. Far more revered than the cops.

I wondered if Paul the jeweler friend of Boob's would talk to me. I walked in to his downtown store and was friendly to him. At first I didn't ask any questions. I just let it come out of him from time to time between customers. The guy was a walking computer on organized crooks. As we talked, I wondered how a guy like him could be so knowledgeable. I didn't know how or why, and I didn't ask him how he obtained his information. His brain was ripe for picking and he eventually allowed me to pick it.

I knew that burglary and home invasions were a big pastime for the St. Louis crooks, but I didn't know to what extent or how lucrative it was for them. In order for a burglary to be successful the thief had to have a place to take his ill-gotten goods. St. Louis was nirvana for jewel thieves because of the Paul Brown Building in downtown St. Louis.

The building had approximately one-hundred jewelers in it, and a large number of them were diamond fences. Boob's jeweler friend always said, "No thanks," to the many people coming into his shop trying to sell him loose stones while I was a witness, but I had a feeling he was a fence when I wasn't there.

He schooled me on the fine art of jewelry. "Diamonds, especially large diamonds are ninety percent stolen gems," he said. "They've been stolen from somewhere, maybe not in St. Louis, but they're stolen. They can't be traced. There's no way to identify a stolen diamond, so actually it doesn't matter where the stone is stolen, or to whom it belonged; nobody can prove who the real owner is. The owner is the one possessing it."

He was a high-volume gem dealer and a wealthy guy. There were brochures in his shop touting computerized, laser identification of the stones he sold, and he had a laser machine, a fancy gadget, sophisticated and expensive. "If you get your stone laser-treated then you can identify it, right?"

"Wrong," he replied. "It's a selling tool, nothing more." I gave him a look of despair. I was wondering if anything was righteous.

"I could buy a stone stolen from you last night, and you could come in here and tell me it was yours, with the police and with a laser identification, and I wouldn't have to return it to you. I wouldn't even have to divulge to the police where I got it. Possession is nine-tenths of the law, and with gems, it's one-hundred percent of the law."

"What about the setting? If the stone is still in the setting can that help identify it?"

"Yes. Most folks who own fine diamonds have them in a setting for that reason, not to mention showing them off at cocktail parties. The jewelry is photographed in the setting for insurance purposes. But good burglars remove the stones from the settings almost immediately, sometimes while they're in the getaway car."

"What do they do with the settings? They're expensive, right?"

"They hit them with a hammer and sell the metal for scrap gold, or platinum or silver. All of this stuff is fenced at the Paul Brown Building. Every big-time burglar in this country has come through the Paul Brown Building at one time or another. It's a monthly event. They market their goods there. And by big-time burglars I mean a million or more per heist."

"Million dollar burglaries?"

"Yeah," he replied with a smile. "Home invasions and burglaries. It's what organized St. Louis criminals do for a hobby. It happens all over this country. You want to see some organized crime folks, just start driving around the Paul Brown Building. All of those so called Mafia types and those tough-guy Eastside folks working for Art Berne, they're burglars in their spare time. It makes them rich."

"And there are fences for all of these stones?"

"The economy's bad right now. There's high interest, high inflation, gold is making a strong comeback and there's nowhere for folks with cash to put their money for investments. The stock market stinks. The people with moxie and cash buy stolen diamonds. They can sit on them for a month and double their money, especially with large stones. It doesn't make them criminals, they're just exercising their God given right, making a living in America. Everybody's supposed to be rich here. It's one of the avenues to wealth, or in most cases, more wealth."

I waited and listened while my friend spoke. He was the consummate salesman and he liked talking about what he was an expert in.

"You like cars, right, sports cars?"

"Yeah," I replied. I wondered how he knew that fact about me.

"Let's say hypothetically that you stole a new Corvette, maybe it was worth fifty-thousand dollars. What would you do with it?"

"I don't know."

"Would you drive it?"

"Maybe, part of the time, but I would probably have to hide it. There's vehicle identification numbers all over it, most of them hidden, and the owner would probably know the car if he saw me driving it."

"Exactly, but if you were in possession of a stolen diamond, which would probably be worth five times what a Corvette's worth, you could stick it in your pocket and walk around St. Louis trying to sell it. You could take your time and meander the halls of the Paul Brown Building, chat with some of your jeweler friends, gain insight on who was wearing what stones at what gathering, find out who your next victim would be, and maybe already have the next stolen stone sold before you steal it."

"I see," I replied.

"And, if the police for some reason would stop and frisk you and find the stone, there's no way they can implicate you in any robbery or burglary, unless of course you are identified while you snatch the stone, or you leave incriminating evidence at the scene. It's the perfect crime; lucrative, clean and precise."

I watched him. He was a rare find, a wealthy Jewish jeweler who liked cops, and who liked me, but not as much as he liked Boob. In his mind he and Boob were fellow warriors tracking the synagogue sniper. Actually they were playing each other, waiting to see where the next turn in the road would lead them.

He had given me a PHD in diamonds in the fifteen minutes I had been with him. He was reading me. It was part of his shtick, being able to read the person standing in front of his display case. But I didn't care, I wanted him to know and trust me.

The Intelligence Unit job was intriguing to me. I could be stopping cars and pulling guns off of the street in north St. Louis, guarding United States Congressmen and presidents, or future presidents, and chatting with a millionaire jeweler who educated me in the fine art of diamond fencing, all in the same week.

I watched him, in awe of his knowledge. He had the look of the modern-day entrepreneur: Polo jersey, Polo khaki slacks and Italian shoes. He was tanned from going to Florida whenever he felt the need, and he drove a big Mercedes. His hair was slick and combed back but he wasn't in shape; his only mistake in life. He wasn't a physical guy and I figured someday that might come to haunt him.

Intimidation is a major factor in dealing with scum. They all have the schoolyard bully syndrome to rely on. They have to, or they wouldn't be thieves, killers and gangsters. Maybe that's why he liked cops and agents. He felt he could call one of us and we would come to his rescue. I would have.

"You see, Detective, there's a "stone fetish" going on in this country at this time. Legitimate business people are going to bed with the dregs of society to get their hands on those diamonds, and the bigger the stone the better. Everybody wants the biggest stone, just like the biggest yacht, or the biggest house, or the broad with the biggest tits. It's all about perception, and people with cash are able to get what they want."

"So, the Mafia faction here on this side of the river and the Chicago organized group on the Eastside, headed by Art Berne, are freelance burglars?"

"Yeah."

"What about the Syrian faction on this side of the river?"

"Murderers, mostly, but they'd knock over somebody for jewelry if they had a chance. You've got to have information on who to knock off, and you've got to do surveillance and plan for the event. I can't see Paul Leisure planning for a burglary. He'd plan for a murder. But his brother Anthony, he would probably plan for either. He's a big-time home invader with his friend, Ray Flynn. Anthony's smarter than Paul, but not as treacherous. If either of them came into my shop I'd call the police. I don't like them. You know they're wired in with City politics, don't you?"

"I had heard," I replied. "Cousins, right?"

"The Syrians are all cousins. They're big-time clannish and they're as cold as ice. I wouldn't cross them."

I must have had a look of despair and as usual my friend picked up on it. "Why are you in the cop business?"

I didn't want to tell him my background so I shrugged and said, "Interesting way to make a living."

"You can work for me if you want." He had tossed the carrot out there and was waiting to see my response.

"I don't know," I replied, as I looked around the shop. I couldn't see myself standing in such close quarters waiting for someone to come in so I could talk to them. I wanted to go to people and talk to them. I had grown to love the interview, and I was good at it. I could ask pertinent questions without turning off the person I was interviewing. The more I did it the better I got at it. But I was well cribbed before I ever entered their domain.

I couldn't figure why my friend asked me the question, unless he wanted to get me off-guard for some reason. "Are you wanting to expand?" I asked.

"I could use another shop in this vicinity," he said. But I could tell he had read my thought process and knew I wasn't going to bite.

"Why me?"

"Because I know you're honest," he replied.

It was his thing, he could read whomever came through his door and he had read me accurately. I was flattered but I wasn't anxious about his offer. I wasn't going to leave the intelligence unit on my own. I loved it and I couldn't think of anything I would rather be doing at this point in my life. "No thanks," I calmly said. He smiled and rushed to a customer who had just walked in. I quietly walked out and trudged to the detective Chevy, fired it and headed north.

I had been driving around in north St. Louis looking for gun carriers. You can spot them as you drive by them. They see the cop detective car and divert their eyes away from you. It means they've got something to hide. I would make a tight turnaround and head after them, toss the red light on the dashboard and pull them over.

It was sort of like something out of a Mississippi State Highway Patrol training film. I would saunter up to their drivers' side window, tap on it, motion for them to roll it down, and say, "Step out."

They always complied without much fanfare because they thought they could trick me into thinking they're just good, law-abiding folks on their way to work. I would only ask one question; "Are you strapped today?"

I could tell if they were telling me the truth in one second. The eyes, they would divert them again. "Turn around and put your hands on the roof of the car," I would command them. I would cuff them behind their backs and then pat them down for their piece. It was hardly ever on their person, but usually in the seat beside them, or in the center console or the glove box. Sometimes they would toss it under the seat when they observed me turning around. It was a felony then. It isn't a crime now.

But I would have a felony arrest for the week and then I could screw with the union folks, after I had lunch. I had cultivated a friend at the Missouri Athletic Club and I ate lunch there most days, gratis. It was great food; rich folks' food, and it was another perk to being a big-time intelligence unit dick in the mediocre City of St. Louis.

It was a great weather day, low eighties, sunny with a light breeze. I had taken my plain Jane Chevy to the police garage and talked the supervisor there into putting whitewall tires on it and placing a white pinstripe all the way down the sides.

I knew a junk dealer on the north side who had piles of spoke hubcaps that had been taken off of totaled cars. I asked him to sell me four, and he gave me four Oldsmobile spoke hubs. Instead of the little two-way radio antenna, I had a citizens-band type antenna installed in the middle of the trunk lid, just like all of the cool guys had in the day. I was styling in my freebie Chevy, and the brothers on the north side knew who I was. The Teamsters knew of me too.

I was on Lindell near Forest Park studying the drivers' eyes of the oncoming cars and was about to stop a blue Caddy when Guido got on the police radio and asked me to switch to the private channel. It was rare for him or Stretch to contact me. It wasn't that they didn't like me, it was just that I wasn't an "in" guy and they didn't want to be a part of my dilemma in the unit. If I couldn't conform, it was my business, not theirs.

"Meet us at Lemay Ferry Road," he said, giving me a specific location on the street.

"Clear," I replied. That was a long way off and I sped through traffic to get there. I knew it had to be something important for them to contact me, the outsider.

They were on a medical building parking lot in their cop funny-car Mercury Montego. I parked my obvious cop detective car several slots away, walked to them and slid into the backseat when Stretch opened the door for me, and scrunched up so I could fit through the opening.

"We were checking the airport," Guido began. "We didn't see anyone of interest there so we were heading to the Hill area hoping to find Mike Trupiano. As we were leaving we observed Mike Trupiano on the outer road heading toward the airport in his black Oldsmobile Local 110 car. We turned around, parked and went into the terminal. He picked up two guys, slick guys, Mafia types. He took them to John Vitale's house, near here. See that subdivision?"

"Yeah," I replied.

"They're in there and that exit is the only one. Stretch and me parked a block away and snooped up to John Vitale's backyard. They're all having a big pow-wow on John's patio. Hank Slay's with them. You know who he is?"

"No, not really."

"Syrian truck company owner. He's a hang-out guy with the big time Mafia types. Close friends with John Vitale, politically connected."

"Okay."

"Everybody's seated but Trupiano. He's acting as if he's a servant, getting them drinks and standing around like a barmaid. We'd like to know who these guys are but we can't stop them in this car. We don't want to burn the car, or ourselves. You want to stop them for us?"

"Yeah," I instantly said.

"Okay, set up over on that side of Lemay Ferry and when they come out we'll contact you. We'll be in the subdivision with surveillance on Trupiano's union Oldsmobile. We want them identified, that's all. Okay? You don't have to arrest anybody, unless you see fit to do so. Any questions?"

I thought for a second. "There's four gangsters in that car, most of them probably made guys. If I get into a jam will you guys be close by?"

"Yeah, we'll have you and them under surveillance. We'll come to your assist if you need it."

"Okay." I slid out and walked to my car, entered it and cranked it, then waited for Guido and Stretch to get out of sight in the funny car. I slid across Lemay Ferry and parked on the shoulder about a half-block away from the intersection.

I was only there for about two minutes when Stretch got on the air. "They're leaving the house now, coming your way."

"Clear," I replied.

The gangster filled Oldsmobile came out of the subdivision and turned back toward the City, toward the Hill area. Guido and Stretch kept it under surveillance and I laid back so I wouldn't be seen and blow the operation.

They toured the Hill area and then Trupiano went north onto Kingshighway, cut over Delmar and continued north. "They're probably heading back to the airport Stretch said.

"Clear," I replied.

They wormed the Oldsmobile through the ghetto and were on Goodfellow Boulevard, an industrial area, four busy lanes of traffic, high curbs, and a typical mean St. Louis street. They continued going toward Interstate 70. "I'm going to stop them before they get to the interstate," I advised Guido and Stretch.

"Clear," Stretch replied.

They backed off and I came up on the Oldsmobile at about seventy-five with my dash light revolving. I got right on the Oldsmobile bumper and sounded my horn. Mike Trupiano was looking at me through the rear view mirror. I yelled, mostly for my own benefit, "Pull over," and motioned with my hand and arm.

He pulled to the curb in front of the federal Small Arms Plant. I pulled my Mississippi State Highway Patrol routine, sauntering to the window. I was dressed in Levis and a Polo shirt, and I was in fairly good shape, although the free lunches at the Missouri Athletic Club had put some pounds on me. I knew I was in better shape than any of the gangsters in the car.

Trupiano rolled the window down and sneered at me, just like the

Teamster gangster had done. He was trying to be scary but he couldn't pull it off. "Who you got in the car with you, Mike?" I said in thug fashion.

"They're friends of mine," he snarled at me.

"I need to know their names," I thug-talked back at him.

"I don't know their names," he snarled and stared.

I could see this was going nowhere fast. I walked to rear of the Oldsmobile and pounded on the side of it with my fist, shouting, "Okay, everybody out," as I went to the curb and waited.

Nobody moved. I opened the rear door and looked into the backseat. Two big guys with expensive suits sat there sneering at me. Hank Slay was in the front seat.

"Get out," I shouted at the big guy nearest to me. He got out. He was a big Italian looking guy, taller than me and heavier. He was going to try and intimidate me but he changed his mind after he read me. I was ready to fight. I figured I was short-lived in the intelligence unit and that Guido and Stretch were close by to assist me, but I was in no position to look around for them.

My eyes were glued to the Italian gangster standing in front of me (later identified as Dominic Montemarano from Brooklyn.) I was going to nail him with a straight left hand if he got aggressive with me. What better way to leave the unit. I would be going down fighting, and I would win the battle. I just wouldn't win the war.

"I'm a police detective in the City of St. Louis," I began. "You're in the City of St. Louis and I want to know who you are. Give me some identification."

It was a standoff. He studied me some more and then smiled as he opened his suit coat as to show me he had nothing to hide. "I don't have any identification," he said. His suit probably cost a thousand dollars, but I figured he got it as a gift for murdering somebody, or he intimidated a tailor into making it for him. It was dark wool with a red silk lining. His airline ticket was in the inside pocket.

I didn't want to search him because I didn't want to get that close to him. He was big enough that he could tag me with a right or left and leave me rolling around on the sidewalk. The guy could have been a character actor in Hollywood. His features were photogenic, but he had murdering eyes and he couldn't hide that. But that would be a good thing in Hollywood.

His black hair was combed straight back and the guy was in shape. He wasn't sporting a gut like most guys in their mid to late thirties. He continued to smile at me, knowing I wasn't going to search him by myself, not with three other gangsters in the car wanting to stomp me to death and drive off to the airport.

Mike Trupiano sat frozen at the wheel of the Oldsmobile. I could tell he was humiliated. These guys were his heroes. They were big-time Mafia, not dirt-mob St. Louis gangsters. But Mike Trupiano was being tricked by his Mafia friends. They are all dirt, street gangsters. New York to Miami.

They are just street criminals first, then when they get a big enough reputation, and when enough lowlifes believe the propaganda about them, they become stars. Unless they're born into the life.

I grabbed at his airline ticket and backed away from him. "Stand in front of the car," I ordered him. He turned and looked at the older, fatter guy in the backseat, who was obviously gangster royalty, put his hands palms up, scrunched his shoulders and made a face as if to say, "There's nothing I can do, this cop's crazy."

I jotted his name down (Dominic Montemarano) walked to the front of the car and handed him his airline ticket, then walked back to the Oldsmobile backseat. I started to play the same game with the older fatter guy, but he didn't give me a chance. He handed me his drivers' license and sneered at me like I was an irritating insect who should be exterminated. I jotted down his name and address and date of birth (Salvatore Profaci) then handed the license back to him.

I knew who Hank Slay was and I knew who Mike Trupiano was, so my job was finished. I walked back to my car, but I didn't turn my back on them. I was in no position to search the car for a gun, but there was probably one in it. They all sneered at me as I climbed into my little Chevy and drove off.

I had another good feeling, but I would get no credit for my bravado. Guido and Stretch would get the glory, but they needed it for promotion, not to mention their position on the pecking order list. I was on the bottom, they were somewhere toward the top, but under the stars.

But I didn't care. I wasn't even in the running for pecking-order stature as far as I was concerned. I was the loner from East St. Louis. All I wanted to do was to investigate organized criminals. The pecking order was an invisible list made by participants' peers. I had no peers in Intel 210. I was on my own.

Stretch got on the radio, "Meet us at headquarters."

"Clear," I replied. I took my time driving downtown. My day was over and I was going home to my wife and kids, barbecue and slam some beers. I was relaxed. I pulled onto the lot and waited for Guido and Stretch.

They were there in two minutes, parked and motioned for me to come with them. I figured they would want to peruse the names before we went up to the office, but they asked me who they were as we walked. I tore off the piece of paper from my note pad and handed it to Guido.

Guido was the guy who knew all of the Italian Mafia folks. He knew most of the names of every big Mafia type in every City in the United States. "I've seen the names," he said.

We walked into the office. Guido and Stretch went to their desks and I went to mine. Guido was on the phone with a friend of his with the FBI, but it wasn't Sam Thompson. We kibitzed for a while and I went through the car stop and my conversation with the big-wig crooks. We all had a good laugh about it, but I knew it was big time dangerous, but if that's what I have to do to get by, then so be it.

My desk phone rang. It was the unit secretary. "Boob wants to see you," she quietly said.

I wandered into Boob's office. He was smoking a cigar and leaning back in his chair. He had a file with him, one of the secret files he kept in a file cabinet in his office. I looked at the name on the file and read it upside down. It was John Vitale's file.

There was another guy with him, but Boob didn't introduce him to me. "Who were those Mafia types you made the car-check on this afternoon?" Boob asked. He glanced at the John Vitale file, then stood and slid it back into the file drawer behind his desk while he waited for my response.

"I've got their names written down, Lieutenant," I said. "Oh, I gave their names to Guido, I'll go and get the page from my note pad. I walked back to my desk and Guido and Stretch were gone. The names of the gangsters were on my desk. I grabbed the page and returned to Boob's office. I handed the torn out page to him. He glanced at it and handed it to the stranger.

The silent guest reached into his briefcase and handed me some pictures. "Pick the guys out that you stopped," he said.

The pictures didn't have names on them. It was a lineup with pictures.

"This one, and this one," I said. The guy didn't say anything else, just nodded, turned and walked out of the office. "Who was that guy?"

"Federal agent," Boob replied.

"Unfriendly fellow," I muttered.

"You stop these guys by yourself?"

"Yeah, but I had Guido and Stretch as backup. They had them under surveillance and asked me to stop and identify them. They didn't want to burn their car, or themselves. Mike Trupiano was the driver. Hank Slay was riding in the front seat. They had gone to John Vitale's house for a meeting."

"The one guy is the Capo of the Colombo crime family in New Jersey. He's a big shot, his daddy was a big shot gangster. He inherited his power," Boob told me.

"I figured he was high up in the Mafia," I replied.

"The other guy is a made guy, a big time killer. He's right up there with Paul Leisure as far as ruthlessness is concerned."

"You know these guys, Lieutenant?"

"Yeah, I know who they are. I've been working organized criminals out of this office for twenty-five years, Detective. All of the organized crooks come through St. Louis at one time or another. Why, I don't know."

I was impressed with his knowledge and it showed. He smiled at me and didn't blow cigar smoke my way. "You can go," he said.

Five o'clock rolled around and I strolled out of the office, took the elevator down to my little detective Chevy and headed for home. It had been a strange day, not productive but not counterproductive. So some big time Mafiosi were in St. Louis to see John Vitale. What did it prove? Nothing!

And why was the federal agent so covert with me? He could have been friendly to me. I know one thing; he was prompt in responding to the office for me to look at the gangster photos. And why didn't Sam Thompson come to our office? Guido, Stretch and I are friends with him. And if it's such a big deal for these two Mafiosi to come to St. Louis, why didn't the FBI have surveillance on them?

These Mafia jerks no doubt ride around New York City and New Jersey, and the surrounding area all hours of the day and night, and probably never get stopped by a crazed cop. They are regarded as criminal royalty.

I pondered all of the questions I posed to myself and came up with an answer. John Vitale was a federal snitch. That had to be the answer. I would sit on that thought and see where it played out.

It was past five o'clock and I wondered if the office would be empty. The stars had a search warrant to do, and Captain Bud wouldn't be in the office if they weren't there. He would have no one to talk to, or about.

Boob didn't hang around the office. When the clock hit five, he was out the door. I turned the little Chevy around and headed back to the office. I let myself in with my key, deactivated the alarm and went straight to Boob's office. The file cabinet was unlocked, so I fished out the folder of John Vitale. I sat at his stinking desk and read it.

John Vitale was a federal snitch, but I wondered how Boob found it out. Boob wasn't exactly a guy with a top-secret clearance. John Vitale started out by snitching to the Feds about the Leisures. He once tried to hire Jesse Stoneking to kill Paul Leisure, but for some unknown reason that plan did not come to fruition.

I continued to read. John Vitale told the Feds that Anthony Giordano was the guy who set Jesse Stoneking up at the Kracker Box Tavern on the Eastside to be killed by the two guys. They were there to kill him. Jesse killed them. They were paid assassins hired by Anthony Giordano.

So, John Vitale wasn't just snitching on the Syrian faction. He was snitching, period. Nothing is sacred.

7

The seasons in St. Louis beat you into submission. The winters are brutal; the icy wind bites into you and lets you know you're supposed to be indoors. The summer is different. The mornings are cool and you get lured into thinking the living is easy. By noon, it's ninety and by late afternoon, it's in the hundreds. By then, you're tapped out, if you aren't in air conditioning

November is the beginning of the cool weather in St. Louis. Early November mesmerizes you into thinking everything's all right. You don't need heat and you don't need air conditioning. The trees are a golden brown and folks are laid back. You relax, let your guard down and daydream. It's kind of like California but without the beaches, the mountains, and the natural disasters. I was daydreaming, acting like I was reading crime memorandums at my desk when Guido cruised by.

He stopped at my desk and I was surprised. He didn't wish to align himself with me and I understood why. I was always going to be the outsider. He was always going to be an inside guy, but with an outsider heart. It was fate, and he and I understood each other.

He looked around to see if the other inside guys were watching or listening. "T.J. Harvill died last month. You remember him don't you?" he softly muttered.

It was a game in the unit to see who could stump whom in the organized crime world of identification. The trick was to act like you know the guy, and then through casual conversation, try and pick up some clues to spark your memory. Then you try to think of some bizarre fact about the criminal that wasn't already in file. I didn't feel like playing the game on this morning.

"Who's he?" I asked.

Guido gave me a perplexed look. "He was the boss of Laborers Local 42. He's been dead for a month and the position is still open. There's going to be a war to see who gets the job."

I stared and tried to shake the November blues from my brain. "Whose side was he on? Was he an Italian faction guy or an Art Berne guy?"

"Both," Guido whispered, "but he was mostly an Art Berne guy."

"So, why a war? What's going to happen?"

"Ray Flynn wants the position."

"Ray Flynn? I don't recall him," I muttered.

Guido was beside himself. "These are names you should know by now. You been doing your reading?"

I was embarrassed. "Yeah, it's just the November blues, I'll be all right. Humor me."

"Ray Flynn's a union official for Local 42. He wants to be the president of the local."

"Oh, and which side is he on?"

"He's kind of both, Art Berne and Tony Giordano. But he's got to be close with Tony Giordano if he wants the position, and he's got to have Art Berne's Chicago ties with Aiuppa to fight for him to get the position. Tony Giordano wants his protégé and bodyguard, John Paul Spica, to run the local. There's going to be a war."

"John Paul Spica? That's another new guy for me, I don't recall him."

Guido moaned. "No wonder the bosses don't like you." I turned red and he laughed.

"Ray Flynn's a burglar, he's made a lot of money doing it and he's good at it, but he got caught once and he's a convicted felon, so he's going to have a hard time getting through the federal process of running a laborer's local."

"I remember," I muttered.

"John Paul Spica's a convicted murderer. He's going to have a problem, too. But it won't stop one of them from gaining control of the local. It's the way the process works, the American way. Money and violence talks, bullshit walks. The guy left sucking air by the time the position's filled will be the head of the local."

I hesitated for an instant. "Is Ray Flynn close with Jesse Stoneking?"

"No," Guido replied. "He's close with John Paul Leisure."

"Paulie Leisure? What's that connection?"

"They're two of a kind," he replied.

"Two murdering monsters?" I exclaimed.

"Yep!"

The unit secretary shouted toward us, "Guido, line two."

Guido picked up as I listened. "Yes, no kidding, you sure, okay all right, this should be interesting. Okay, thanks."

Guido looked pleased at the information he had just acquired. "Art Berne went to Joey (Doves) Aiuppa in Chicago, and they told Giordano they were going to put Ray Flynn in T.J. Harvill's spot in Local 42. Giordano's upset, because John Paul Spica is his choice. It's a big power play, and now he's got a lesser position in the local. Jimmy Michaels is pissed because he wasn't notified or his opinion requested. He doesn't want Flynn in control of the local. He contacted Aiuppa because he feared Flynn. Aiuppa told Flynn he'd back him in the takeover of 42 but he'd have to leave Jimmy Michaels alone because he was close to Giordano."

"Oh," I muttered.

"It boils down to this. Giordano, Vitale, Michaels, they're all getting old, and when that happens, they naturally lose some of their clout. These younger guys, Ray Flynn, Paul Leisure, John Paul Spica, they see a chance to move into the locals, and then the door is opened for them to take over the rackets. It's a natural organized criminal progression. They're going to be killing for these jobs."

"How do you get this stuff?'

"Informant," he replied. "Now I'll ask you a question." He paused as I waited. "Are you the only white guy who ever lived in East St. Louis?"

"No, there was Buster Wortman, me and my parents."

He walked away from my desk, so I went to the files and pulled the ones on Ray Flynn and John Paul Spica. It was like cramming for a test but it was interesting reading. Paul Leisure had aligned himself with Ray Flynn because he didn't want him as an enemy. Flynn offered Paul Leisure a high-paying position in Local 42 if he was loyal to him.

I got out my crib sheet, which was by now a loose-leaf binder, and began taking notes. Ray Flynn, convicted burglar, caught ransacking a home in Ladue. Organizing agent for Laborers Local 42. Local under the control of Anthony Giordano, leader of the Italian crime faction, but also under the control of the Chicago mob, The Outfit, headed by Joey (Doves) Aiuppa. Flynn desires to be the head of Laborers Local 42.

Ray Flynn was at one time, in his youth, a driver and a bodyguard for Jimmy Michaels. It was the equivalent of an ambitious young man starting in the mail room of a major corporation, gaining knowledge, meeting the right people, learning from the bottom up. In many ways, the comparisons are the same in principal; do what you have to do to get what you desire.

John Paul Spica, Anthony Giordano's driver, bodyguard and protégé, was a contract killer who at age twenty-five was charged with killing real estate agent John J. Myszak. His wife wanted him dead. The wife said she had paid Spica five thousand dollars. Myszak was shot and killed in front of his home. Spica was convicted of the murder and sentenced to life in prison. He did ten years and was released.

While in prison he befriended James Earl Ray. The House Select Committee on Assassinations investigated Spica as being the broker for the killing of Reverend Doctor Martin Luther King. No conclusion in the investigation. Spica, backed by Anthony Giordano, one of the elderly heads of organized crime in the region, desires to be the head of Laborers Local 42.

A maze of ghostly facts, and all of this killing and confusion just because thirty years ago somebody decided St. Louis needed to be connected to East St. Louis by another bridge. Couldn't some law enforcement organization see this coming? Every labor organization in the region is mob controlled. Ludicrous!

Guido walked back in. "It might be interesting for someone to get on Ray Flynn for a while. Think you can do it?"

"Maybe," I muttered. I continued to cram the information from the files. There was too much information, so I grabbed the files, stuck them under my shirt and strolled out. I jumped onto the elevator, made my way to the parking lot, and climbed into my little detective Chevy. I headed for mid-town, where the Local 42 union offices were located. They were situated in a short block between Grand Boulevard and Spring Avenue, across from the Veterans Hospital.

It was bright and cool, and I could see Ray Flynn's laborers-local

Oldsmobile parked near the door. The parking lot was surrounded by a ten-foot chain link fence, and kept locked. There were surveillance cameras watching the parking lot and the street.

I sat and watched. A security guard from the hospital came to my car and asked me why I was there. "Looking for car clouters," I advised him. The cars parked at meters were broken into at regular intervals. Window glass was strewn about the streets and sidewalks from the cloutings. The guard smiled and walked away.

The surveillance camera panned my way, as if the hospital parking lot was in range and it was watching me, so I moved to a parking spot deeper in the lot. I had binoculars, and I was watching the people coming and going from the union hall.

A large black man, probably six-foot-six, at least three-hundred pounds, walked out into the lot and stared toward my detective Chevy. He was dressed in a shiny tailored suit, probably five-hundred bucks, I figured, and he moved like a dangerous animal. I felt like I was at the zoo watching this predator move about behind the ten-foot chain link fence.

I got my binoculars on his face. He had a look like Sonny Liston, the ex-St. Louis world heavyweight champion. An intense, angry look, the kind that causes the average man to have nightmares. Sonny was a St. Louis product. Born here, raised in incarceration, he hooked up with the mob and became a professional fighter. This guy could have been his twin brother. I panned down and looked at the guy's hands. They were like Easter hams hanging out of his shiny suit sleeves.

I placed the binoculars on the seat and tore into the file on Local 42. There was a separate envelope containing pictures of all of the officers in the local. I sifted through them and came to the picture. It was Willie Washington, an on-site organizer, which meant he went to the job sites and controlled the laborers.

He was muscle for the local, plain and simple. They had picked the right guy for the job. I read about him: he started as a ditch digger, showed loyalty to T.J. Harvill, was introduced to Anthony Giordano and was used by Giordano to intimidate whomever he wished to intimidate, physically.

If Giordano wanted someone killed he called Paul Leisure. If he wanted a debt collected, or a leg broken, he called Willie Washington. He was like Sonny Liston in more than appearance; he had modeled his life after him.

Willie was still staring at my car, but he couldn't make me out, not without heavy lenses. A guy like Willie was easy to figure out. He used what God had given him to succeed in life. He used his brawn.

Being a hired gorilla to the low-life union thugs was success to him. He grew up poor, but tough. It was his college degree, being tough. I looked at his hands again. I couldn't imagine being smacked with one of those hands closed into a fist. It meant instant brain damage, unconsciousness, and maybe death.

But maybe a guy being attacked by Willie Washington could see the punch coming and dodge it. Willie wasn't in shape, just big. If a guy could dance away and let Willie wail at him, Willie might get tired and maybe let his guard down. You would have to watch him, listen to his breathing and his grunts and groans. He would be swinging with everything he had, and he was probably always successful in his fisticuffs.

But if he couldn't hit you, that experience would work on him mentally as well as physically. I doubted he had heart, and that's something a man needs if he's going to be an enforcer, either law or criminal. Willie didn't have heart. He was just a machine, a menacing, intimidating robot being used by the controlling criminal faction. He was used and abused by the union thugs. He knew it, but if the job was easy, why not do it? He may have had heart at one time, but not anymore. The thugs took his heart away, his brain, too. He only followed orders, harmed, intimidated, destroyed those who laid down with the thugs and thought they could come up without infestation.

He would never have to ask himself why he was doing it because he was so intimidating nobody ever challenged him. When somebody saw him coming they'd no doubt say to themselves, "Oh, God, Willie's coming to kill me. Maybe if I let him beat me up and break my legs he'll go away and never come back."

Nobody ever danced away from him and peppered his big face with straight punches. It's what Muhammed Ali did to Sonny Liston. What little heart Sonny had left from shooting heroin was dispatched by straight punches. It would be the same way with Willie Washington. He didn't know how to lose.

It was lunch time, and I was wondering if Ray Flynn would be leaving the office to go to The Edge for lunch. If he did, I would follow him and have lunch at the buffet while Ray dined off of the menu at the bar and ogled the barmaids.

Right on cue, Ray came out and entered his Local 42 Oldsmobile.

This was the first time I had ever seen him. I was used to guys who were perceived as tough, as being in shape, jock-type guys. Ray wasn't. He was tall, but bowed over, and he walked with a limp.

He was a big-boned guy, big hands and shoulders, but he was soft in the belly. I could see Willie Washington holding someone while Ray Flynn banged on him with those big hands. Kind of like an aged police commander trying to keep his reputation intact, putting his cigar in the ash tray when his detectives brought some scum-bag into him for his fair share of City abuse.

The old commander would bang on the guy until he couldn't raise his arms anymore, then he would kick him until he could no longer kick, and then he would order the detectives to take the guy out of his office, as he walked into his personal restroom and puked.

To define Ray Flynn as tough was a mistake. He was a dangerous man, the kind of guy who would hide in the bushes and shoot you in the head at your house, like some of the cops in the unit office. It seemed that most of the union thugs came under that description. Not tough, but dangerous.

Ray hit the electric gate opener and drove out onto North Grand Boulevard. I drove after him in the detective Chevy, staying about a half-block behind him. He led me on a tour of the inner City, the old Gaslight Square entertainment district, the area around St. Louis University, and the Central West End, but Ray didn't stop for lunch, he continued to drive.

I kept checking my rear view mirror; paranoia runs deep. Willie Washington was behind me in his Local 42 Oldsmobile four-door. He had gotten right on my bumper and was staring at the back of my head and my eyes when I looked into the mirror. He didn't want to hide the fact that he was tailing me while I tailed Ray Flynn. The overt act angered me.

Willie, the predator, was too close for comfort. I had been set up. He had gone into Ray Flynn and told him somebody had the union hall under surveillance, and they had hatched this scheme to find out who I was.

They would have to know I was the heat. My detective car verified that fact. I couldn't figure out why they even cared if I followed them. I was a cop detective, they were crooks. What's the big deal? But they did care, and there had to be a reason. The surveillance was over, for now. I pulled to the side of the street and watched as Willie Washington came to my car window and stopped. He gave me a long and intimidating look, but I wasn't intimidated. I was the good guy, he was the bad guy.

But, discretion overcomes valor. I looked back at him and nodded, as if to say, "Okay, Willie, you got me this time, but I'll get you next time." It was all a game for Willie and Ray Flynn. They thought they had won it, but they hadn't.

In actuality they had played their hand and showed their hole card. They didn't wish to be followed, and there was a reason for that. But one thing for sure. I would never forget Willie Washington, and he would never forget me.

This day was all but shot. I drove around for a while, had my free lunch, and made social calls to possible informants. It was time for me to make an appearance at the office, so I drove to headquarters, parked the detective Chevy, took the elevator to the fourth floor, walked in, and plopped at my desk.

It was nearing five o'clock. Captain Bud strolled in, gave me a dirty look and went back to the big office. He would sit and talk to the stars, and anybody else who would listen, about the unit, the detectives who were the good guys, and who he was going to transfer for not conforming. That was me.

He had made some snide remarks to me that I should stay after hours and kibitz with them, that it was a career builder, but I knew what it was. It was a snitch festival. He would bring up a name and the guys in attendance would character assassinate the guy who wasn't in attendance.

But I had an excuse this evening. Bob Hope was in town and staying at the Chase in the Central West End. He was secure in his room, servants and the like, but he enjoyed a cool walk in the evening hours.

I would head to the Chase, have a gourmet meal in one of the restaurants, gratis, meet up with Bob at his room and take him for a stroll. I liked the guy, but who didn't like Bob Hope? One thing I noticed about him: he never offered any insight into himself. He didn't tell me anything about his life. Most guys of his stature like to talk about themselves; not Bob Hope.

And he never offered any advice to me. Most important people are so full of themselves that they feel compelled to tell the less fortunate, or their servant cops how they can improve their lifestyle; investing, being creative, education, changing careers. But Bob never did.

But there was one thing I gleaned from Bob Hope's persona, something he could never hide; he was a non-violent, gentle man, something I had never seen before.

We just walked and I was his armed guard, courtesy of the City of St. Louis. I often wondered if the Los Angeles cops had to perform this service.

Bob loved St. Louis. We would walk west on Lindell Boulevard, with the stately granite mansions on our right, and the historic Forest Park on our left. He always had a look of glee on his face. He would stare at the mansions and their huge front porches and large wide windows and try to peek inside.

The homes were built for the 1904 World's Fair and were cared for like art treasures, for that is what they are. Nothing in Los Angeles could have matched these mansions. I felt he was trying to go back to a time when there was some honor in life, not just money and power. As we walked I observed his transformation; it was the early 1900s and he was living in St. Louis, owned one of the mansions and was walking with his manservant and bodyguard.

I doubted there was any honor in the entertainment business in Los Angeles. There wasn't any honor in my vocation, but I didn't ask about honor in his business. I didn't want to break the spell for him, the one where he was entering the time machine and going back.

He said St. Louis was clean and beautiful and he loved the architecture. I didn't offer him any insight into myself, but he was an intelligent man and he knew what he saw was what I was: a cop detective, struggling with bills, life, the mini-bureaucracy, asshole bosses and egotistic co-workers. He had seen it all and he knew me. What good would have come from discussing his life, or mine?

It was the next morning. I had overslept after walking with Bob and I was speeding toward work on side streets trying to make the nine o'clock deadline. Boob watched the door like a security guard at a floating crap game. It was part of his thing, making sure everybody made it in on time. It was the ultimate attitude test.

I heard Guido on the radio calling out of service to an address on Claytonia Terrace in Richmond Heights. He sounded stressed, which made me search the coffers of my brain to try and figure what was there. I thought back to my notes of the day before. It was John Paul Spica's residence, a two-family flat he rented with his girlfriend.

I turned the little Chevy toward it, then thought I had better check in with the unit secretary and have her tell Boob what I was doing. I stopped at a pay phone and took care of that business, then continued on. It was

November 8, 1979, the day the bombings began.

I idled up the street and was stopped by a Richmond Heights cop. I flashed my credentials to him and he told me to park and walk up to the scene. I double parked, shut it down and locked it up, then strolled to the murder scene.

It was a big car, a Caddy, but it was completely destroyed. The first responders were removing Spica's blown-to-bits cadaver as I walked up. His legs and parts of his body were missing. It was over-kill, but all car bombings are.

I had seen car bombings before in East St. Louis. I was with my parents at a family friend's house when one went off just a block from our location. The gangster was still in the car, slumped at the wheel. I presumed the lower part of his body was gone. It was as if he had been stopped by a traffic cop and was reaching for his wallet in the left rear pocket of his trousers and was leaning to the right; that was the position of his body.

The scene here was packed with Alcohol, Tobacco and Firearms Special Agents, FBI agents, St. Louis County cops, and Richmond Heights cops. It was another dark day for the safe little burg of Richmond Heights, Missouri. I stayed back out of the way. Guido and Stretch were hanging around with FBI Agent Sam Thompson gauging the scene and conversing with him.

It wasn't City of St. Louis's jurisdiction and even if it was, the Feds would take control of it. Guido, Stretch, Sam Thompson and a score of other law enforcement types knew who had done this, they knew it was coming. Luckily no innocent bystanders were killed or maimed.

Detective Sergeant Steve Sorocko from the City bombing and arson unit, the plodding investigator, was milling around, out of his jurisdiction, like the intelligence unit guys, but it didn't stop us from observing. The unions were in the confines of the City of St. Louis. Most of the thugs lived outside of the City, but they were still our thugs. We were the experts on them. The other jurisdictions came to us when they wanted to know something about them.

I marveled at how quickly things change when violence takes control. Less than two miles away from this location, and twelve or so hours past, I was walking with a famous movie star and marveling with him on how great the old St. Louis architecture was. Bob probably heard about this violent act but he wouldn't be able to put together how close it was to our walking place.

I was almost embarrassed by the killing, and by the method used to accomplish it. I thought about it in an instant flash. It's a class fight in this town. There are rich folks and poor folks and not much middle class. The middle class folks who stay in this town and try to make a living are people who live off of the trade unions.

It made sense that organized criminals would want to be the leadership of these trade unions. It's the only control they have over working-class folks. The rich folks are as ruthless as the union thugs. Nobody cared about the plight of the poor folks. They were the responsibility of the federal government.

It's what the union thugs wanted; control and they got it through fear. What other reason is there for the overkill of John Paul Spica, convicted murderer, on this cool, calm November morning.

I knew then why Ray Flynn didn't wish to be followed by me. They had overreacted, and this bombing was the reason. Ray Flynn could have given the order to shoot John Paul Spica when he came out of his house, but it wouldn't have had the same terrorist effect. It wasn't just money for the gangsters. They demanded conformity, just like Captain Bud demanded from me. Do what I say or I'll transfer you back to the uniform patrol. But I defied him. It was the East St. Louis thing to do.

The union gangsters say, "Do what I say and follow me or I'll blow somebody up who is close to you." Same principal, different group of organization men. Most folks are looking for someone to lead them. It just takes a little threatening, an incident like this bombing, and then the ordinary man follows the schoolyard bully and gives him his loyalty. It's a scary thing. The common man doesn't defy, he conforms. He's shouting for guidance. It's why Joey (Doves) Aiuppa, Art Berne, Tony Giordano, John Vitale, Jimmy Michaels, and the like are in business. They demand they be followed. The trade unions are just a tool for them to lead. Just like the guys in the police department.

A couple of weeks zoomed by. I had heard, through Guido that Ray Flynn had been elected by the officers of Laborers Local 42, as the new leader. The swing vote was Willie Washington. He was ordered by Anthony Giordano to vote for Ray Flynn.

As usual, I asked Guido where the information had come from, and as usual, he said, "Informant." But I knew that Guido didn't want anybody in the unit to know his secrets. He was the secret guy in the unit, the invisible man. Guido was in possession of union jackets for all of the locals. They're proudly worn by the loyal union members, have their names embroidered on the front, and have the name of their locals on the back in bold lettering.

When there was an important meeting in the union hall, Guido would don a jacket and walk in like he was a member. He would always take a seat at the back of the hall and he would watch and listen. FBI Agent Sam Thompson told me Guido was in a meeting of Local 110, and before the meeting, Mike Trupiano instructed the rank and file guys to look to their left and right and to make certain there were only union brothers in attendance.

Guido was spotted as an infiltrator, but he used his wit by smiling, referring to folks as brothers, shaking hands and backing out of the meeting, saying he thought this was Local 42's meeting. The guys in the audience were just working stiffs. They didn't come after him. The thugs were in front, on stage, and by the time they realized what had transpired, Guido was high-tailing it toward his funny car at a full run.

On the surface, the swing vote by Willie Washington was no big deal. But as I pondered this secret fact, it angered me. Willie Washington was nothing more than a lackey for Italian organized criminals. These Mafia types were the ones who had targeted and hooked his race with heroin. They had made slaves of the black folks in St. Louis, all over again. Willie must have had relatives who had been poisoned by their European imported drug.

And Laborers Local 42 was a racist local. It was a bastion of white supremacy. Willie was one of the few black guys working at the local. He was a turncoat, a step-and-fetch gorilla in a suit, doing the bidding of the Italian Mafia. It angered me, and I drove by the complex wondering if Willie was roaming on the parking lot.

I drove around the block for an hour, and finally he showed up, all six-foot-six, three-hundred pounds of him, in a brown silk suit, strutting in the lot behind the ten-foot chain link fence, scaring everyone who glanced his way.

I slowed the detective Chevy, rolled the window down and shouted to him, "Hey Willie, you still step-and-fetching for Tony Giordano? I heard he got your momma hooked on heroin. You're a sell-out."

I was stopped in traffic, but there weren't any cars behind me. It took about five seconds for my insults to hit his primate brain, but it finally sunk in. He had never had anybody disrespect him as bad as I had just done.

I continued to look him in the eye, and it infuriated him. He ran for the fence, jumping on it, pushing his giant fingers into the chain link and trying to climb over it to get to me. But, the fence did its job. It was made so big folks couldn't climb it, and it sagged under his weight. He hit the asphalt on his knees, tearing his silk suit.

He knew he couldn't get to me, to rip me from limb to limb, and it was hurting him. He would have tried to kill me had he gotten his fat hands on me, but I was ready for him. I was prepared to fight with him, and as displeased as I was with his ilk, I might have given him a good fight.

I drove off laughing and pointing, and showing him that I disrespected him, and had gotten away with it. I despised the guy as much as I hated the corrupt union system. But, it was the way it had to be. If a group of men get together and endeavor to do something, no matter what it might be, the toughest guy, or the most dangerous guy, comes out as the leader. People desire to be led. It stinks.

8

I had been shaking the trees of the union thugs, something a lowly cop detective isn't supposed to do in this town. We're supposed to be subservient. In the cop/crook pecking order, cops, even intelligence unit cops are lower than union thugs. I kept my eye on my rear view mirror when I drove, and I kept alert when I got into or out of my detective Chevy. I knew there were union guys who would beat me to a pulp, just for a pat on the head. So would a cop. If you're gotten from behind in a parking lot, you're at the mercy of the attacker. I wasn't going to allow that to happen to me.

The days after the bombing of John Paul Spica were strained. Guido and Stretch were never in the office, and my FBI friend Sam Thompson was working day and night to try and find who the next victim was going to be. We all knew another bombing was forthcoming, but where and when was the question. Nobody in law enforcement cared about the gangster victim. We were concerned with collateral damage, the innocent kid waiting for a school bus, or the husband coming home from work. Dynamite is hard to aim.

I had read the preliminary report on the Spica bombing. It appeared that someone put eight to ten sticks of dynamite with an electric blasting cap hooked to his Caddy's brake lights. When he stepped on the brake, it was all over for him.

It was easy for me to rationalize this death. Informants told Sam Thompson and Guido that Spica had confided in Anthony Leisure that he was going to whack Ray Flynn. Anthony told Paulie Leisure, his brother, the deadly rumor. Paul advised Ray Flynn. So Spica signed his own death warrant when he mouthed off.

Paul Leisure had allegiance to Ray Flynn for the promise of a high-paying union job at Local 42. Rumor had it that once he got the job, he would probably blow up Flynn to gain complete control of the local. Dog eat dog.

I wondered why the Buster Wortman gang was allowed to flourish in the days of my youth. I thought about it and came to the conclusion that the problem was jurisdictional. East St. Louis, is in a state where only one town matters. Chicago is where the action is and I figured nobody cared about the East Side. But there's always been big-time organized crime in Chicago, and there are thousands of cops and federal agents there.

But the Chicago mob sent its heavy hitters to East St. Louis, and then eventually to St. Louis to take over the trade unions. Wasn't there enough corruption in Chicago for them? It's just like big business. They're always looking for new customers.

I was questioning my dedication level. I had painted myself into a corner by not wanting to fib about an informant on a search warrant affidavit. Do you have to be a crook to catch a crook? Is that what the system is about? But search-warrant swearing about the informant is just a local cop, State of Missouri procedure. I had been present when an agent got a federal search warrant and the federal magistrate didn't make the agent swear about the informant.

Maybe my dedication factor was lacking. Maybe the guys in the unit were right, and I was wrong. I was probably dissecting the judicial system when I shouldn't have been. It's just law enforcement. It's archaic on the local level and streamlined on the federal level. Why did I have to examine the search-warrant procedure so closely?

It's a trust thing. Falsely swearing is against the law and the Constitution of the United States of America. Those restraints are in place for a reason. The way gossip travels in the City of St. Louis, anybody could be deemed a criminal, and be in file in the intelligence unit. Most of what I had read was just gossip, probably flowered up to make some boss happy. What if the recipient of an unlawful search was innocent? It would be a nightmare. My main problem was that I wasn't a "made" guy.

In organized crime the "made" guys are taken into the organization, trusted because of someone vouching for them, or for making their bones with the bosses; killing somebody, making a big score in the crime world. If they do this long enough they are made, they're management, and they reap the benefits of management.

In the cop business it's the same thing. If you've got outside influence and you come to a unit like intelligence, you're automatically a made guy and you reap the benefits. You get the best assignments, the best vehicles and the best partners. I was getting a partner, but I felt sorry for him. He was going to be burdened with me. His name was TJ, short for Tijuana.

T.J. wasn't made; he got me. I wasn't made; I got him. Now Captain Bud and Lieutenant Boob had control of us. They knew they couldn't intimidate me, so they would beat up on T.J.to get to me. T.J. didn't delve into the psyche of intelligence management; but I did. It was a scary thing, but I felt lucky to have him as a partner.

I got a call from Detective Steve Sorocko, city bombing and arson unit. He told me he had received some information on a partner of Paul and Anthony Leisure, a guy by the name of Fred Prater. Steve was a non-stop, plodding investigator. He went over every piece of evidence, continually, piecing them together to come to a conclusion. In a town like St. Louis, bombing was no big deal, it happened all the time.

Steve was unrelenting in his quest to catch the bad guy. He would interview informants, make reports pertaining to information, have meetings with prosecutors and Feds, and he made it a point to personally get to know all of the folks involved; bad and good.

I envisioned him sitting at his desk while we talked. Square-faced, full head of hair, smoking and drinking coffee, deeply thinking before speaking. He plodded along while he spoke to me just like he did when he interviewed suspects.

Bombings leave evidence. The bombers know it, and they're paranoid about it. They always feel that there is some fragment of evidence that is going to put them in prison. Steve played on their paranoia. He would call them and tell them to come into the office and talk with him. It was a simple request, if you weren't the guilty party. But everyone involved in a bombing is a guilty party.

Everyone involved with the bombers knows something, because they nervously chatter about their feats of terror. It is pillow talk, the most damaging to the talker, and people incriminate themselves during their casual conversing. Steve was always determined to find out what everybody knew. He would start with a girlfriend of a suspect, and then work his way up the chain of guilt.

People on the fringe talk when they're nervous, and Steve's demeanor allowed them to be frightened, and talkative. All he had to do was to keep them on the subject at hand. Who was the bomber?

Sorocko advised that Fred Prater was a legitimate businessman who had been a truck driver for Yellow Freight, but saw a business possibility with the repair and sale of the tires for eighteen-wheel trucks.

He quit the truck business and went into the tire business, and because he was a workaholic, the tire business flourished. Paul and Anthony Leisure approached him. They owned a towing service with a lot on Chouteau in the City, and they wanted to expand, but they needed someone like Fred Prater to help operate the business while they continued their avocation of being gangsters.

Fred knew the Leisures were connected politically, on the City and state level, and that there was a lot of money in the towing business. He sold the tire business and joined up with the Leisures.

Sorocko advised me he couldn't figure out why Fred Prater joined that group of crooks. Fred had a good reputation as an honest, hard-working businessman. His wife had a good job with the telephone company, and he was stable in the little City of St. Louis.

He told me he had gotten word that Fred Prater had made a bomb out of dynamite, and that the bomb was ultimately placed at the side of a house near Tower Grove Park, and detonated. It damaged the foundation of the house.

He said the reason for the bombing had to do with the purchase of a building near the downtown area of the City. The Leisures wanted to purchase it to warehouse some of their equipment used for the towing business. The person whose house was bombed also wanted it, and subsequently purchased it. The Leisures felt the guy had been disrespectful to them for buying the house out from under them, so they had Fred make a bomb and Anthony planted it next to the house and detonated it.

I asked Steve Sorocko how he had obtained this information. "Informant," he advised. He went on to say that their towing business was successful due to Fred Prater's work ethic, but they had some competition on the north side.

Prater, Anthony Leisure and David Leisure burglarized the competing towing business, pulled the drain plugs on the truck engines and started them. The engines burned up, and the competition was out of business.

"Same informant?" I asked.

"Yes," he replied.

"Why are you telling me this?"

"I need somebody to place Fred Prater under surveillance for me. I'm too busy with the John Paul Spica bombing to do it myself. Will you do it?"

"Yeah," I replied. "I'll let you know the outcome."

T.J. and I acquired a funny car from Boob, a Chevy Monte Carlo, two-door with whitewalls and big hubcaps, and we began our surveillance of Fred Prater, good guy workaholic who was in cahoots with the gangsters.

He had never been arrested, so we had to resort to his Missouri drivers' license picture as a means of identification. The tow lot was situated at twentieth and Chouteau, fenced in, private, and frequented by gangsters, politicians, people wanting to get their cars back and insurance adjustors. Fred Prater didn't leave the office. He showed up in the morning about eight and he stayed behind the fence all day.

We occasionally caught glimpses of him, working in the tow yard, inspecting some of the trucks and cars, and then he'd scoot back into the office.

Boob called T.J. and me into his office. "What's with the surveillance?"

"The guy never does anything overt," I said. "He comes to work, works for twelve or sixteen hours, and then he goes home."

"Get off of him," Boob said spitting tobacco at me and hitting me in the chest with a gob.

"What about Detective Steve Sorocko? We're doing this for him. Shouldn't we give it just a little bit longer?"

"No, what did he ever do for you? What did he ever do for the unit? He's Guido s friend. He gives him information, but he doesn't give it to me. I'm the deputy commander. I should be the one assimilating any and all information coming in to this unit. Did he call me? No, he called you. Dismissed!"

We walked out of Boob's office brushing tobacco gobs off of our shirts. I called Steve Sorocko and advised him of our findings. Steve laughed it off and thanked us. His unit actually had a mission: investigate bombings and arson. That was the end of the Fred Prater surveillance. But his name would come up again.

The mission in Intelligence wasn't clearly defined. Mainly, it consisted of satisfying the bosses, in whatever way they deemed necessary on any particular day. I felt we should have been assisting the other bureaus with their investigations. We knew the bad guys, they didn't. But it wasn't my call.

9

I never could figure why gangsters and union thugs worked so hard at their fields of endeavor. If it was broken down to an hourly wage, they didn't make much more than a cop detective. It was a twenty-four hour a day job for them, and it was damned hazardous. I figured the long hours sent the message they were serious about the labor movement. But in my mind they were serious about stealing, killing and leading. They were crook management. Like being made guys in the Mafia, or the police department. I never desired to be a" made" guy. I was happy being what I was.

Like all non-made guys, T.J. and I worked the streets. I was correct in my assumption, Captain Bud beat T.J. up whenever he got sight of him, and Boob beat him up every morning. He would walk into the office and Boob would start in on him about statistics, then T.J. would walk to my desk, pale and frightened, and tell me we had to get out on the street. In his cop brain, he knew that the pinch that was going to make him a made guy was out there waiting for us.

We would hit the streets and frantically drive on the north side looking into the eyes of on-coming traffic, arguing about which car we should stop. The captain and Boob had placed a quota on us as a team: one felony pinch a day. So we would leave the office and look for the morning pinch, then we would have the rest of the day to shop and eat lunch.

It turned out to be a real good gig, except on those mornings and afternoons we couldn't get a pinch. Then the paranoia would set in and we knew Captain Bud would be waiting for us when we came in at five o'clock without a prisoner. Bud had changed his routine so he could terrorize us. The good gig would turn sour and we'd start bickering with each other.

Captain Bud wanted search warrants. T.J. and I both knew why. Search warrants beget contraband. I couldn't bring myself to lie, and then swear to God I wasn't lying on a search warrant affidavit.

T.J. and I talked about it. He wanted to please the captain. I didn't. You don't just lie on the affidavit. You lie at the grand jury, and you lie during the trial, and most times there's a retrial because of some stupid mistake in the law, then you have to lie all over again. For what? To be a "made" cop? It wasn't worth it. T.J. reluctantly agreed.

Occasionally we would get some dope off of some Mississippi State Trooper car stop victim, pressure him and find out where it had come from, and use the informant to obtain a search warrant. It always ended badly for us. First off, we would have to execute the search warrant by ourselves. It was every man for himself in intelligence. Captain Bud wanted it that way. If the crews worked as a team, they could possibly turn against him as a commander, his worst nightmare.

But we had the Congressman Dick Gephardt detail to fall back on when it seemed like things couldn't get any worse. Dick was gaining international prominence and the power brokers came to St. Louis to see him.

He didn't live here, he lived in the Washington, D.C., area, but he had a congressional office here, and this was where his constituency lived, so whenever a dignitary wanted to see the real Dick Gephardt, they came to St. Louis.

Dick's long-range goal was to be the president of the United States. Communist Russia recognized this and they courted him. He brought a contingency of Supreme Soviets to St. Louis. That's the equivalent of our United States Senate. They were in town for four days and T.J. and I, and State Department Security, as well as KGB security, rubbed and bent elbows and had a great time.

The congressman's staff in the St. Louis office were like the detectives in the intelligence unit. Their mission was to satisfy Dick Gephardt. So they constantly scrambled to show him they were trying to serve him at one-hundred percent, which was like trying to drive one-hundred and fifty in a Yugo.

All of the action was in the congressman's Washington, D.C., office. There was nothing going on in sleepy old St. Louis. The only thing here for Dick Gephardt was his constituency. His vigilant staff noticed I had a vague resemblance to Dick Gephardt. I observed them comparing the two of us. The only real comparison was the color of our hair.

I figured in their paranoid St. Louis way, having nothing to do but watch television all day, waiting for Dick and his D.C. staff to come into town, which was only about once a month, they figured the congressman's life might be in danger someday, and it would be beneficial to the congressman's safety if he had a cop at his disposal, preferably one who vaguely resembled him. Maybe the nut assassin would shoot me instead of their beloved politico employer. I saw the window of opportunity opening for me and T.J. and I played to the congressman's staff.

The congressman had always been stand-offish to us and I understood why. He had grown up in the City of St. Louis and he was an extreme liberal. Anybody with those credentials automatically distrusted St. Louis cops. It was like people in Alaska being untrusting of Grizzly Bears. But his chief of staff in the St. Louis office liked us. He was the one who always called the chief's office and asked for us. He was using me as a possible spear-catcher, and T.J. as a baggage handler, but it gave us leverage with Captain Bud and his ilk. It was our gig, mine and T.J.'s, and it didn't give us made-cop status, but it gave us a break from the mayhem prevalent in the intelligence unit offices.

Dick brought a contingency of Russians to St. Louis. The Supreme Soviet, which was like our senate. We warmed up to the KGB operatives who shadowed the chairman of the group, Vladimir Alkhimova, an old guy, maybe seventy, who was sour and looked upset all of the time. He was an important guy in Soviet Russia, Chairman of the State Bank, analogous to the Federal Reserve Bank in the United States. One of the KGB guys, the one with the briefcase and the concealed pistol, never got more than ten feet away from the chairman.

We gave the Russians the usual tour of St. Louis: the brewery, Shaw's Garden (Missouri Botanical Garden), and an official sit-down dinner in the evenings. T.J. and I mostly just stood around, but we ate with them, and tried to be cordial.

Even though there was a language barrier, T.J. and I managed to get to know these guys. They were like robots; faceless, speechless robots waiting for a command. But as the detail went on, we were being accepted by them.

To be completely accepted by a Russian, you have to drink with him. So, T.J. and I did. There wasn't any vodka. I wouldn't have drunk it, anyway, but there was complimentary beer, supplied by the local brewery.

Before supper one evening, we drank at a cocktail party. The staff of the congressman acted like they couldn't do their jobs without us, and T.J. and I played to them like Hollywood actors, while we played to the Russians, drinking and trying to speak to them through an interpreter.

I handed one of them my business card, which boldly displayed I was in Intelligence. It was an overt act by me, and I knew it was going to cause a stink, but I couldn't squelch the desire to screw with a bureaucrat. It didn't matter he was Russian; he was still a bureaucrat.

The Russian read my card, which I thought was strange since we had been speaking through an interpreter for three days. He turned pale, stared at me and said, "What kind of intelligence?" in English. The guy thought I was CIA. He probably thought I was trying to get him to defect.

I had pulled his hole card, and he was embarrassed. The KGB robot with the briefcase quickly walked toward us, his hand under his coat. They conversed in Russian, but I figured all of the delegation could speak English. It was a Russian ploy to make us believe they couldn't understand us so that we'd speak freely in front of them.

A couple more days went by and the Russians were slated to go to Colorado to visit another Democratic congressman. We drove the delegation to the airport in a bus, walked in and were placed in a hospitality suite while waiting for their plane to fuel.

There was more drinking. It's what Russians do, and by the time the delegation got onto the airplane, we were all great friends. Russians are big on hugging, and I got hugged by all of them, except the KGB robot with the briefcase. Even Dick Gephardt smiled and shook hands with us. T.J. and I figured these Russian bureaucrats weren't any smarter than their counterparts in St. Louis. The only smart guy in the group was Dick Gephardt. He didn't trust anybody, and he didn't use alcohol.

An FBI Agent called me at home to debrief me on the Russian visit. He told me the guy with the briefcase was a KGB killer, and the briefcase was rigged with a device that would give exact coordinates of any location when a certain button was pushed. He told me they were spies, trying to get coordinates to bomb sleepy old St. Louis.

He went down the list of the Russians, wanting my opinion of them, asking me precise descriptions, what their personalities were, how they acted, where we went while in St. Louis. I told him everything I knew. Then I told him about giving one of the guys my business card with Intelligence on it. He laughed until I thought he was going to cry. FBI agents don't laugh much. They're like KGB spies, there's nothing funny when the safety of the world rests on your little shoulders.

I thought I would test his knowledge of Russians, so I told him we drank together. “They hate beer,” he advised me. “They only drink vodka. Beer is too mild for them.”

“Right,” I countered. His credibility as an expert on Russians went out the window. He was as inept as all of the other stereotypical bureaucrats. If these guys were spies then why weren’t there some FBI operatives in the group? The FBI was relying on a couple of City cop detectives to brief them on KGB spies. It figured!

Dick Gephardt sent word to us, via his chief of staff, that he wasn’t going to get involved in police department politics, which meant, he wasn’t going to make a telephone call for us to get us on the promotional list.

I wasn’t expecting any favors from Dick Gephardt. I had heard stories about his disloyalty to his friends, but I wasn’t a friend, I was a cop/ servant. Dick told me one time that his only friends were lawyers. That certainly left me out. T.J. was upset. It brought out “Why me,” syndrome in T.J. and I don’t think he ever got over it.

I felt leery about being a servant to the congressman. He was aligned with the Syrian political coalition on the south side. The Syrian criminal faction guys were related to the Syrian political coalition.

These folks all came from good families. Most of their offspring went on to become lawyers and business folks, but St. Louis was a town with a complex. The folks here and elsewhere drummed the town down, so whenever there was a chance to show that this town had heart, they would brag about the organized criminals here.

All first class cities in this country had Mafia types, killings, shake-downs, bombings, and colorful gangsters. We had more than our fair share and the City fathers accepted this fact. It was almost as if the City fathers were proud of it. The demeanor here was, hey we’re a first-class City, too. We’ve got first-class criminals here.

When these ethnic families talked about their children and their nephews, and cousins, they bragged about people like Paul Leisure, Anthony Leisure and David Leisure. It gave them status on the playground of life. Who would want to mess with someone who was related to a madman murderer like Paul Leisure? He had only to suggest that he wanted someone killed and David Leisure, who had the I.Q. and disposition of a pit bull, would do his bidding in one day.

The successful businessmen, lawyers and politicians were lower on the status scale than the gangsters. It's one of the reasons St. Louis had so many super criminals. They were socially accepted.

Dick Gephardt's chief of staff was the brother-in-law of Hank Slay, one of the guys riding around with the Capo dei Capi of New Jersey (Salvatore Profaci) and his henchman, (Dominic Montemarano) when I did the car-stop on Mike Trupiano for Guido and Stretch.

People in this town talked to each other about episodes with St. Louis cops. They would brag, take notes and complain to each other. I felt strongly that Hank Slay complained to Gephardt's aide about me.

I was known as an Intelligence Unit Detective, as a friend of Gephardt's chief of staff and as Gephardt's bodyguard. The same folks who were mystified by the gangsters were also mystified by the cops who investigated the gangsters.

Hank Slay was a wealthy man and I had seen him at Gephardt fund-raisers. He knew who I was when I stopped the gangster car and demanded identification. I felt weird about the association, but I knew a good gig when I saw one and I would do almost anything to be able to thumb my nose at Captain Bud and Lieutenant Boob.

So I played the servant, bodyguard role and bided my time until I could again start harassing the local gangsters, because I knew nothing was permanent. I had to live for the moment. I compared my situation to cops in other parts of the country and wondered if it was the same in Los Angeles, or New York City, or even in Chicago.

Cops don't want to admit it, but we're just tin soldiers being manipulated by the powers that be. It's their hobby, manipulating cops, and it goes all the way down the line from local politicians, to federal politicians, to the office of the Chief of Police, to Captain Bud and Lieutenant Boob and to me, and to T.J.

They own us and we do their will, as long as we agree to. When we don't do someone's will along the chain of command, then we get replaced with someone who is waiting in a dark corner of a police district for his chance to be a "made" cop.

When these guys replace T.J. and me, Dick Gephardt will play the same role, being stand- offish then gradually warming to them and then he'll get the word to them that he won't help them with anything concerning the police department. And the beat will go on. It's kind of like being an undercover cop. You can only work it for so long and then you get burned. I understood it and I accepted it.

But it wasn't only local politicians I was chosen to protect. Boob advised me I had a weekend detail to protect Henry Kissinger, former Secretary of State. He was in town to address a group of bankers from Southern Illinois. T.J. wasn't on the detail for some unknown reason so another unit detective took his place.

Kissinger's bodyguard was a young man, heavy and not in shape for being a bodyguard for such an important person. He showed me his gun, a Walther PPK, just like James Bond carried. I was embarrassed by his efforts to impress me, but he didn't pick up on it. He obviously felt I was a rube, but I didn't care. I would be rid of him and Kissinger in four hours and then I would have the rest of the day with my wife and kids.

"Doctor Kissinger's in the adjoining room," he told me, "and he wants to meet you." I acted impressed, so the bodyguard taps on the door and in comes Kissinger as if he was making an appearance on a late-night talk show. I stood and shook his hand. It was like shaking the hand of a dead man, and I noted it. He couldn't have cared less if I lived or died, and after the handshake I felt the same way about him.

But I smiled and acted super-subservient and after about thirty seconds he turned and retreated to his room. My partner for the day was a "made" cop, he had a funny car, worked organized criminals and he was unhappy about being there on a weekend day.

We examined the stage for show, as if we thought something could go amiss. It was a high stage with chairs lined parallel with a curtain at the back. We walked to the back of the stage and the bodyguard advised me that I was going to be assigned to guard Doctor Kissinger's back, at the rear of the stage.

"Cool," I said.

The bodyguard continued by telling me there were several heads of state who wished the now retired Kissinger dead and I should be ever diligent in protecting him from a rear attack. I nodded, and he and my backup went out to the front of the stage where they would stay during the presentation.

I wandered around backstage in obscurity while another guest speaker gave his speech. Then it was Kissinger's turn. He tried to stand, but before he did he shoved his chair backwards and it, and Doctor Kissinger, came tumbling through the curtain backwards, sailed the nine or ten feet in front of me and landed at my feet. It was a terrifying thing to see; he landed on his head and it sounded like a watermelon had fallen from a pickup truck and landed on concrete.

I wondered if he'd been shot but I didn't see any blood and he appeared to be conscious. "You okay?" I asked.

"Yes," he replied, "don't stand on my glasses." I backed away and his bodyguard stormed stage rear with his Walther PPK drawn. It was the topper for a boring assignment.

I walked my associate to his funny car, a blue and white Mercury, as I proceeded to my little Chevy. I had two great days off with my family and returned to the office on Wednesday. The detective who assisted me with the detail got shot in the face later that evening. He was tailing Anthony Leisure, stopped at a red light when a street hooker jumped into his car, grabbed his pistol, and shot him in the face. We got his funny car. We were on our way to made cop status.

Our first day with the funny car was remarkable. We got into a shootout with two rapists in a stolen car. But there was a problem. We ran out of ammunition, and the transmission in the funny car slipped so badly we couldn't keep up with the stolen Caddy. Two lowly juvenile cops arrested them. We were humiliated. T.J. and I felt it was time to regroup.

We openly discussed our problems at our desk. He wanted to appease the captain. I didn't. We both knew our partnership was going to be short-lived. The stars listened to every conversation then reported to Captain Bud what we said about him. Bud was out to get us, we knew it. The little star had struck again. I wasn't surprised. Snitches are crooks and crooks are snitches. It's the silent code of the underworld.

We had partnered for about eighteen months. It was another experiment in law enforcement that didn't work. Captain Bud split us up. T.J. didn't get his wish. He wasn't a "made" cop.

10

Being a loner cop wasn't all that bad. Without T.J., the bosses didn't have a handle on me. I respected T.J. and I knew what goals he had made for himself, so I went along with the program. Besides, T.J. was a smart guy and we played off of each other well. But being alone all of the time wears on a cop after a while. I was ready for another partner. It was like the bosses waited and gauged me and knew when I would be vulnerable again.

I had heard the office rumors that Captain Bud and Boob were going to bring someone into the unit to be my partner, someone who would sit on me and be loyal to them, not me. I hated the rumors, and I didn't like the fact that the captain and Lieutenant Boob were trying to contain me.

To me, the rumors meant that I had set the standard on non-conformity in the unit and that the only reason I was still in the unit was because someone in the chief's office felt I had some political clout with Dick Gephardt. Maybe that was a good thing.

The little star came to my desk, not laughing and slapping his knee, not being obnoxious or slap stick. He was acting like my unit friend. I tried to read him as he stood and talked. "We could be partners," he said. "Just let me know, I've already spoken to the bosses and we're in if you say so." He waited for my response.

This was a turning point for me, in the unit and in my career. If I said, "yes I'll be your partner," I would be a "made" guy, sure to be promoted. I would have star stature within the unit, and the department. I had the Eastside gorilla sitting on my back telling me not to do it. I turned down the offer of greatness.

"Why?" he said. "Is it because of my reputation?"

"No," I replied. I ran the rumors of murder and drug dealing through my brain. "I never believed any of that stuff. If I thought any of that was true I would never have spoken to you. I just want to be on my own for a while more." He walked away angry. I knew I had probably made a lifetime enemy.

It was mid-summer and hotter than any human should have to endure. Poor and old folks were dying in their homes. Homeless people were dying on street corners. Anthony Giordano died in August of cancer. That left John Vitale as the sole leader of the Italian faction in St. Louis.

Guido and Stretch were beside themselves. Anthony Giordano was the guy keeping Paul Leisure from killing Jimmy Michaels, the charismatic leader of the Syrian criminal faction in the region. Ray Flynn had wormed his way into the leadership of Laborers Local 42 and given Paul Leisure a representative's position within the local. Now Paul Leisure also wanted to control Laborers Local 110 through his brother Anthony.

Guido had been told by an informant that Ray Flynn had contacted Joey (Doves) Aiuppa in Chicago concerning the now ended friendship, through death, between Giordano and Michaels. Aiuppa allegedly told Flynn any arrangement Giordano had to protect his friend Michaels was cancelled out by Giordano's death. August quickly melted into September.

It was a great day in September in St. Louis. Sunny, breezy, mild. By September 17th you know deep down inside of you the killing heat is about gone for another nine months, and I wondered if that's what Jimmy Michaels was thinking when he was leaving St. Raymond's Church after lunch.

I had seen him there before. I had eaten lunch at the table next to his. He was always politicking, acting like the gentle hood. He had a full head of white hair, a smile and a quick wink and nod, and was the kind of guy anybody in St. Louis would have liked to have had lunch with. He would have kissed babies had he had the chance. He was like a celebrity shaking hands, going through the cafeteria line, talking and laughing. But he wasn't a nice guy.

His criminal career went back to the 1920s. He was an armed robber, murderer, drug dealer, jail bird, and a member of Frank "Buster" Wortman's gang. My hobby as a youngster in East St. Louis was to throw at the gangsters' cars, and them personally if I had a chance. The hoodlums patrolled the streets like the cops were supposed to do, terrorizing the working stiffs of that little town.

I had chucked brick-bats at two thugs in an old Ford one summer evening then ran into some weeds. They stopped and got within my killing zone, got out of their Ford and I pelted them again. I ran into Jones Park and hid in another weed patch. They didn't catch me. I still chuckled about it.

I wanted to take my cafeteria tray and muscle in on him while he ate and politicked with his bevy of friends. I would have said, "Hey, remember when you worked for Buster Wortman? Those were the days, right? Do you remember when some crazy kid tore your car up with brick-bats? He bounced one off of your chest, too, didn't he? Those were great memories, right?"

Then I would let him stew while I ate some of my lunch. "You know why that kid pummeled you assholes with brick-bats? It was because you screwed with the frightened poor folks in East St. Louis. They were meek little people, afraid and unable to defend themselves from you organized creeps. I was the kid who beat your ass with the bricks. What would you like to do about it?"

That's what I wanted to say to him, but I didn't. I was satisfied he was the one who was riding shotgun in the Ford. He looked right at me when they pulled by me on Douglas at North Park Drive. I thought maybe he was Italian, but I was wrong. He was Syrian.

Jimmy Michaels left the church and entered his Chrysler Cordoba. He didn't realize David Leisure, retarded cousin to Paul and Anthony Leisure, had crawled under his car and attached a bomb to it, under the drivers' seat.

He took off as he usually did, driving Interstate 55, southbound in South St. Louis County near the Reavis Barracks Road exit, when Anthony Leisure detonated the bomb. It was every cop's and federal agent's nightmare come true; a bombing in a highly populated area.

The Cordoba bounced three feet in the air, according to witnesses. The force of the explosion tore Michaels legs off and part of his body was hurled against a passing car. The scariest part of the scenario was what was going through the minds of the cops and special agents. You live by the bomb you die by the bomb. We all knew there would be chaos in the town of St. Louis.

In the fall of 1980 there was another notable event in the annals of crime. Joseph Paul Franklin was arrested in Florida. The FBI had gotten information on some of the killings he had committed. The murderer had a bald eagle tattoo on his arm. A nurse taking blood from him noticed the tattoo and contacted the FBI. He was arrested and confessed to several high profile murders, but not the synagogue killings in Richmond Heights.

I mentioned his arrest to Boob. I also checked our files, and he wasn't in them. Boob told me he and Paul and David were on top of it, and that Franklin wasn't the synagogue sniper. He wasn't from around here and nothing placed him here at the time of the murder and shootings. "The guy we want is in our files, I know it," Boob said blowing smoke in my face.

Organized crooks were patrolling the streets of St. Louis just like they had in East St. Louis when there was still something to steal there. And to add insult to injury, there were gangsters being released from prison and returning to the area. Norman (Bosco) Owens, a world renowned safe-cracker and hit man, burglar and soldier of Art Berne, slid into town from a federal-paid vacation.

Bill Politte, union thug, burglar, home invader, from Hoisting Engineers Local 513 returned to the area, fresh from prison. He had considerable influence in the local and was trying to take it over from Jack Martorelli, an honest union representative. Bosco Owens got a job with the local as a shop steward.

Politte was as violent as Paul Leisure and Ray Flynn. He lived in Illinois, near a slough of the Mississippi River where a canal had been built for the barges to navigate. The location was like something out of a New Orleans crime novel. River, canal, and houses owned by his relatives. We tried to make surveillance on it, but his relatives burned us instantly.

Politte was determined to get control of the Hoisting Engineers Local five-thirteen by hook or crook. He had the backing of some of the members who were also Illinois crooks. It took the proper amount of votes, and the rank and file needed something to substantiate their voting power.

Politte figured if he could get a big labor job for the local, one that would bring a lot of jobs and money, he would get the backing of the union members, and he could oust Jack Martorelli.

Politte had a scheme wherein Local five-thirteen, a Missouri local of hoisting engineers, would get part of the work at the Alton, Illinois, lock and dam project. It was a gigantic job, federally funded by the Corps of Engineers, and sanctioned by the labor council in Illinois.

His plan was just like the stars' plan. Get a big job, versus get a big case, then go to the heads of the international and tell them he was better equipped to run the union than Jack Martorelli. With some intimidation and a vote from the rank and file, Billy Pollitte was sure he could gain control of five-thirteen.

He met with opposition from Hoisting Engineers Local five-twenty in Granite City, Illinois. They objected through the International Hoisting Engineers Union, stating the Missouri Local didn't have jurisdiction to work on the Illinois side.

Politte became enraged, and he threatened several of the officers of the Illinois Local. A hand grenade was thrown through the window of the Illinois Local, doing severe damage. The word was out that Pollitte had thrown the grenade, but nobody could prove it, so the case lay dormant.

Jack Martorelli, the head of Local five-thirteen, was elated. Pollitte's big attempt to gain notoriety within the local rank and file had backfired on him. But Pollitte pressed on, threatening Martorelli and flexing his mobster muscle. He was backed by Joey (Doves) Aiuppa and Art Berne. We all expected another bombing, with Martorelli being on the receiving end.

Bosco Owens was a cocky, greedy criminal, a home invader, murderer and union thug. Sam Thompson told Guido, Stretch, and me that Bosco Owens was in a tiff with an international burglar who had come into possession of items stolen from Howard Hughes' safe in Hollywood, California (another St. Louis burglar who'd made it to the big time.) The big-time burglar was back in town and Sam Thompson had us checking his house on regular intervals.

The international burglar came back to town cocky, and with cash. He bought and sold cars and jewelry like there was no tomorrow. He worked the street, and he wasn't affiliated with anybody, not the Syrians, the Italians, nor Art Berne. But nobody touched him.

He had this big reputation of being a successful crook; the one who had beaten the FBI. The FBI paid him for the return of some of Howard Hughes' papers pertaining to a deal struck between Hughes and the federal government for the salvage of a Russian submarine that had sunk.

The FBI, CIA and LAPD detectives couldn't solve the burglary of Howard Hughes safe, but an investigative reporter, Michael Drosnin formerly with the *Washington Post* and the *Wall Street Journal*, found the person who had committed the burglary.

Drosnin gained the thief's confidence and was given access to ten-thousand secret documents. He wrote a book, Citizen Hughes from the information he had received from the St. Louis crook.

The guy never admitted to any crime, but he did admit that he had some of Hughes property. The Feds paid to get it back, and this guy came back home to St. Louis, victorious. Sam Thompson and every other FBI agent hated him. He had beaten their system.

The tiff between Bosco Owens and this big-time criminal, burglar, jewel thief, came from a trust between two crooks. Bosco entrusted the other crook with a bevy of diamonds to hold for him while he was in prison. Bosco apparently had not heard the old creed, "No honor amongst thieves," and when he got out of prison he went looking for his prize. The diamonds were gone. Sam Thompson told us it was only a matter of time before one of them turned up dead.

Sam Thompson was right in his prediction. Bosco Owens, career crook, safe-cracker and murderer, was found in the trunk of his car, parked in the parking lot at Lambert International Airport. He had been shot in the back of the head. After he was shot he must've grabbed the back of his head with his hands, and he was shot again, this time the bullet went through his hands and entered his brain.

County homicide worked the case and eventually came up with a scenario. Bosco was lured to a house in St. Charles County and shot while he was using the toilet. They went to the house, but it had conveniently burned to the ground. You live by the gun, you die by the gun.

I had gotten my new partner, an older guy, and a made guy. He had been in a black district his whole career and he had befriended high-ranking black cops. They were sure to get him promoted, so he just came in and settled down with me, after being cribbed by Captain Bud and Lieutenant Boob.

We started out slowly in the friendship aspect of our partnership. I knew he was working with Captain Bud and Boob and that I was just a pawn in his career enhancement program. The funny thing about it was that he didn't realize I had figured out the program and the captain, and Boob didn't know I knew the drill, either.

We ate well. I knew many restaurant owners and he knew his share, and we were always trying to outdo each other in the art of getting good food at a decent price, free most of the time. I had a friend who had a restaurant on Euclid in the Central West End. I had eaten there for years and I liked the food and the owner. He usually charged me half-price. I never knew why, but I kept going in, and he kept feeding me.

It was a buffet, and we were moseying through the line, cracking jokes to each other, with our police radio on the tray so the cashier would know we were cops and give us the half-price cop special.

My restaurant owner friend was Jewish, and he hired Russian Jewish immigrants to work in his business. They were smart, trustworthy and cheap to hire. A young woman was on the register and she was staring at us. My partner and I were both fair, with combed-over hair, muscular and cocky. When we got to the cash register, the lady shouted "KGB" and ran into the kitchen.

My friend came out and apologized, he told us she had just left Russia and she was still leery of cops. I figured St. Louis was a lot like Russia, a police state, bad winters and crazy cops wanting something for nothing. Cops are the same everywhere. I had flashbacks of the Russian delegation, and I realized that the Dick Gephardt Russian detail was an experience of a lifetime for a cop, especially a St. Louis cop.

So my new partner and I referred to ourselves as the KGB and spent most of our time following around this international burglar, writing down where he went, documenting his life in this crooked little City.

He was difficult to follow and he knew we had him under surveillance. He would sometimes pull over and shout to us where his next destination was going to be. He would call us whores for the FBI and shake his head in pity for us. I figured folks in Russia didn't act that way to their cops.

The funny thing was that I knew he was right. But I didn't really care. Surveillance with a cop car, without lights and decals, was ludicrous. We were in reality harassing this crook. But it was the only way we could keep a handle on him; constant harassment, constant surveillance.

Following this famous burglar and harassing him and his girlfriend was kind of like Captain Bud and Boob always wanting to keep tabs on me. I could relate to the guy, and the girl.

We were whores for the FBI, and my new partner was a whore for the captain and Boob. But one thing about my new partner, he took his days off when they came up, and he had a lot of vacation days because he had over twenty-years on. So I was alone a lot of the time, and I relished those days.

I couldn't believe how having scruples, a conscience and being affiliated with Dick Gephardt made Captain Bud and Boob so leery of me. But the Dick Gephardt affiliation worked in my favor. Police management feared politicians like a cobra fears a mongoose.

Ten months had gone by since Jimmy Michaels had gotten blown up on Interstate 55. It had been a long time for retribution to make its appearance, and we were all waiting for the inevitable. The Michaels clan took their time planning their attack. They enlisted friends to help them, people they had helped in the past. One of those friends was the Chief of Police of the little municipality of St. George, in South County, Chief Milton “Russ” Schepp.

On the morning of August eleventh, Chief Schepp, Johnny Michaels, Sonny Faheen, (Michaels cousin), and a sheriff’s deputy for the City of St. Louis, and a couple of other political losers, had surveillance on Paul Leisure’s Local 42 union Caddy. It was parked in front of his mother’s house at Nottingham and Kingshighway, quiet tree-lined streets with tidy brick homes and impeccable lawns.

It never came out who snuck the bomb under Paul Leisure’s car, but whoever did it didn’t do it right. They didn’t attach it to the vehicle, like David Leisure did when he placed the bomb in Jimmy Michaels car.

They just placed it on the pavement presumably under the drivers’ seat, but it wasn’t. It was forward of the drivers’ seat, under the cowling of the vehicle, so that when Paul came out and entered his vehicle, and when someone pressed the button to explode the bomb, it didn’t kill, but maimed. Detective Sergeant Steve Sorocko was advised by an informant that Paul Leisure backed up before someone hit the trigger to explode the bomb. It was a classic example of buck fever. Amateurs trying to be trained killers.

I was kibitzing in the office when I heard the radio call come out for an explosion at Nottingham and Kingshighway. I knew what had transpired. My partner was off for the day and I was unencumbered.

When I got to the scene, Paul Leisure had just been taken out of the car and was being placed on a gurney and wheeled to the EMS ambulance. He was ashen, breathing through his mouth because of facial trauma, his shirt was off and his huge chest was heaving, fighting off the grim reaper. His dark eyes were darting around, as if he was looking for the face in the crowd of the person who’d done this to him. He was already thinking, revenge.

I wondered if he thought back in time to the dozens of people he had sent to the promise land. I wonder if any of them fought the reaper, like he was doing then. Did they speak to you, Paul, when you dispatched them?

Some of us don’t die instantly, we have time to make a statement, try to instill guilt, call for our wives, our children, our parents, even our pets. Could their dying declarations be going through his killer brain at this moment? The word on the street is that he had killed over twenty people for Anthony Giordano, John Vitale, and anybody else who had the cash to pay.

He was a killing machine. Did he actually think he was immune to a violent demise? Foolish thinking on his part. He had to know the end was near, that the game was over for him. No more scary killer. No more gangster leader, except maybe to delegate a killing or two.

His days as a dominant physical force in the game of cops and robbers and union thugs was over. EMS personnel and firefighters were scouring the area looking for body parts and fighting off stray dogs also looking for some of Paul's fingers and toes to eat.

His mother was there for him, crying and consoling his blown-up body. He just looked at her, the way a child who was injured during a football scrimmage would look at his mother. He wanted her help, I could see it. He wanted to say, "Help me mom," but he didn't. The faces of his victims had to be going through his brain.

He had lived with his mother for his entire life. When he plotted and planned murder assignments, in her house, in her presence, did she know it? If so, then she was as much to blame for this bombing as the relatives of Jimmy Michaels.

What did Paul Leisure tell his mother he was doing when he planned these murders for cash? Did he say, "Bye mom, I'm going out of town for a few days on business. Have you cleaned my gun lately?" She had to know.

His legs were mangled and parts of them were missing. His face was deformed and his hands and arms were missing parts. He had internal injuries, but he fared better than Jimmy Michaels, one of the victims of Paul's hatred.

The cops and special agents knew the violence was going to move quickly now. Revenge was something the Leisures cherished. It was what they were about; their creed. Paul's Local 42 construction helmet had been blown out of the car and into his mother's front yard. I retrieved it, and tossed it into my little detective Chevy. After the scene was secured, and after I had gotten bored with the federal agents, cops and firefighters rummaging through the car, I headed for the office.

I inspected the helmet as I drove. It was brand new, and it had his name emblazoned on it: PAUL LEISURE, LABORERS LOCAL 42, BUSINESS AGENT. The man was proud of his achievement, and he obtained his success by using what he had been trained to do; intimidate, murder, maim. It was all in a day's work for him.

I envisioned how the laborers on the job must have felt when he walked onto a job site. They all knew what he was, and they all knew what he was capable of doing. He was every working man's nightmare. He was Count Dracula and the Wolfman all rolled into one politically backed monster. He was the Bela Lugosi of organized union thuggery in the little City of St. Louis, Missouri.

I imagined him strutting around with his white helmet, staring and intimidating. It was the same with any profession. When someone gets what they want out of life, they flaunt it. Doctors do it, lawyers do it, cops do it, and gangsters do it. Murderers who live by the bomb don't flaunt it for long, though.

But why do they do it? What makes someone over-extend themselves to claim leadership? Why is it that important? The cops lie, cheat, brag, talk down and talk themselves up just to get a little promotion, so they can be leaders.

The crooks kill and maim to gain leadership. I can't figure the lust for leading. But, in St. Louis, in the labor movement, leadership means power, and control of the rackets. But it has to be shared with Joey Aiuppa in Chicago, Art Berne in East St. Louis, and with the Italian Mafia in St. Louis. It couldn't be worth it after everything's cut up and distributed.

It's got to be an ego thing, the chance to say, "Hey I'm the one in charge. I run things. I'm the toughest. I'm the smartest. I'm the most ruthless. If you don't play ball with me, I can have you eliminated with a snap of my fingers. People will do my bidding just for a chance I can get one of their relatives hired on as a laborer down at the union hall."

I placed the helmet on top of a file cabinet as a trophy for anyone who wished to observe it. The monster's helmet, barely used, and I thought it was a fitting tribute to violence, and what it brought to the violent ones.

Boob came out of his office, blew smoke in my face and asked about it. I told him I collected it at the scene. He walked away in a cloud, and an hour later a Fed came to collect the helmet. My trophy was gone.

A couple of slow weeks went by. The little star had convinced Boob this was the best time for him to get a police discount on his hair transplant. The little star's ex-partner had set the discount up for him, and made the appointment. Boob was elated that in a short time he would be a young man, again.

He was waiting for me when I strolled into the office. He motioned for me to follow him into his office, covertly almost, so I followed him. He was wearing his best Brooks Brothers suit, pin striped, tailored with a Brooks Brothers button-down-collar shirt and brown slip-on shoes, with tassels.

He got this stuff for free. He told the Brooks Brothers manager cop stories and the guy believed him and gave Boob free clothing. "I need you to take me out to West County this morning, I've got a doctor's appointment. Understand?"

"Yes, sir, Lieutenant," I replied. I knew what was going on, and I knew the little star was laughing in the back room at Boob's naivete. Boob wasn't a healthy guy and the chances of a hair transplant working for him were slim to none.

"We're going to be leaving in about ten minutes," Boob said. "I'll give you the high-sign."

I waited around the office, then remembered Boob's cigar problem. He always smoked in the car and he never lowered the window. When the driver lowered his window, the cigar smoke would come through his breathing area before leaving the car. It was hideous, and torturous.

I told Boob I would be waiting for him in the car, and I walked out of the office and took the elevator down. The little detective Chevy had wing windows in the rear doors. I swung both of them open before Boob came down.

He walked to the car and waved to me, happy to be on the way to the fountain of youth. He started to close the wing window on his side, but I quickly started the car and placed it in gear which made it lurch backward, and he changed his mind and climbed in.

He directed me to the doctor's office, which was in exclusive Frontenac where only the wealthy reside, or seek physicians. I parked and we went inside. Boob was flirting with the nurses, and they were flirting back with him, and he knew them by name. They left us alone for an instant. "They love me," he assured me.

The nurses called him Lieutenant, and asked him to extinguish his cigar so they could prep him for surgery. "Watch closely at this procedure, you'll be having the same thing done in the near future," Boob said to me.

"Yes, sir," I muttered.

There were pictures of Porsches adorning the walls, a car I always dreamed of owning. "Are those the doctor's cars?" I asked.

"Yes," a nurse said, "he has a collection of them."

I couldn't figure this guy giving any police discounts to Boob or anybody else. They took Boob into a room where he changed into medical procedure garb and I asked the friendly nurse how much the procedure was.

"About ten thousand," she replied.

"But cops don't pay that much, do they?"

"Yeah, Porsches are expensive," she said with a laugh. Boob had been duped by the little star.

"Does the doctor pay for referrals?"

"Yes, he's always looking for new customers. Do you know of someone? He'd pay you ten percent."

"I'll keep my eyes open," I muttered.

They brought Boob back out. He was acting like he was a celebrity, still flirting and being brave. He had been had by the little star. "Shall I hang out in the waiting room?" I asked.

"Oh, yeah, just wait for an hour or so. This is nothing, just a little procedure. It's like getting a tooth pulled. I'll be up and about in no time," Boob said.

"It'll take about three hours," the nurse said. "The Lieutenant won't be able to do anything for a while. Can you drive him home?"

"Yes," I said.

"I won't need to go home, I'll go back to the office and resume my daily duties," Boob said.

The nurses gave me a knowing look, and I said goodbye to Boob and the nurses. I drove around for three hours, then strolled back into the doctor's office. The nurses had worried looks, and the young Porsche collector was speaking sternly to Boob, who seemed to be incoherent.

They were trying to sit him upright, but Boob couldn't sit. He was wearing a huge turban of bandages, and blood was running down his cheeks and the back of his neck. He was pale like he had fainted and been brought back around with smelling salts. The nurses were wiping the blood away, and Boob was moaning and groaning like the victim of a drive-by shooting.

"Take him straight home," the doctor said. I nodded, and the nurses and I helped Boob out to the parking lot and secured him in the detective Chevy. He still wasn't coherent, but he was able to keep his head up and wipe the blood away.

"We contacted his wife, and she'll be waiting for you when you get to his house. She'll have to help you get him into the house," a nurse advised.

I nodded and Boob and I headed for North County. Boob moaned the whole way home, but he wasn't smoking a cigar and that was a good thing. I watched him, wobbly-headed, old and pasty, mouth open and drooling, and I wondered if he was going to die in my little detective Chevy.

He started sobbing and I felt sorry for him. "What's up Lieutenant?" I asked him. "Are you in pain?"

"No," he said, "every time I think about what the Nazis did to the Jews during the war it makes me cry. The damn Holocaust, it was horrible."

I knew Boob wasn't Jewish. He'd told me he was Southern Baptist, but he hadn't been to church in decades. He'd told me a story, months earlier, that I wasn't ready to believe when I heard it. An aunt of his persuaded him to go to church with her. He had just gotten promoted to Lieutenant and was appointed Deputy Commander and he was feeling important.

His aunt, and his wife and he entered the church and sat at the back. As the service got started Boob said he inadvertently lit up a cigar. He told me he had a lot on his mind, with the new position and such, and that he didn't see anything wrong with lighting up. He was asked to leave, so he waited in the car, smoking and thinking about the unit files and the surveillance in intelligence.

When he told me that story I figured he was trying to make a correlation between being a cracker-jack investigator and smoking cigars. He wasn't an investigator to look up to. He wanted me to be like him; a cigar smoker who ponders the unit files twenty-four hours a day.

"John Doherty smokes cigars," he told me. "If John Doherty does it then it's got to be all right." I couldn't figure the alignment between Chief of Detectives, John Doherty and Boob. But they ate lunch together at least once a week. If the Chief of Police got word of the friendship Boob would be transferred back to a north district.

Boob wasn't a bad guy. He had just been a boss for too long in a specialized unit. He wasn't seeing the world realistically. He was led to believe he was special. It is the mindset needed to do the day-to-day job of a detective lieutenant in a unit wandering with confusion. He was just a mini-bureaucrat in a political, investigative unit. A unit that in reality had no mission.

I pulled into Boob's driveway and waited for about thirty seconds, but his wife didn't come out. I walked to the door and rang the bell. His wife came out and she was upset, and embarrassed, but she helped me get Boob out of my detective Chevy and into the house. It wasn't five o'clock yet, but I headed for home. I pondered the day's events.

The next morning at the office I described to my partner the outcome of Boob's hair transplant surgery. I didn't pull any punches. I gave him a blow-by-blow description. My partner acted as if he was stunned. He respected Boob and thought of him as a friend. None of us knew what to expect; it was a brutal procedure. "Boob will be off from work for weeks. He may never return," I told him.

I could hear the laughter coming from the star's office. The little star had been eavesdropping, just like he always did. He was howling and slapping his knee. Boob would never put it together. He was certain everybody loved him.

Boob never took his vacation. He gave it back to the City. I could never figure how or why someone would donate their vacation time back to the company. This was a job to me; a high-stress cop job. But it wasn't a job to the stars, or Boob. It was their religion. It was sexual gratification. It gave them purpose in life, because it was all they had. Their families meant very little to them. Being a big City cop was their priority. Nothing else was important, except promotion. Their attitudes were foreign to me.

11

I was always scrounging for a morsel of a clue on Jesse Stoneking, my targeted organized villain. I knew he was in and out of St. Louis, even though he lived in O'Fallon, Illinois, a metro-east burg. Whenever there was a horrendous unsolved crime in this jurisdiction; murder, burglary, home invasion, I suspected Jesse was the perpetrator. I never observed him.

It was early in September when I got the bad news. FBI Agent Sam Thompson had arrested Jesse Stoneking in O'Fallon, Illinois, for auto theft. An FBI agent in deep Southern Illinois, which is so backward it makes Appalachia seem like Miami Beach, had arrested the leader of a stolen car ring. They were stealing the vehicles in the sticks and then transporting them to St. Louis for sale. The guy brokering the sale of the vehicles was Jesse Stoneking.

It is a federal offense to transport stolen vehicles across state lines. Jesse should have stuck to stolen diamonds, his specialty. The Southern Illinois agent contacted Sam Thompson and asked him if he had ever heard of Jesse Stoneking. It went downhill for Jesse after that conversation.

They incarcerated Jesse in the St. Clair County jail awaiting disposition of his case. Sam Thompson went to talk to him. Sam told me he walked in and it was just Jesse and him in the room. Jesse was cordial, gave Sam a smile and held up his hands. "I'm not telling you anything," Jesse stated.

Sam played the good-cop role and told him he just wanted to talk a little. They talked about both of Jesse's families, his responsibilities in life, his past and his future. Jesse confided in Sam that he had been a police officer at one time, in a little railroad-track burg near Brooklyn, Illinois.

Jesse and Art Berne's top Lieutenant, Don Ellington, devised a scheme so they could steal from the railroad cars at night. Jesse didn't last long.

He severely beat up an informant for DEA who was selling drugs on his beat.

Don Ellington became uncontrollable and surly to Art Berne. He turned up dead, shot with a forty-five in Jefferson County, Missouri, after meeting with Jesse Stoneking for lunch. Jesse conveniently took his place as the number one soldier for Art Berne.

But there is another side to the Don Ellington murder. George Eidson, safe burglar and stick up man, specializing in gems, and a long-time associate of Jesse Stoneking, advised me that Jesse wanted to make a move on the Fairmont Race Track on the Eastside. Possibly a robbery.

Ellington was a union steward at the track. He was loyal to the track owners and the workers there. He told Jesse to stay away from the race track.

In Jesse's mind, nothing was sacred. A score was a score no matter where it was or who was involved. There was big money at the track in the evening hours. Jesse wanted it.

Jesse and Don Ellington met in Jefferson County, Missouri, in a rural location. Jesse allegedly climbed into Don's Caddy, and after some conversation, Jesse shot Don Ellington with a 45-automatic handgun. Don's foot went down onto the accelerator; Jesse jumped out. The car went against a tree and eventually caught fire.

"Art Berne and the organization will take care of my two families while I'm gone," Jesse told Sam Thompson during their impromptu meeting. He said it was the unwritten creed of organized criminals. Sam walked out and Jesse was subsequently sentenced to 3-years.

Jesse was the super criminal I had dreamed of nabbing. I was shocked he had been a cop. But I was shocked I had become a cop.

I knew there were going to be more bombings. It would be something to do for a while, but the Feds were going to clean up all of the organized crooks in the region, sooner or later. They were too brazen, there were too many informants and the crimes had gained national attention. The bombings were horrendous. It was terrorism in middle America. The strange part of the bombing and violence cycle was there didn't appear to be anything here worth killing for.

But, if being a cop is like being a career criminal, then why didn't I go to Los Angeles, or San Diego to be a cop? They pay more, and it has the beauty and the weather. But it isn't home. We all desire the feeling of being home. It's what makes us drive ourselves in our pursuit of happiness. It has to do with place. We all have something inside of us dictating where that certain place is that we should be.

My dilemma was: what would I do when the union crooks were dead, incarcerated or out of the crook business? There was no super-criminal for me to think about. All of the other crooks were blasé compared to Jesse. He had panache.

But there would always be the stone fetish. Home invasions, burglaries, and armed robberies of jewelry stores would always be prevalent. It's where the money was. It was the crooks' avocation, right behind being murdering power brokers.

Charles "Johnny" Michaels, one of the conspirators in the revenge bombing of Paul Leisure, was a card-carrying Local 562 pipefitter. He had a good job at the brewery and he was a product of the prestige bestowed upon him from his bloodline. In St. Louis he was royalty.

The word on the street was that he, his cousin, City of St. Louis official, Sonny Faheen, Chief of Police of St. George, Missouri, Russ Schepp and some of Johnny's loser friends had bombed Paul Leisure for the revenge of his uncle, Jimmy Michaels. If the cops and the special agents got word of it, then Paul, Anthony and David Leisure knew what had transpired.

The Edge Restaurant, Chouteau and LaSalle, was the lunch meeting place of the union hoodlums. It was a classy mobster-decorated type of place: dark wood, red flocked wall paper, and elaborate back bar, where you could order off of the menu or go through the cafeteria line.

Local businessmen usually went through the cafeteria line. These were business owners in the neighborhood, and from throughout the City, who on a daily basis had to do business with the union hoodlums.

The waitresses were dressed like Playboy bunnies, and the barmaids bore cleavage like strippers. The union hoodlums would sit at the bar, order off of the menu and drool at the cleavage, spend money on drinks, tip lavishly, and talk about how successful they were. It was a contrast of ideology, and I would often go in there for lunch just to watch the two sides glare at each other.

On September eleventh, shortly after Jesse Stoneking got popped by the FBI, Charles "Johnny" Michaels, not a hoodlum, but someone who lived off of the legacy, and an innocent associate, Dennis Day, had eaten lunch at The Edge. They were walking to their car in the parking lot, which was near a line of abandoned houses.

Anthony and David Leisure were hiding in the vacant house that Fred Prater had selected for them. It was closest to the lot. Prater even cut a hole in the chain link fence so Anthony could stick the barrel of a shotgun through. They fired at the duo, injuring but not killing Michaels and his friend.

It was a stupid attempt at murder. There was bird shot in the shotgun and it wouldn't have killed anybody unless it had been fired at point blank range. Paul Leisure wouldn't have made such a feeble attempt, but he was crippled with mangled legs, recuperating at his mother's house and would never be a threat to any human again, except to give the orders to kill.

All Paul Leisure had now was a big reputation and a murdering mind. He prayed that God would give him the ability to walk again so he could kill people. The FBI taped that statement shortly after he got blown up at his mother's house. But Paul the brain was working overtime thinking about revenge, and liabilities. He knew he was vulnerable, for the first time in his life.

Johnny Michaels went into hiding. His cousin, Sonny Faheen didn't and he wasn't so lucky. On October 16, 1981, George "Sonny" Faheen climbed into his Volkswagen Bug, which was parked in the Mansion House subterranean garage, a fashionable upscale apartment complex overlooking the Mississippi River.

David Leisure and two associates, Michael Kornhardt and another gangster, had placed a dynamite bomb in the trunk of the Volkswagen, near the gas tank. When Sonny Faheen hit the ignition the bomb exploded the gas tank, which was in the front of the vehicle. The explosion and fire ignited gasoline, cooking Sonny Faheen to death.

I went to the scene shortly after the call came out. Sonny Faheen was sitting at the wheel of the Volkswagen, cooked like a ninth-inning ballpark hot dog. Another horrendous bombing in a highly public location.

The Feds had an informant on the inside with the Leisures. They were advised Ray Flynn had assisted David Leisure with surveillance of Faheen's daily schedule. The Feds had also been advised Ray Flynn had provided the dynamite used in the Sonny Faheen murder. He had brought the dynamite to the White Castle lot at Vandeventer and Chouteau the day before the bombing and had given it to Anthony Leisure.

Paul Leisure, who by then frequented his tow lot in a wheel chair, with half of his massive body blown to smithereens by Charles "Johnny"

Michaels and Chief Russ Schepp, had time to think and contemplate his next move. It appeared the Feds had an informant on the inside of his gang, and if they didn't, they soon would have. It's the way the system works.

He knew the weak link in his organization was Michael Kornhardt. He was the only member of the gang who wasn't actually a criminal. He had assisted with the placing of the bomb in Sonny Faheen's Volkswagen. But to him, being a gangster was a hobby.

This whole scene was a joke to him. I had had him under surveillance. He was gangly, with a full head of hair and dressed like a guy who worked in a tow lot, for that's what his job was. He had apparently never had any friends in his life. He walked around, slumped over, drooped shoulders, looking down, with a smirk on his face, like he was trying to tell the world he had finally arrived, that he was a part of something, and he knew something nobody else knew, except his brother gang members. He thought he was an insider, a made guy. I had seen the look in my office.

He had come from working folks, was impressionable, and just wanted to be a member of something, anything that would make him somebody. He chose the wrong crowd to hang with.

The Leisures were too stupid to out-think the United States government. Listening devices were placed inside the towing office. They were damaging to everyone who ever made a statement in there.

Paul had given the order to kill Michael Kornhardt. Anthony, David, and some of their loser friends openly discussed the murder, in the presence of Fred Prater. Prater objected, and was heard on tape telling the misfits if anything happened to Kornhardt, he was out of the business.

But the murder order had been issued by Paul Leisure, and when that's the case, it is etched in stone. They assured Fred Prater that they wouldn't harm Kornhardt, and he acted as if he bought it. But he didn't.

Michael Kornhardt was arrested for the bombing of Sonny Faheen and was being held in the St. Louis City Jail. Records obtained by the FBI showed that Sorkis Webbe Jr., the seventh ward Democratic alderman for the City of St. Louis, had made inquiries about Kornhardt through deputy sheriffs who work at the jail. Sorkis Webbe Jr. wanted to know if Kornhardt had made any incriminating statements to authorities.

Sorkis Webbe Jr. apparently reported his findings to Paul Leisure. Kornhardt was bailed out of jail. Paul Leisure gave the order for Michael Kornhardt to be eliminated. David Leisure gave the contract to two of his associates.

Kornhardt was so trusting of his gang buddies he willingly went with them to St. Charles County and walked into a field with them, under the pretense of walking through a cornfield to gain access to a farmhouse they had planned to burglarize. They shot him in the head and left him to die.

Fred Prater went to the FBI and turned informant. Prater knew that the only gang members immune from the maniac murderer Paul Leisure were Paul's relatives. Everybody else was an outsider, just like Kornhardt. The Feds immediately placed his family into the witness protection program, sold their home, and hid them. Fred wasn't just a workaholic, mechanic, and businessman, he was also a bomb maker.

The FBI debriefed him; he admitted to making the bomb that killed Jimmy Michaels. He had practiced detonating the device with a remote control transmitter he had fabricated. He and Anthony Leisure rode around the City with Fred's practice bomb detonator in hand, activating it and watching the tail lights go on on Anthony's car, a Chrysler Cordoba they had purchased to practice the deed, just like the one Jimmy Michaels drove.

They went through the drill of attaching the bomb to the Cordoba, crawling under it and timing themselves. They got it down pat, and David Leisure, the retarded one, was adept at attaching the bomb in about one minute. Everybody's good at something.

The FBI phone taps on Paul Leisure opened the door, along with Fred Prater's cooperation, for a successful prosecution of all parties involved. In taped conversations with Sorkis Webbe Jr., Paul Leisure was taped saying, St. Louis cops were pussies and that if they went to the penitentiary they'd turn into punks. He wanted to kill cops, beat them with his fists, then stomp them to death. He talked about shooting it out with the cops, "Just give me two forty-fives, I'd eat them like hamburger."

Sorkis Webbe Jr. responds, "You know they're gone. Bye-Bye Birdie."

United States Attorney Tom Dittmeier, a fighter in the courtroom and in the boxing ring, had what he needed from the FBI. He had informants. He had tape recordings, and he took them to the grand jury. David and Anthony Leisure, along with several of their gang members, were federally indicted. As is often the case in a little City like St. Louis, where everybody knows everybody, the indictment information leaked out.

David Leisure sought refuge in the Mayfair Hotel in downtown St. Louis which was owned by power broker and fellow Syrian politico Sorkis Webbe, and operated by his son, Sorkis Webbe Jr., the St. Louis City alderman who had already been taped by the FBI talking to Paul Leisure.

Little Sork was coddled and spoiled for his entire life. Clean cut, suave and handsome, but small in stature, he could have written his own ticket to anywhere, but he chose to stay in St. Louis.

When ordinary folks in his age group were delivering pizzas and newspapers, cutting grass, or waiting tables, Little Sork was driving roadsters and dating beautiful, young girls. And he was a scratch golfer. His future was secure no matter what tack he took, but he went into the family business; hotels, casinos and organized criminal associates. Had he grown up in Los Angeles instead of St. Louis, he would have been in the movie business, maybe a leading man.

Junior Sork hid David Leisure in a laundry basket while the Feds searched the hotel for him. The Webbes also owned the Aladdin Hotel and Casino in Las Vegas, with Peter Webbe, local politico and relative. It's where Elvis and Priscilla were married. It's the casino where the first million-dollar slot machine was hit. It was the casino the St. Louis and Detroit mob controlled.

They were old power and old money, but Sorkis Webbe Jr. couldn't say no to the animal, David Leisure. His compliance was instinctive; it went back centuries to Syria where the only people you could trust were the ones with the same bloodline.

You dealt with your own kind, traded camels with them, sold rugs to them, hid them from their enemies. Everyone in your clan was a cousin, and sometimes you married them. David Leisure was no doubt a product of that, somewhere a long time ago.

The Leisures and the Michaeles were royalty, but the Webbes were the kings of the clans. Sorkis Webbe Sr. had only to say, "Stop the killing, the bombings," and they would have stopped, but he didn't, even though he had said he had.

That irresponsible act led to the crumbling of his empire. He set his son and himself up for scrutiny like never before. It was the swan song for the Webbes. Death to one. Senior died at age fifty-five. Painful incarceration to the other.

But Sorkis Webbe Sr. didn't go down without a fight. He grabbed onto a faithful friend and dragged him down with him. Senior was being investigated by the Nevada Gaming Board and the United States Attorney in Las Vegas. Chief of Detectives John Doherty went to Vegas and was a character witness for him.

The newspapers in St. Louis had a field day with the testimony. There was a picture of Colonel Doherty stating to the United States Attorney, "I'm not a gangster." And an association between Colonel Doherty and an area businessman, Eugene Slay, came out. Doherty was on his payroll as a security consultant.

Eugene Slay was the brother of Henry, (Hank) Slay, the guy riding in the front seat with Mike Trupiano while the New Jersey gangsters were in the backseat when I made the car stop for Guido. And Stretch. When I read the article I felt like I got kicked in the gut.

Colonel Doherty was called on the carpet by the Board of Police Commissioners. As he spoke with them he testified that he had checked with the deputy commander of Intelligence about the character of Sorkis Webbe Sr. and was advised he was an honest attorney with political ties.

Boob was interviewed concerning this information. He told the board that Sorkis Webbe Sr. wasn't in file in the unit records. It was now the swan song for Boob. It was just a matter of time before he would be gone from the unit. John Doherty was too powerful and well liked to be moved or forced to retire. Boob was the likely scapegoat.

The Webbes rubbed shoulders and broke bread with some of the most powerful men in the world, but when the United States Judicial System wants you, there's no place to hide. The machine devours you, piece by piece.

Little Sork's assistance with the hiding of the fugitive David Leisure brought federal attention to him. He was later indicted for a cable television bribery scam, the hiding of a federal fugitive, David Leisure, and incarcerated federally after pleading guilty. He and his dad were involved in the City of St. Louis cable television scam with Mike Trupiano and Art Berne. They were extorting money from the cable television companies for the promise of influence.

They were already wealthy; business owners, casino owners, successful politicians. But the scam was too appealing to pass up. Not just a television scam, which would have probably netted them millions, but any scam. It was their heritage, the American way. They believed it was the right thing to do.

His father was indicted with him, but he conveniently died before he could go to trial. Little Sork was sentenced to eleven years and sent to a federal prison in Florida. His mother wrote a sad letter to the *Post-Dispatch* in defense of little Sork.

She was alone, now. She had been a part of the vast empire, brought down to rubble by criminal loyalty, poor choices, and braggadocio. Sork bragged he was raised on the streets of St. Louis and he'd killed before, and that he was a tough guy. He was fooling himself and anyone who was listening. The problem was the FBI, a federal prosecutor and the United States Attorney were the only ones who believed him.

Little Sork, the privileged gangster wannabe with a pedigree, went off to federal incarceration. His mother purchased a condo in Florida near the penitentiary so she could be close to him.

David Leisure was still in hiding. My partner and I had information about an old girlfriend of David's who lived in south St. Louis. It was a hunch, but we had nothing better to do. One afternoon we had just gotten into the detective Chevy with nothing to do and nowhere to go.

I had dug the girlfriend's name and address out of the files. It was in an old memorandum written by a detective who was no longer a cop. We drove by the place, stopped and went to the door.

We were playing it by ear. A homely, chunky woman came to the door. "Where's David?" I asked. I didn't know what the response would be. She was terrified by our presence. I shoved the door, and her, out of the way and we walked in, like the KGB.

"We're searching your house," I informed her. She didn't object, so we searched. I didn't think we would find him, but it was fodder for a memorandum to Captain Bud and Boob, so we looked around.

We were about to leave, when I opened the hall closet. He was hiding in there, like a small child playing hide and seek, in a fetal position. His parents had kept him in a cage when he was a youngster. He was used to being confined. He had long brown hair, not long like a hippie, but scraggly like a street person. He had a bloated belly, like a dog that would eat until it foundered. He wore dirty jeans and a T, and he stunk. The seriousness of being captured hadn't made it to his damaged brain. He smiled, but I could tell he was scared.

It scared me, and I reacted. I grabbed him by the shirt and dragged him out into the hallway, cursing him and shouting. I figured he would have a weapon, at least a gun and that he would start shooting us.

He cowered like a street dog who was used to being beaten, covering his ears and jaw. He apparently thought we were going to kill him, or at the very least, beat him. He didn't resist as we cuffed him and walked him to the little Chevy. We turned him over to some Fed, never even got his name, and we were written out of the equation. We told Captain Bud and Boob about it in a memorandum, but we didn't receive any accolades for our stellar detective work.

It kind of dawned on me why the stars bragged about their police work. It took a braggart to survive in this game. There were too many player cops who would steal your thunder in a heartbeat. David Leisure never breathed the air of freedom again, and he was eventually executed.

Paul Leisure had problems on the state and federal level. He was on trial in state court for the conspiracy to murder and the subsequent murder of Sonny Faheen. All of his associates had snitched on him. Once one of them goes down, all of them turn on the leader. Fred Prater was the one who pulled the plug on the ill-fated ship. It started sinking and all of the rats leaped off, seeking refuge anywhere they could get it. The FBI was waiting for them, but that agency didn't need more snitches. They wanted blood, unless the information they got was better, or different than Fred Prater's.

It was them or you syndrome, and the band of murderers, thieves, bombers, home invaders, and pimps were scratching their heads to gain prominence with the FBI, the thing they had hated the most for their entire adult lives.

Lady Justice doesn't see or hear, but she knows what's going on. She patiently waits for the career criminal to pass by her statue as the scales of justice vibrate with excitement.

I went to the courthouse, just briefly to see who was in court. You never know who you might see there. Paul Leisure was sitting in court, at the defendants table, shackled to a wheel chair, pale, gaunt and bitter.

He had been incarcerated without bond for his involvement in the Michael Kornhardt murder, but was on trial for the Sonny Faheen bombing. I had heard that while he was awaiting trial his sisters, cousins and family friends brought him Syrian food to get him healthy. There were several unattractive, chunky women in the courtroom crying and making eye contact with him. I wondered if they were the food providers. As soon as he got convicted and transferred to a penitentiary, their job would be over. Paul wouldn't be royalty in the joint.

He was a wounded vampire, partially maddened by incarceration, totally insane from genetics. I watched him as the procedure went on. He was obviously not recovering from being blown up in the Caddy in front of his mother's house.

He was having difficulty breathing and he breathed out of his mouth. He had the look and sound of Satan when he breathed. It was like a horror flick where the person playing one of the vampire roles suddenly turns into the monster vampire who kills everybody he sees. I always thought it was strange nobody ever tried to fight off a vampire.

But it would have been the same with Paul Leisure, when he was in his prime. You could try to fight him, but it wouldn't have done any good. He was strong like an animal, and bloodthirsty like Count Dracula.

Paul started making hissing sounds, and looked around the courtroom as if he was going to stand and kill everybody in attendance, ripping their heads off, or worse. It was a frightening bit of theatrics, but nobody seemed to be impressed with his scariness, except maybe me.

I had seen similar charades in East St. Louis, Illinois, and in the Marine Corps. Guys in the Marine Corps went through some of the same antics trying to get a crazy discharge. It was amusing watching them, but they were nutty Marines wanting to go home.

Paul Leisure was the real thing, and I was taken aback by his performance. But as I thought about it, the judge wasn't impressed, and the prosecutor wasn't impressed. I think he thought that maybe someday he would get out of prison and come back to St. Louis, and that if he put on a vampire, killer act, now, maybe someone would remember it and be fearful of him.

You have to know your enemy, his strengths and his weaknesses. Paul was now a vampire in the sun, shackled and dying. He would never kill again. He was incarcerated for life on the state charge, and soon after he died in jail.

My partner and I had to do our turn at the night watch, which meant we were scheduled to work from six P.M. to two A.M. It's a pretty good gig, mainly because all of the bosses are gone when you get to work. It's like having the evening off.

We strolled into the office and Boob was still there. We were shocked and let down. We didn't want to see him and the indication was that he was checking up on us to see if we would get to the office by six o'clock.

He wore his south side gangster hat to hide his scarred head. As I figured, his hair transplant didn't take. Most of the plugs had fallen out, leaving small, oozing divots all over his head. He was too old and too unhealthy for it to take on him. The doctor knew it, but Boob was ten grand on the hoof. Now he would not only act like a Boob and be called a Boob, but he would look like a Boob. Disgusting! "Here's a test for you boys," he said. We stared and waited. "Where did Ray Flynn grow up?"

I waited for a second to see if my partner could answer the question. "Pine Lawn is where Ray Flynn grew up," I replied. Guido had told me that historical revelation. "He was a street gang member, car thief, burglar and tough kid. He was so tough that Jimmy Michaels heard about his capabilities, and hired him as a driver and bodyguard for him. He'd turned on his mentor for Paul Leisure." Boob stared.

"It's the irony of the crime business," I continued. "Anthony Giordano heard about John Paul Spica in the same manner. He hired Spica as his driver and bodyguard. Both Flynn and Spica went to prison, Spica for a contract murder, and Flynn for burglary. Both of them wanted control of Laborers Local 42. Flynn crossed the finish line a winner. Spica ran his mouth and was eliminated by a car bomb."

Boob acted impressed. "You get the gold star for today, detective," he said. He winked, turned and walked out. "What was that all about?" my partner asked. He was upset. Hours in a police car give insight into your partner. I knew him well. This cloak and dagger office politics environment wasn't for him. His skin was too thin for it. He took it personal. Boob was trying to turn us against each other. Divide and conquer, it was their creed, but my partner wouldn't understand the concept if I explained it to him. I had to explain it away and get on with our cop livelihood.

"Who knows," I muttered. "You knew this was a strange place to work when you came here. I didn't know, but I learned quickly. These supervisors have complete control over us because we like it here. Most of the rank and file guys would do anything to stay here for their entire career. You and I are no different. Realize it and get over it, or go back to the black district you came from and resume your life there. But you won't, because you're hooked on this lifestyle just like the rest of us. Here, when you're the low man on the totem pole you're still head and shoulders above the guys in the districts. The system's made that way, it's how they control us and make us do their bidding. Let's go and eat a free gourmet meal."

12

Things had slowed down in the little burg of St. Louis. My new partner and I were interviewing Teamster officials. The interview was my mainstay. I came about it naturally, and I enjoyed it. It was partial intimidation, partial intelligence, partial moxie. I wasn't afraid of the union thugs. I held contempt for them and they sensed it.

Even though my partner was a "made" cop, he worked the street with me like he was a street guy, because at heart he was. My only problem with the new partner was, he felt he was in charge of me. He didn't know anything about being a detective in an intelligence unit. I knew all about it. I taught him everything I knew, and he acted like he appreciated it.

But during my interviews with the union thugs, in their own offices, on their turf, I would get one of them against the wall with questions and fear, and my partner would jump in with some strange utterance or question that would break my rhythm.

There was a knack to interviewing union officials. You had to walk in like you owned the place. These guys were insulated from the everyday run of the mill straight guy. I'd walk up to their secretary, ask for the guy and then walk into his office without being announced.

I would smile, like I was trying to sell him something, then I would sit down and start talking to him, maybe say something that evoked a smile from him. They knew you were there to lock them up, and they also knew it wasn't going to happen, but there was still intimidation and fear being absorbed by them through your presence.

The subject matter I always began with was honesty in the labor movement in St. Louis. It made them feel you cared about their plight, because deep down inside, they felt the same way you did. But they didn't want to tell you anything for fear of being bombed, or worse, having a family member killed or injured.

The Teamster officials I dealt with, through my interviews, all handled money. They were the secretary-treasurers and presidents of the locals; the only folks I would interview. They all had self-imposed guilt. So, all I had to do was start talking about something I had heard through some form of intelligence, usually information from another union official told to me to get me out of his office, and into another local's office.

So, I would hit them with the question about a meeting where a death threat was made, or about the intimidation of a businessman by a union official, or of the rumor funds were being diverted to organized criminals. That was always a good one, because funds were always being diverted to someone's pocket. It freaked them.

I had been to the FBI Interview and Interrogation School. I knew how to interview. I didn't want to tell my partner to keep quiet when I was interviewing someone. He had a right to join in the questioning, but he was ignorant of the art form, and it was displeasing to me.

I had asked Lieutenant Boob to ask Captain Bud to enroll my new partner in the class. He took the class and things began rolling along better.

We made a game out of the interview. I would interview one guy, and then he would have his turn with another one. There were plenty to go around. I had dug some information out of the files pertaining to the building of an old sports stadium. It pertained to payoffs being given to local politicians by a corporation doing business in St. Louis. They ran the concessions at the stadium. I was skeptical about political information in the unit files. Cop detectives would write anything to appease the bosses.

The little star eavesdropped on me and went to Lieutenant Boob with my idea. He came storming to my desk and ordered me to cease and desist. He spat a wad of cigar at me and walked back to his office. I rationalized my predicament. It would have been entertaining but nothing would have come from the investigation. There was cash flowing to the members of the blue ribbon committees chaired by the ruling class of the City. In their minds, it is their birthright to be bribed by organized criminals. The birthright bureaucrats are probably all dead. The money has been passed on to their heirs. It's a waste. It's all about the money. Nothing else matters.

Old money is always looking for new ways to make more money. It doesn't have to be legal, preferably not legal is the best kind. It's tax free. They've got all of the bases covered in this town, and they don't mind doing business with the union thugs sometimes, if it benefits them personally.

My partner and I were back to looking for something to do. We were milling around the office getting ready to go out for the day, without any plan, just working the street. I got a call from a cop in a Metro-East jurisdiction seeking assistance. He had arrested a burglar, and upon interviewing the thief, he was told that the jewels he had stolen were sold at Lordo's, a jeweler in downtown St. Louis. He wanted me to meet him at the jewelry store to retrieve the jewelry.

I thought it was a great idea. I was aware of the store, and its owner. It was exclusive, and the owner was close friends with the Chief of Police and every other high-ranking cop in the City. He gave lavish gifts of rings, watches, and items of intrinsic value to the chief, and most of the deputy chiefs. I didn't have a problem with his generosity toward the brass. If he wished to give his fortune away to cop managers, then that was his business.

I told the out-of-state cop I would meet him at the store. I briefed my partner and we were walking out of the office when Boob came out of his office, blowing cigar smoke in my face. "Where are you going?"

I ran it down to him. "No, you are forbidden to go to that store. That guy's best of friends with the Chief of Detectives, the Chief of Police, and all of the deputy chiefs." I stared at Boob. My partner went back to his desk.

"The guy's a fence," I said to Boob. "Who cares who his friends are? There's a victim of a burglary wanting his jewelry back. A cop's going to be waiting for us at the store."

"The owner's got a pawn-shop license," Boob replied. "He committed no crime. State statute gives him the right to buy anything he wants through his store. Let the bureau of investigation handle it. You're not going."

I went back to my desk and telephoned the out-of-state cop. I told him to call the bureau of investigation, that the guy has a pawn-shop license, and the chances of his victim getting his jewelry back were slim. I was embarrassed, but that's life in the big City. Hey, it was the 5th of June; summer in St. Louis, I was able to shake it off and look ahead to the rest of the season.

My partner and I did paperwork for the remainder of the morning. Guido came in and stared at me. It was his way to communicate with me before he started to speak. It was an Italian thing. "John Vitale died this morning," he solemnly said. He smiled, "you remember him, don't you?"

"Yeah, Guido, are you going to be one of his pall bearers?" I was smiling. He laughed it off. "Another federal snitch bites the dust, Guido. Where are you and your Fed buddies going to get your information now?"

"There's more where he came from," he said with a laugh.

We worked John Vitale's funeral as a unit, doing surveillance of the funeral home, taking pictures, gathering license numbers. I sat in a surveillance van in a large rotating leather chair, with a periscope like a nuclear submarine, taking pictures and reading off license plate numbers while my partner wrote them down.

The union gangsters knew we were there. They were paranoid crooks with high-ranking friends within the police department. They were no doubt given the description of our van. Two of them walked over to it, banged on the side and shouted, "Have you no respect for the dead?"

We didn't respond. It reminded me of submarine sailors hiding from Japanese destroyers in the Pacific in World War II, slowly breathing and sweating, being cautious not to make a sound for fear the enemy boats would hear the noise and drop depth charges.

The exercise was ludicrous. Who cared about who attended John Vitale's funeral? Is association that important? I was all for crawling out of the van and slugging it out with the goons who were banging on it. Their act was more disrespectful than taking pictures of a gangster associate. But we didn't, we hid like submerged little rabbits, until the big bad wolves went inside of the funeral home.

It turned out to be a good month for crime. On June thirteenth, three masked gunmen barged into Lordo's, the exclusive jewelry store in downtown St. Louis, the one that I was forbidden to go to for the retrieval of stolen jewelry. They pistol-whipped the security guard, terrorized the well- connected owner and stole over a million in jewelry, stones and wristwatches.

The owner must have been beside himself with despair. He had given away millions over the years to the upper echelon of the police department, presumably buying protection, influence and prestige, in the not-so-prestigious jewelry business. It was all for naught. But if you lay down with dogs you'll come up with fleas. The robbers got away scot-free.

We were told to stay away from the investigation. The Bureau of Investigation had taken the case. It was clear to me the robbers were the union gangsters we were dealing with on a day-to-day basis. They were enjoying their hobby and satisfying their fetish, robbing for gems. It was the irony of the crime business.

Matthew "Mike" Trupiano was now the reputed head of the St. Louis Italian faction. The cops and Feds nicknamed him, Mike the inept. He wasn't a bright guy and he didn't have the backing of the rank and file gangsters in the region, but he had the blessing of Joey (Doves) Aiuppa in Chicago, and that's all it takes to be the boss here.

I had bumped heads with him and I wasn't impressed with his response. But I wasn't impressed with Salvatore Profaci, the Capo from New Jersey, or his body guard henchman, Dominic Montemarano, either. I had so much hatred for the organized gangsters that I took chances to get to screw with them. I knew I was tempting fate, but it was the only way I could let them know there was somebody somewhere who disrespected them enough to risk getting into their faces and defying them. It was the same with Captain Bud and Lieutenant Boob. It was martyrdom, an East St. Louis thing.

The Syrian faction blew each other up and the ones who were still standing went to prison, Tony Giordano, before he died was the guy who made Mike Trupiano the head of Laborers Local 110. So Mike had a good job, a car, expense money, and what was left of the rackets in St. Louis.

He ran a sports gambling ring and tried to get the local hoodlums to hustle for him, but they didn't respect him enough to go out of their way to please him. He was referred to as a whiner, not a good leader, and stupid.

Guido told me that Trupiano had gotten into the massage parlor and topless bar business over in the east side, my old home town. I perked up at the news and my partner and I started driving over there on sunny afternoons to see who came and went from the sex businesses.

A new name came up, Nando Bartolotta, allegedly a made guy by Tony Giordano before he died. We did some investigating on Nando. He was the son of a tailor who was a lifetime associate of organized criminals, and was being trained to be a tailor by his father when he came into contact with Giordano, through his father's introduction. He was whisked into the gangster business by Giordano and placed under the tutelage of Trupiano.

I envisioned his tailor-dad bragging at family reunions. "Yeah, little Nando couldn't make it in the tailor business, but I took care of him. I got him into the Mafia. He's a made guy. He doesn't have to work the streets, he gets the best assignments."

My partner and I figured the organized criminal bosses were grasping at straws, frantically trying to find someone who would follow Mike Trupiano into the darkness of the criminal world. It was all but washed up on the St. Louis side. The Eastside was again the future for organized crime. The Mafia in St. Louis was a joke.

It had always been that way. It breeds and grows over there, on the Eastside, until it becomes strong, like a deadly germ, and then it makes its way across the Mississippi River into St. Louis through some crack in the wall of despair, like a bridge project and union infiltration.

Before the folks in St. Louis figure out what's happening, it's a full-scale epidemic controlling and ruining their lives. They look across the river at the squalor; they curse and spit, but there's nothing they can do. The gangster germ controls them.

Then, after decades of carnage, the germ is weakened, injured, but not eradicated. It swims back across the Mississippi, into East St. Louis where it is nurtured and given another disguise. This time the new disguise is sex.

Another new name popped up, Dennis Sonnenschein, a St. Louis man with massage parlors in Jefferson County, Missouri, as well as East St. Louis. Somehow, Nando Bartolotta had wormed his way into a partnership with Sonnenschein at the Golden Girls night club in East St. Louis.

My partner and I had driven around all of the massage parlors and night clubs. They were lucrative, twenty-four hours a day. Sex was big business. But what Sonnenschein apparently didn't realize was that organized crime traditionally ran sex-for-cash enterprises, not greedy young businessmen.

We set up surveillance on Golden Girls. It should have been called Gold Rush girls. It wasn't opened yet, and had liquor license problems (looking for the right person to bribe), but there were people coming and going. We did some background on these places. Some were makeshift portable buildings, slapped together on a vacant lot with gravel parking lots and weeds surrounding them.

Others were existing dwellings that had been abandoned, enlarged, remodeled and turned into sex clubs. They were owned by businessmen throughout the country. A large group of lawyers in Colorado owned some of them. Silent partners from St. Louis, doctors, lawyers, legitimate businessmen were investing in the East St. Louis cash-for-sex trade.

All of them were paying protection to Art Berne, with the largest part of the proceeds going to Joey (Doves) Aiuppa in Chicago. Mike Trupiano got his share through Nando Bartolotto and Dennis Sonnenschien.

Nando was allegedly Sonnenschien's bodyguard, but my partner and I came to the conclusion he was his handler, the way a pimp covets a whore. It proves the adage that we are all whores for somebody.

We wanted to interview Nando Bartolotta. It was more of a harassment interview than anything else. We hated him, even though we had never met him. The word on the street was that he was an aggressive little gangster who would do anything, anytime. Murder, extortion, burglary.

We were out of our jurisdiction, but I didn't care. My partner was a bit anxious, but it was old home week for me. I grew up at twenty-first and State Street. I was right at home at Golden Girls.

We walked in like the KGB on a bright afternoon, and the place was packed with construction people making the last-minute changes before opening day. Somebody had just thrown a fire-bomb onto the roof, again, and it took extensive repair to bring it to code.

Strippers were doing their things on and off the stage, auditioning and practicing on the poles. I asked a nice-looking young lady where Nando was, and she pointed to a table in the back. It was so pat. These guys played the game like a cheap movie, they always sat at a table at the back of the place.

We walked over to him. He was checking us out, but I was sure he knew who we were. Mike Trupiano had doubtless given him my description and name, and described to him how I had disrespected him in front of the New Jersey gangsters.

Nando stayed seated and we sat down at his table without being asked to. He should have stayed with the tailor business; he looked the part. He wore the Sonny Bono haircut, big-collared shirt, European-style clothing, shiny pants, Italian shoes (no diamonds, though). He wasn't a big guy, and he wasn't imposing or intimidating. He had clearly chosen the wrong vocation.

He smiled at us, which I thought was an intelligent thing for him to do. He wasn't going to play the tough gangster role. He was taking a more educated approach. He knew we didn't have anything on him, and that we were out of our jurisdiction, so he figured he would go through the routine for us and maybe we would leave him alone after that.

"City Intelligence," I said to him offering him my card. He took it, read it, and placed it on the table in front of him. "We thought we'd pay you a courtesy call, Nando." He didn't respond, he just smiled and waited.

"We hear you're a gangster, a made guy. That true?"

"No," he began. He slid out of his chair and did a standup comic routine on us, and by the time we left him we were laughing. He was the tailor's kid, the one who could tap dance and sing and was an altar boy. His mom and dad had no doubt doted on him as a child. Little Nando, the talented entertainer.

He shook our hand, wanted to buy us lunch, wanted to give us free passes to his club, and probably would have had our detective car washed for us if we'd asked him. The guy had been cribbed, and he knew how to respond. He and Trupiano and Sonnenschien were making too much money to be concerned with a couple of KGB agents from across the Mississippi River. We were old hat to them and they felt safe and secure.

The problem was that we had played our hand. Now everybody in the sex business was expecting us to pay them a visit. So we did. At every club, we were met by gorgeous young women who said they were the managers.

I could never figure where these gorgeous gals came from. There were so many of them, and they weren't trashy looking, they were first-class, clean-looking women; the kind every red- blooded young American boy desires. They were like Hollywood starlets. They were too beautiful to be true. But, that's the kind of gals we encountered at the clubs. It was confusing. We never got to interview Sonnenschien.

So, we continued with surveillance and got tons of names of patrons of the sex clubs, and we wrote memos to Captain Bud and Lieutenant Boob about the surveillance and it kept them off of our backs for a while. I often wondered what Captain Bud did with the information we gathered. It had to be damaging to some of the patrons.

The summer flew by and mid-September was upon us. My partner was on one of his many vacations and I was happily alone. Guido asked me if I wanted to go to lunch with him and Stretch. I gladly accepted. Lunch usually meant surveillance. We drove over to Belleville and walked into Augustine's Restaurant. They had a buffet lunch which was excellent, and most of the gangster big shots ate lunch there.

We were on our second helping of pasta when Guido nudged me. "Look over your left shoulder, the table by the door and tell me who you see." I complied; there was a muscular looking guy with a lady there and they were having lunch. There was something familiar about the guy, but I didn't put it together.

"So what?" I muttered.

"It's Jesse Stoneking," he softly muttered.

I snapped my head back to look at him and he was looking back at me with an "I'll kill you if you look at me," look. I took a mental picture of him and tried not to visually respond to his kill look.

I was amazed at how close I was to him. I could have thrown a garlic roll and hit him in the face with it. And I was shocked at how much alike we were. He was about my age, size and build. His mannerisms were a lot like mine, but he had more hair. He had my attitude. Eastside syndrome, and we dressed alike, Polo, khakis, slip-on shoes.

We finished our meal and wandered out to the parking lot. We set up surveillance on a lot adjacent to the restaurant parking lot and waited. Jesse and his girlfriend came out and got into a late model four-door white Lincoln Town Car, and drove off. We didn't follow him.

We wondered how he got out so soon. He had only been in prison for a year or so. "Somebody should inform Sam Thompson that Jesse's out and about," I said.

"I'll do it," Guido replied. "You know Sam's been transferred. He's in the Belleville office now."

"No, I didn't know that. What's up with that?"

"Don't know, but that's where he is. I'll call him."

I sat in the back seat and watched the landscape. Most of my East St. Louis relatives had moved to Belleville. I knew the area as well as I knew East St. Louis and St. Louis. It was still old home week for me every time I went over there.

We all come back home. It's like we all have an inner magnetic draw to our birthplace, or where we eventually settled. East St. Louis and Belleville were still home to me. The gangsters had ruined it. I had a burning desire to keep the union thugs and the street gangsters from ruining the west side. It was home to me now, and home to my children.

I didn't want my kids to have to be refugees like my family and my relatives. But it's the American way, move every five years and upgrade your real estate investment. I looked upon Jesse Stoneking the way I would look at a dangerous animal in the zoo. Interesting species, deadly, but not a worry to me or mine. He's on the Eastside and my family's on the west side. I figured I would probably never see him again, unless he drives Art Berne to the pipefitter's complex. Maybe then I would pull him over and do my Mississippi State Trooper routine on them.

It had been a couple of days since our Jesse Stoneking sighting. I was sitting at my desk waiting for my chance to escape the office. It was late afternoon and I had a protection detail for Congressman Dick Gephardt. I figured I would sneak out early, head for home for a couple of hours and then go to the detail. It was at a famous surgeon's house in the Central West End.

I had been there before. He had a full human skeleton in his living room. I had my picture taken hugging it, showing off for the congressman's staff. It was a classic turn-of-the-century home, with a big front porch, gigantic rooms, high ceilings and even higher payments. It was the type of house Bob Hope loved and ogled when he came to town.

Guido stopped at my desk. I knew it was some news I would be interested in because he didn't start talking right away. He usually just let his presence soak into you and then he would clue you in on what was bothering him.

"I got some information a couple of minutes ago," he began. I watched and listened.

"Jesse Stoneking's got a house in south St. Louis County, Oakville. You know where that is?"

"Kind of," I muttered.

"You know where Telegraph Road is?"

"Yeah,"

"Okay, take Telegraph to Becker Road. Turn left and go for about a half-mile. You'll see a street called Armona Place. He's supposed to have a new house toward the end of the street, on the right-hand side, before you get to the cul de sac. I thought you'd be interested."

"You don't know the address?"

"No, I thought maybe you could drive by and maybe see his car, then get us an address. You interested?"

"Yeah," I muttered, "I'm interested." He walked away and left me to stew.

I was fidgeting in my seat, nervous like a racehorse at the gate. I checked my wristwatch. I had time to drive by the house before my detail. I didn't walk by Boob's office, I went out the back door by the stars' desks. They were too busy analyzing telephone records to notice me, or they would have snitched on me to Boob for leaving early.

I quickly went to the detective Chevy, climbed in and cranked it. I felt like I had pulled off some great coup, sneaking out early to look for the super-crook, Jesse Stoneking. I wondered if crooks have the same feeling, the feeling of "getting over on the system" when they pull off some criminal enterprise. For the union thugs it must be a constant twenty-four-hour-a-day-rush.

I sped to South County and turned onto Armona Place. It was a good street in a great neighborhood. I had hoped that one day I could move my family to such a neighborhood in Oakville. Safety, security, good schools, and close enough to the City to still have easy access to it.

I slowed down, hoping I would see the white Lincoln parked in the driveway, then I would memorize the address, head for my detail and tomorrow I would write a scathing memo to Captain Bud and Boob, and I would be safe for a couple of days before they attacked me again for being a non-conformist.

I drove slowly toward the supposed location of the house. Jesse was standing on the front porch. He eyeballed me and I eyeballed him. I had to go to the cul-de-sac and turn around to get out of the subdivision. I did it, and rode by his house again.

We were staring at each other. The cold-blooded killer-gangster and the East St. Louis refugee, martyr, staring hatefully at each other. It had been twice in two days we had locked eyes. His presence in this clean little neighborhood angered me. He had no right to be in this kind of a place. This was the epitome of middle-class America. It's where people who work for a living go to escape the crime of the City. A place where you can leave your door unlocked, or where the neighbors have a key to your house.

His look was threatening, but I could tell it was more of a look of curiosity. He had figured out who I was, at least he now knew I was a cop, not a hit-man or fellow crook. But he still had the murdering look. But I wasn't afraid of him. I felt he read my look, too. The "why are you here?" look.

I had my thirty-eight in my hand and I felt it would be fitting for me to kill him now if I had been given the opportunity. He was a dangerous animal who had escaped from the zoo. No longer entertaining to look at, he was a poisonous snake in the grass, the grass where children play ball and decent folks toss a ball for their dogs.

We had read each other, instinctively. We now knew each other, and it was fitting that it turned out that way. He belonged back in the cesspool of East St. Louis, and I was furious he was here. I knew I would be dealing with him again.

I went to the Dick Gephardt detail, serious and removed from the light-hearted event. The food was excellent and the staff of the congressman treated me like I was the dignitary, not the folks I was providing security for. I got home late, woke up late, and drove like a nut to get to the office by nine.

It had been a wasted day as far as investigating organized crooks, but every day couldn't be a Jesse Stoneking day. Maybe that was a good thing.

I was sitting at my desk watching the clock, patiently waiting for my chance to head for home, my family, my pool and barbecue kettle. Boob slid by, blowing smoke, "You've got a detail tonight." He stared for effect and he gloated on my facial reaction.

"What detail? Nobody told me about a detail."

"I'm telling you, now," he said with a blast of cigar smoke. "John Block, Secretary of Agriculture, you're taking him and his entourage to the ballgame tonight. He's got tickets for you. It's a good detail, free food and beer, just the things you like."

I stared. "Who else is on the detail?"

"Frank Reed," he replied, "he's got the itinerary, check with him. Have a nice time." Boob slid away as I dialed my wife to tell her I wouldn't be home until the early morning hours. Frank Reed was standing in front of my desk as I ran the news down to my wife.

I had known Frank Reed for years, he was a good cop, a killer of criminals, but he was intense to the point of being scary. He wasn't always that way. He never smiled, never tried to give anybody the impression he had a personality or a life outside of the intelligence unit. He carried a big nickel-plated Magnum revolver in a shoulder holster, one with pearl handles that shined through his leisure jacket at whomever he was speaking to.

I reminisced about the first time I had seen him. I was working the evening watch in the unit, six P.M. to two A.M. It was in the summer and I was alone. There's nothing to do on the evening watch during the daylight hours. Hardly anything to do at night.

My little detective Chevy didn't have a stereo so I brought one with me at night. I would ride around and listen to jazz and blues, go by some gangsters' houses, write down some license plate numbers and if possible go home early. It was like having a night off without your wife.

It had just turned seven o'clock, and I was cruising Euclid in the Central West End ogling lady shoppers. An all points call came out for an officer-in-need-of-aid at an apartment complex near Euclid and Forest Park.

A lot of the time these calls are bogus, but the radio dispatcher came back on the air and advised that a plain clothes detective was fighting with a subject armed with a metal rod in an open hallway on the second floor.

I double parked and headed into the complex. It was an open courtyard configuration with buildings surrounding it. I headed to the second floor and came up behind Frank Reed. A whacked out white guy was swinging a steel rod around and at Frank like a baseball bat. The rod was about four-feet long and about an inch in diameter.

Frank, his Bo Diddley hat on his head, was using footwork like a professional boxer, timing his response to the swings of the madman but not backing down from him. The hallway was narrow and there was no way I could get next to Frank to assist him.

The mad man attacker was using deadly force against a St. Louis police officer. That almost always ended with the attacker being shot. Deadly force begets deadly force. I stood behind Frank, supporting him in case he got tagged by the rod. Then I would retaliate with deadly force. It was the way it would have had to have been. I wasn't going to get dinged by the rod. I had too much to live for. I figured Frank was in the same boat as me and I couldn't figure why he restrained himself.

But he did. He expertly danced and avoided the rod and eventually the nut tired himself out to the extent that Frank and I jumped him and got cuffs on him. I was impressed with Frank. Had Frank been a white cop, and if the nut was black, he would have been shot dead.

I didn't hang around, but Frank remembered me and whenever we would see each other he made it a point to acknowledge me. We had been partners in a combat situation and we had bonded. It didn't always happen in the cop game but it did this time.

I followed his career. He was a district detective; always on the front line. He had responded to a robbery call and was forced to use deadly force on that occasion. I heard he had changed after that event. He turned into a brooding, intense gun-guy. I felt badly for him. Shortly thereafter he was transferred into the intelligence unit.

Frank Reed was a real man. He despised the back-biting going on in the unit. He couldn't stand the stars because of their snitching and bragging, and their phony search warrants always used against blacks, but unlike me, he didn't express himself verbally. He was the type of guy who would attack his enemies instead of speaking to them.

I studied him as I spoke on the phone. He was the exact image of Bo Diddley, the blues musician. He was light tan in color. He was the same size, wore the same type of clothing with the shirt out, and he wore the leather brimmed hat, just like Bo Diddley. It was his shtick and he was true to it. The only difference was that Frank was young and carried a magnum.

He stood his ground until I got off of the phone. "You heard about the detail?" he asked.

"Yeah," I said, studying him. "You okay with it?" I asked that question because I didn't want Frank Reed unhappy. He was a cocked gun ready to go off, a hand grenade with the pin pulled, and I didn't want him going off on a dignitary protection detail. I had seen him in action. He was a fighter and now a shooter, a product of St. Louis streets, much like I was a product of East St. Louis streets. Bad situations change cops, mostly for the worse.

I figured he had gone into the service shortly after high school, like me, and had eventually gravitated to the police department. The department is always looking for military veterans, somebody to do the grunt work while they cater to and promote their political cronies' friends. If Frank would have told me, "No, I'm not okay with it," I would have covered for him and told him to go home, and that I would call him if anything went down he should know about.

I had had the John Block detail before. He had his own federal security detail, but they always wanted a local or two with them. It was a good detail. The food was great and the beer flowed like water. But you have to pretend you enjoy the company of these dignitaries and their security guys. It makes for a pleasant event. It's like a group of friends going out to dinner and then the ballgame for a fun-filled evening.

I could and would make them think I liked them. Frank didn't have the wherewithal to pull off that ruse. Frank didn't like anybody, except maybe me. We had the bond.

But, as I delved into the conundrum, I figured Frank knew I was a marked man. I was vocal, rebellious, not a team player, and I disliked the stars and bosses. That spelled disaster in an outfit like the intelligence unit. Frank identified with me. Black folks in St. Louis are marked from birth, just like anybody from East St. Louis. We had something in common.

And I figured Frank knew, as well as everyone else, the lead star would be promoted soon and leave the unit. The only problem was he would eventually come back as a supervisor, and depending on who was the commander of the unit, his word would be gospel.

My life in the unit would be a living hell if that prediction came to pass. I would have to retreat into my corner and cover up while the lead star and everybody else beat me into submission. My only friend would be Frank Reed. Everybody else would rally around the lead star. People want to be led. The lead star wants to lead. Frank and I would be outcasts.

But Frank and I were friends, and he was a real person, not a bureaucrat wannabe, not a snitch or a carrier of false tales, and not a pilferer of contraband. He had character and I liked him.

So we were off, the blonde and blue detective from the Eastside with the Bo Diddley of law enforcement riding together in my detective Chevy toward Kiener Plaza, a gracious park in downtown St. Louis, for a free supper, catered, in the park, all of the beer we could consume, and a free ballgame, the last game of the season.

Frank even wore his Bo Diddley hat in the police car. People stared, and probably thought Bo was in town. I was surprised that local folks didn't come up to him and ask him for an autograph. The hat was a bit much, but I wasn't going to be the one to ask him to remove it. He even wore it in the office.

I had met his girlfriend. She was an employee of the department, a clerk. They lived together in a rented flat in central City. I never got the nerve to ask her if Frank took his hat off while he was at home. If it got back to Frank that I was asking about him, then I would be his enemy, like the stars, and I didn't want to be Frank Reed's enemy. At this point in his life Frank killed his enemies. A pity!

We met the security guy and John Block in the park, ate some good food, drank some cold beer and eventually strolled over to the ballpark. Our group was about twenty in the park, but only about six or seven had tickets to the ballgame.

We entered and advised security that we were at the park on a protection detail and then we headed for our seats, box-seats at the third-base line. The group went down to the boxes and the security detail guy for the Secretary of Agriculture advised me that there weren't enough tickets for all of us.

I didn't wish to hurt the feelings of Frank Reed, so I said, "I'll stand topside and watch from up there." I walked back to the top of the section and prepared to watch the game from the aisle-way.

I had gotten another beer from the concession stand and was sipping it and congratulating myself for joining the police department, and for getting into the intelligence unit, and I was regretting how I had spoken to Lieutenant Boob when he advised me of the detail. I shouldn't have questioned him about his directive. I had decided that I was going to show more respect to him in the future.

I had only been away from Frank and the dignitaries for two minutes when the federal security guy came bounding up the concrete steps toward me. "You'd better come down here," he began with a worried look on his face. "Frank's gotten into an argument with a guy. He's in one of our seats and he won't leave. Frank identified himself as a police officer and showed the guy his tickets for the seat, but the guy accused Frank of being an East St. Louis, Illinois, cop and won't move. Frank's got his gun drawn and is pointing it at him."

I walked down expecting to hear the crack of a magnum. Frank had the guy at bay and the guy was beginning to become rational. The sports fans had cleared the section while the standoff continued.

I strolled up to him, "What's up, Frank?"

"This motherfucker didn't want to get out of my seat," he said in a low voice. "I told him I was a police officer, I even showed him my badge, but he said I was an East St. Louis cop and he wasn't moving."

The drunk south-side reject wanted to move now, and I could see it in his eyes. "You'll move now, won't you?"

"Yes, sir," he said.

"So, go ahead and move," I said. The gate-crasher climbed over the seat, ran up the steps and was stopped by stadium security and carted away. Frank and the dignitaries slid back into their seats and started watching the game as the other fans regained their seats. It was just another exciting evening at the old ballpark, something they could talk about at the water cooler in the morning. Bo Diddley draws his magnum at the ballpark.

It was a three-inning game for John Block and his pals. We escorted them back to their hotel and we were free. There was no discussion about the gun incident in front of thousands of fans. It was as if it never occurred. Another successful dignitary-protection detail.

13

I had been fretting about Frank Reed. He was almost too dangerous to be out and about in a free society. The gun deal at the stadium clinched it for me. I kept wondering what would have happened if he would have killed the fan over a seat mix-up. He would have gone to prison, for sure.

But his violent side was bound to come out again. It was too easy for him to revert to the gun. For him it answered all of the questions a cop is bombarded with. In most instances, the gun paralyzes the person it's being pointed at. Especially if the gun yielder looks like a crazy man. But it isn't one-hundred percent. Some people try to take the gun away from the gunman. That almost always ends in death. One person goes to jail, the other goes to his grave. I didn't want Frank Reed to go to either place.

He was my compatriot in a place where there were none for an Eastside outcast. If I asked him, he would stand shoulder to shoulder with me in an attack against the stars; or the bosses. He was a loyal compatriot, and that was scary. It meant I was imposing my will upon him. Something I didn't wish to do. It meant I was leading and he was following; another frightening thought.

My partner came back from his vacation and we resumed the interviews of almost any criminal associate we could trap in an office to interview. It was still fun, and we still laughed when we walked out of their offices. I felt the crooks thought we were insane, and unlike any cops they had ever come across. Captain Bud and Boob were seething about the interviews, but I didn't care.

It was okay for me. I had set a course for myself, subconsciously, for disaster. Being a detective in intelligence was like a kid sneaking into Disney World, knowing that soon he was going to get caught and tossed out, so he rode every ride he could while he looked over his shoulder for the local gendarmes. I was riding every ride. I knew my time was nearing an end, so I was going to shake the politicos' trees while I was there. I was a congenital shit-disturber, the one nobody wanted around.

My partner, on the other hand, was a career minded guy, a made cop. His promotion was forthcoming, if he could keep me in check. But he enjoyed screwing with the untouchable, invisible crooks as much as I did.

We didn't have any more Jesse Stoneking sightings. My partner had never seen him, and I described to him the way he acted and the threatening glares he aimed at me. He wanted to kill him, too. He lived not far from where Jesse had taken up residence. His kids played in the grass where the snake was hiding. He tossed a ball for his dog there.

Guido advised me Jesse had gone straight, and he was a card-carrying Local 562 pipe-fitter employed at the brewery. I pondered this alleged fact and tried to come up with a reasonable hypothesis. Maybe he had gone straight. Some nuts do. I did. But I wasn't a crazed gangster, murderer. I was just a nut from the Eastside.

December rolled around and there were no more car bombings, no home invasions and no jewelry store robberies. The stone fetish had subsided. Jesse had been out of jail for about three months.

I had read in the St. Louis paper about an armed robbery of a fellow in Brussels, Illinois, a guy I had known through the years. I knew his girlfriend, too, Jane Stewart. She could have been a poster girl for an AARP magazine; old, but well preserved. But Carl was well preserved, too. Brussels is a peninsula between the Illinois and Mississippi Rivers, about an hour's drive from downtown St. Louis.

Two guys broke into his restaurant, the Wittmond Hotel, and hid out in a room by the kitchen. They rushed Carl and Jane late at night, just after closing, and beat them up. But they didn't just beat them, these guys pistol-whipped them. The victims were elderly, early seventies, but wealthy. Carl Wittmond, the owner, proudly wore a sixteen-carat diamond solitaire ring in a platinum setting.

He flaunted the ring, for he also had the fetish. The hotel was more of a restaurant than a hotel. Carl had inherited it, although he had worked there since his youth. It could have been a movie set for a western flick. It was red brick, two-story with a balcony overlooking the country road rolling through Brussels. It had the old front porch with rocking chairs and sleeping hounds. It looked the same as the day it opened in 1874.

The specialty was family-style fried-chicken dinners, and it was reasonable. There was a big bar at one end, but not where the restaurant was, and there was a gift shop with expensive, unusual items, like whiskey decanters, antique silver, gold coins, out of circulation paper money and just about anything someone would want that was out of the ordinary.

On the weekends the place was packed, and old Carl Wittmond worked hard, as did his girlfriend, Jane Stewart. Carl watched every cent as if it was going to be the last one he would ever make. He cherished money, diamonds, and his business.

I would take my wife and kids over to the hotel and we would have Sunday family-style chicken dinners. It was a neat trip. The ferry ride over thrilled my kids, and the rolling hills and the miles of corn fields, the peach orchards, cattle ranches and pig farms. It had eye candy for all of us, and it was close to St. Louis.

Carl always had his eye on us, sizing us up. I had my eye on him, sizing him up. The difference was he was a famous guy, a rich restaurateur, working the tables like a college kid, serving and bussing, courteous and kind.

The ring gave him away. What waiter or busboy wears a sixteen-carat diamond ring? He was an ex-politico, a retired state legislator from the Illinois General Assembly. That alone made me leery of him. I couldn't help it. I had grown up hearing about Illinois legislators. They were rumored to be as crooked as Buster Wortman, but in a different way. They controlled state money.

Carl was a big-shot politician in Illinois. He served as an arbitrator for the Illinois Industrial Commission, and he was a state representative for eighteen years. He was instrumental in getting ferry service to the peninsula of Brussels, and he was part of the development of the Great River Road Project.

The River Road, in that part of the woods, runs from Alton to Grafton, goes through Grafton and then continues north along the Illinois River. For years it followed the scenic Mississippi River toward Grafton, but stopped about seven miles from Grafton.

It was a big construction project to continue the road north, to where it meets up with the Illinois River. But it was vital to the economic expansion of the area of Brussels, Grafton, Jerseyville, and Hardin.

There's a lot of pork in southern Illinois. Not all of it is restricted to hog farms.

Carl was a crusty old man, thin and tall, a full head of hair, not white, but brown, full and styled, and he had shifty eyes, always scanning and measuring. He was big-time curious about my family. We looked like surfers, all of us blonde and blue.

What was interesting was the irony that both of us were cunning observers of people. I knew he was studying me, and he knew I was studying him. We were like two wild foxes who had met up on the same path to the chicken coop.

My kids were three and five, feisty and curious, and he would watch them while we ate, their eyes scanning, just like his. He had a Polaroid camera and he would take our picture and talk to us. I finally told him what I did for a living. I gave him my business card, and he acted impressed. But I knew he wasn't. Politicians aren't impressed with cops. They know they own the cops. We're indentured servants to them.

I read his thoughts. Why are you a cop? You should be more, work harder for your beautiful family. You're wasting your life. But, my ancestors didn't leave me a legacy, an established business. My inheritance was a bad attitude. He didn't know I was a street kid from the Eastside. I didn't impress him, but my wife and kids did. He didn't have children. But there wasn't much that would impress this old multi-millionaire. He had it all and he wanted more.

His nephew, Charles Burch, the State's Attorney for Calhoun County, worked at the restaurant with Carl. He bussed tables, washed dishes, served fried chicken and slung booze for Carl on the weekends.

Charles was the only prosecutor I ever heard of who could serve you chicken, buss your table, get you drunk, on Sunday, and then arraign you for DWI on Monday. But he was Carl's right-hand man, his trusted relative, the son he never had, and his heir of choice.

Charles fashioned his life after Carl. He worked seven days a week, had a profession, and had tried to get elected to the same legislative seat Carl had held. That ambition did not materialize for Charles. But he still had power, the State's Attorney job, and he was wealthy, due to his relationship to Carl. It was no secret that when Carl cashed in his chips, Charles would get everything Carl owned.

Carl's girlfriend, Jane Stewart, was his constant companion. She was in her seventies, like him, but she wasn't as cunning as old Carl Wittmond. He had cultivated her, even dated her while he was married, before his first wife died. He gave her jewelry, diamonds and gold, and he got her a job with the State of Illinois, until she could get a retirement and join him full-time in Brussels.

She sported an eleven-carat European-cut diamond in a platinum setting. A gift from Carl. It was a nicer stone than Carl's, clear and perfect.

Carl's big stone was about the size of a dime in diameter, and it was yellowish, and not attractive to me. But it satisfied his fetish. The robbers didn't get her ring. I wondered why.

There was cash in the restaurant, too. The day's receipts and probably a lot of cash in the restaurant safe. They didn't go for that, just went for Carl's ugly ring. They beat both of them, pistol whipped them, injured Carl's foot and ankle, pummeled them like street people.

The injured foot and ankle, it was a convict's way of getting someone weaker than them off of their feet. They sweep with their right foot like an athlete kicking a soccer ball, from the outside in. The weaker victim's feet go out from under them and they land hard on their hip. It's debilitating and cruel, but, it's one of the moves convicts practice in prison. They go through the moves with their fellow convicts so it is perfected. I figured one of the robbers had just been released from prison.

Paul Powell, Secretary of State for Illinois for decades, was a close friend of old Carl Wittmond. Carl told me that fact. They served the State of Illinois at about the same time. Carl had a special blend of whiskey distilled especially for Paul Powell. Paul had the bad luck of dying suddenly in his hotel home in Springfield, Illinois. Somebody called the cops because of the smell, and they entered to search. Their search revealed Paul Powell's body, and hundreds of thousands of dollars in cash, all concealed in shoe boxes for distribution. When you made a check out for your taxes, or license plates, you made it out to Paul Powell, not the State of Illinois. I had done it since I was old enough to drive when I resided in Illinois. Nobody thought anything of it.

The cash caused a stink worse than Paul Powell's rotting carcass, but the folks in Illinois forget quickly. It was considered one of the perks of being a politician. People understood. It's what they were trained to do. Forgive and forget. Illinois politicians make Louisiana politicos look like Sunday-school teachers.

Carl founded the Bank of Kampsville. He bragged about the bank, telling his customers how much the bank had in holdings. He always had ready cash to buy the farms on the island, for in reality, it's what Calhoun County is. It's thirty-seven miles long and is surrounded on the south, east and west by the Illinois and the Mississippi rivers, and three ferries, and one road connecting it with Hardin, Illinois.

The mostly German Catholic folks living there inherited their farms, just like Carl inherited his hotel. The difference between them was that Carl didn't till the soil. He tilled cash. So when the locals needed money, he offered to buy their land. Many sold to him. It was rumored he owned most of Golden Eagle, a farming community surrounding Brussels, with its own post office and zip code.

The County was desolate, accessible by ferry, unless you wanted to take the one road north to Hardin. The folks there didn't particularly trust each other, and they didn't trust outsiders at all. When strangers were in the little town of Brussels, everybody knew it, and they knew what kind of car they were driving, and what they looked like.

Golden Eagle folks were leery about Meppin folks, or Brussels folks. They would do business with them, but Golden Eagle folks weren't thrilled if their daughters went on a date with a Batchtown guy. And with a total population of five-thousand in the whole peninsula, that made for a shallow gene pool. Most of the young people went away to college and only returned for a visit.

Calhoun County was picturesque in the spring, summer and fall, but nasty in the winter, and there were crooks living there. It could have been local talent who knocked Carl down, beat up his girlfriend and stole his gaudy diamond ring, but I doubted it. It was some sort of union-style thug attack. It fit the modus operandi of them.

I had seen aerial surveillance pictures of the island in the winter. The snow covered the beauty, and the tire marks through the snow kicked up the mud on the roads. The snow got dirty and the island looked like a mad cow had dumped on it.

There were burglars, as well as car thieves, dope dealers, and an assorted bevy of criminals living on the island. Why not? It was desolate and safe. It was like Buster Wortman having a moat and a bridge around his property in East St. Louis. The moat in Calhoun County was the Illinois and the Mississippi rivers.

But the crime was out of my jurisdiction, even though the criminals perpetuating it were from the west side. Captain Bud wouldn't allow me to investigate this crime, unless he thought he could, in some way, pilfer some recovered contraband through the investigation. But there was just one diamond ring, a giant nasty-looking diamond which satisfied some politico's fetish for stones. Captain Bud couldn't do anything with it, even if he got his hands on it.

So all of my thoughts on the robbery and all of my insight on the victims and the possible perpetrators was in vain. But, I could call old Carl Wittmond and check up on him. He and Jane were in a hospital in Jerseyville, Illinois. Carl had another house, and I figured if I was ever going to see him again it would be there. It was in Jacksonville, Illinois. I had never seen it, but I had heard it was nice.

Charles told me once that Carl had a burglar-proof safe in the house where he kept cash and diamonds. He told me Carl had a hundred-thousand dollars in the safe, in cash.

Why did he tell me that? I have no clue. Maybe he was just bragging to what appeared to be a broke cop. He is Carl's heir and he will be filthy rich when Carl is gone. And he is a lawyer and a prosecutor. I'm just a big City cop.

Carl was standing there when Charles told me the safe story. He smiled and shook his head, confirming the tale. I couldn't figure why they wanted me to know that little bit of information. Maybe Carl felt like he had missed something in life when he viewed my beautiful blonde and blue children.

Why did he wait tables like a college kid wearing a sixteen-carat diamond ring? And why did he brag about his acquired wealth? His bragging got him beaten and robbed, almost killed. He thought he was untouchable on the island kingdom, where he was the king and everyone else were his serfs.

So I called him. He recognized my voice. He acted like he was expecting a call from me. His brain was working faster than mine. It was as if, when the first blow from the robber's pistol had landed on his skull, he knew whom he was going to empower to help him get his diamond back. I asked him how he and Jane were faring; he didn't answer the question. In his raspy voice he said, "I want my stone back. Can you get it for me?"

I dismissed Carl's request. He had laid down with dogs for his entire life, and now he wanted me to go out on a limb and help him find his hideous diamond. He had cops, the State's Attorney was his nephew, his chosen heir, and the local sheriff was at his disposal. He could hire a private dick to help him, but that would cost money, and Carl didn't wish to pay for something he could get for free. His study of me was not for naught. He knew me well and he knew he only had to charge me with the responsibility of his robbery investigation, and that I would do what I could for him. I was like a Labrador retriever who instinctively retrieves shot ducks. Bring a Lab to the river, shoot a duck and the dog will swim out and get it. He doesn't need any coaxing.

The problem I had was I knew what he was doing. This money grubbing, crusty old man was using me, and I didn't like being used, by ex-politicians or anybody else. But it was an investigation, a conspiracy, and I had no defense against such a scenario. I loved conspiracies as much as I hated authority.

Detective Colonel John Doherty, Cheif of Detectives. Man's man, war hero, killer cop. Picture taken shortly after he testified before the Nevada Gaming Commision as a character witness for Sorkis Webbe Sr. He made cigar smoking fashionable in the P.D. (Courtesy of John Auble KTVI Television)

Photos of the John Paul Spica car bombing. Circa November 8, 1979. (Courtesy of Lieutenant George Venegoni SLPD)

John Paul Spica blown up by Raymond Flynn. Circa November 8, 1979.

Surveillance photos of Ray Flynn. Circa 1978.
(Courtesy of Lieutenant George Venegoni SLPD

Photos of Jimmy Michaels car bombing on I-55.
(Courtesy of Lieutenant George Venegoni SLPD)

Photo of John Paul Leisure car bombing. Author with green shirt, back turned to camera. Circa September 11, 1981. (Courtesy of Detective Sergeant Steve Sorocko SLPD)

Photo of Sonny Faheen's bombed Volkswagen in the Mansion House garage.
(Courtesy of Detective Sergeant Steve Sorocko SLPD)

Surveillance photo of James Michaels Sr.
Murdered in a car bombing by
John Paul Leisure.
(Courtesy of John Auble KTVI Television)

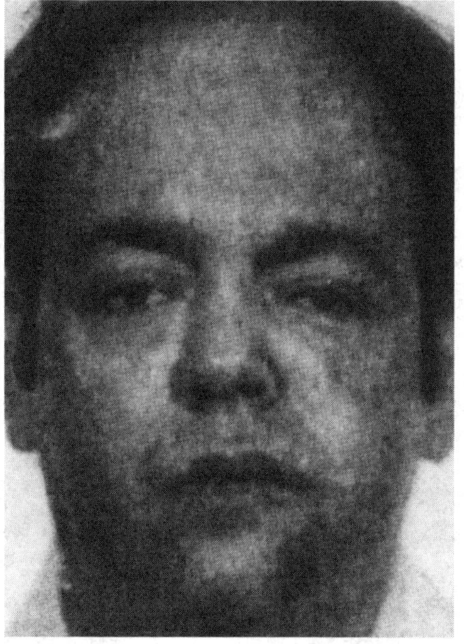

Photo of John (Paulie) Leisure. Gangster, union official and bomber. Died in prison. (Courtesy of John Auble KTVI Television)

Photo of Anthony Leisure. Paul Leisure's brother. Still incarcerated. (Courtesy of John Auble KTVI Television)

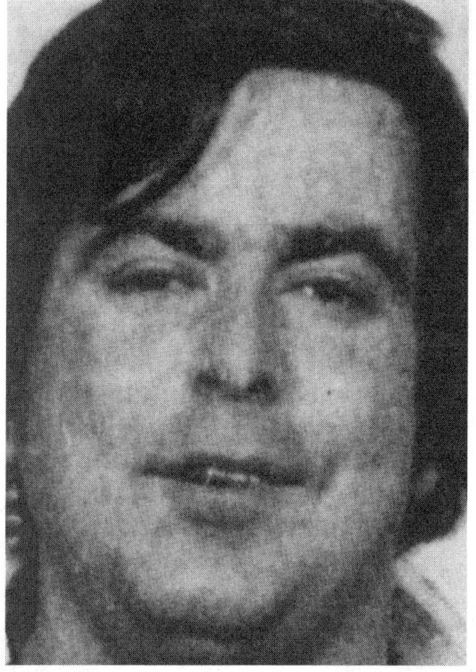

Photo of David Leisure, cousin to Paul and Anthony. Executed in Missouri State Penitentiary. (Courtesy of John Auble KTVI Television)

Italian Mafiosi leader (St. Louis) John Vitale. (Courtesy of John Auble, KTVI Television.)

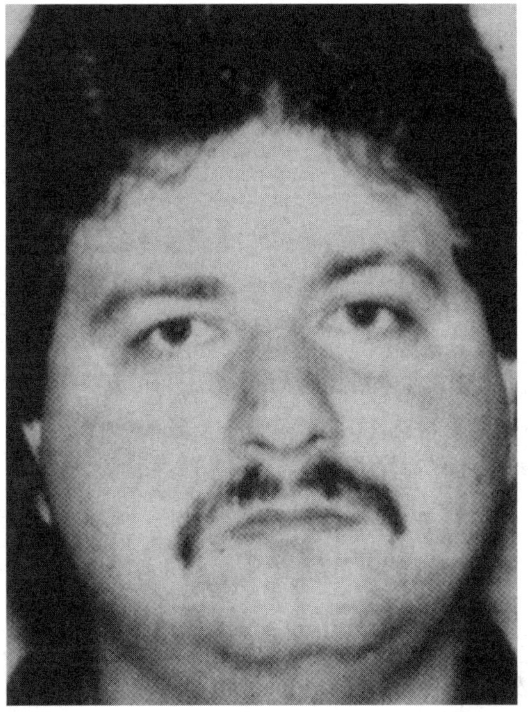

Nando Bartolotta, up and coming St. Louis gangster. (Courtesy of John Auble, KTVI Television.)

United States Secretary of Agriculture, John Block security detail at Busch stadium. Left to right: Detective Frank Reed, unidentified security officer for the Secretary of Agriculture, Fred Bird, and author. (Courtesy of author)

Wittmond Hotel, Brussels, Illinois. (Courtesy of author)

Carl Wittmond. (Courtesy of Calhoun County Illinois State's Attorney Charles Burch)

Photo fo notorious gangster Jesse Stoneking. Taken by the FBI shortly before his snitch fest.(Courtesy of FBI Special Agent Tom Fox, retired.)

14

Everyone has something they covet. For wealthy folks it's their investment accounts, diamonds, yachts, estates. For working folks, it's their families, their cars, their modest homes. Most of my day was spent thinking about my wife and kids. I wanted the best for them. But criminal conspiracies ran a close second to my family. I dwelled on them. I fantasized about them, and I was captivated by the Brussels diamond robbery.

A couple of days had gone by since the Brussels, Illinois, robbery. It was first and foremost on my mind, but I was saddled with my partner, who had no doubt been cribbed by Captain Bud and Lieutenant Boob to keep me away from the investigation, if he could. If there was any pertinent information on the perpetrators, they would expect a memorandum by me explaining what I had found out. If it was good information, they would take me off of the case and place their star search warrant crew on it. It was how the system worked. The stars were contraband reaping machines, and Captain Bud loved them.

My partner was preparing for another vacation and I was seeing the light at the end of the tunnel. I would be on my own for another week or two, soon. We still had not seen Jesse Stoneking, and I was beginning to think Guido might have been right in his assumption, maybe Jesse had gone straight.

We were preparing to go out in the morning for some further harassment of some good old boys. Boob was following us around the office, blowing cigar smoke at us and making cow eyes at my partner, which meant he wanted to crib him some more before we went out. My partner took the bait and followed Boob into his office.

I heard some conversation in the back office, where the stars analyzed telephone tolls for search warrant affidavits. It was a twang that grabbed my attention, an Alton, Illinois, style of dialect that I was familiar with. I walked back there. Guido was talking with two investigators from the Illinois Division of Criminal Investigation. They were true southern Illinois guys, country sounding, fair, German type, probably athletes in high school and still in shape. I could identify with them.

I eavesdropped; they were after some information on Carl Wittmond's robbery. They figured the perpetrators had come from over here in St. Louis, just as I did. "Here's our Illinois expert," Guido said, pointing to me. He was trying to dump them. Mike Fair was the lead investigator. He shook my hand and smiled like he was wanting to sell me something. St. Louis Intelligence was apparently their last resort in the investigation, and I was eager to become a part of it.

Mike Fair explained how shortly after Carl Wittmond and Jane Stewart got beaten and robbed, they ran to the Crystal Room, a secure room behind the bar, and locked themselves in until the robbers left the restaurant. I was familiar with the Crystal Room.

Right after that, they came back out and telephoned the Sheriff's office to report the robbery. The Sheriff's office shut down the ferries and set up a roadblock on the only road leading out of the peninsula. A Hardin, Illinois police officer set up the roadblock.

The police officer advised he knew most of the folks coming through his roadblock, but there were two guys in an old rusty Chevy that he didn't know, so he got their names, dates of birth and addresses. Mike Fair gave me the names of the two suspects.

The first one was Mark Stram. I had never laid eyes on him, but I knew him. He was Jesse Stoneking's right-hand man. He hero-worshiped Jesse, and he would do anything for him. He guarded Jesse at the hospital after he got shot at the Kracker Box tavern in East St. Louis, when he killed the two assailants during the big shootout. Jesse killed both guys, and he took a bullet in the chest.

Rumor had it Mark Stram stayed by his side during his recovery, guarding him and catering to his whims. One of the wives of Jesse's Kracker Box victims came into the hospital in the middle of the night, armed with a handgun, to kill Jesse. Allegedly, she was pointing the cocked revolver at the sedated Jesse when Mark Stram came out of the darkness and took it away from her. The other guy was a guy I had never heard of before, but it wasn't Jesse.

Agent Mike Fair didn't know about the association of Jesse Stoneking and Mark Stram. I was shocked he wasn't aware of the Illinois crooks, but there were so many, and apparently the State of Illinois didn't have an intelligence unit. "If Mark Stram was there, then Jesse Stoneking was there, somewhere," I advised.

"Jesse's in prison," Mike Fair stated.

"No, he's been out for a couple of months, and he lives in Oakville and works at the brewery as a pipefitter," I advised.

Mike gave me a copy of the investigative report and he went on his way. My partner and I went out onto the street with nowhere to go and no plans for the day. It was too close to my partner's vacation time for us to make any plans.

We were contemplating where we were going to have lunch when Guido called us on the radio. He asked us to go to a secure channel, which we did. "Are you guys close to The Hill?"

He meant Little Italy; it's what The Hill is in St. Louis. "Close enough," I advised, "What's up?"

"Mike Trupiano's parked at the curb as if he's waiting for somebody. You guys want to do a Mississippi State Trooper car-stop on him?"

"Yeah, we'll be there in five minutes." I drove like mad to get there. The little City of St. Louis was asleep. It wasn't bustling like it should have been. I was almost embarrassed to be a part of this backward economic disaster, and I blamed guys like Mike Trupiano for the problems of the City. He wasn't a St. Louis product. He was from Detroit, Anthony Giordano's nephew, brought here to be a criminal. The process stunk and it infuriated me. Wasn't there enough to steal in Detroit?

We rolled onto The Hill and I got Guido on the radio for further directions; we didn't observe Mike Trupiano. "I don't have any more information," Guido said. "We're no longer on the scene, or in the area."

It was like Guido and Stretch to do things like that to us. They feared blowing their cover more than anything. Their covertness was almost like an obsession to them. It was like Captain Bud obsessing over contraband.

We started riding around the area, and soon we spotted Trupiano's Laborers Local 110 Oldsmobile, but he wasn't in it. We set up on it and waited. It wasn't long before a familiar vehicle drove slowly down the street. It was the white Lincoln Town Car belonging to Jesse Stoneking.

Jesse was driving and conversing with Trupiano, using his hands to emphasize something. Trupiano was shaking his head, stupid like, as if he was agreeing with Jesse, and he respected and feared him while he was agreeing. It was a moronic scene, and it further reinforced my theory there was nothing in St. Louis worth bragging about. No enterprise, no future, and no competent organized criminal leaders.

Trupiano observed our little Chevy four-door detective car, and he panicked. He said something to Jesse, and then he got out of Jesse's car and ran like a car thief to his Local 110 Oldsmobile. He was in it, had it started and in an instant headed north.

Jesse observed me at the wheel of the little Chevy, and he took off toward South Kingshighway. "Which one of these morons do you want to stop?" I asked my partner.

"It's your call," he replied.

"Let's stop Jesse Stoneking," I said. We headed toward South Kingshighway and eventually came upon Jesse's Lincoln. He was stopped at a red light at Southwest Avenue. The light changed and I got on his bumper and tossed the red light onto the dash. He didn't pull over immediately, but lingered as if he was trying to figure what he was going to do. He was too much of a criminal to run from us. He knew he hadn't broken any law.

He pulled over and then pulled onto the Chevrolet dealership lot at the corner and parked near a string of new Chevys. He sat in the car as we exited the Chevy detective car and walked to his Lincoln.

There was one thing I was certain of, Jesse Stoneking hadn't gone straight. If he had, then why was he meeting and instructing Mike Trupiano on something? I was furious at Jesse Stoneking, master gangster, killer, and person from East St. Louis living and driving the streets of St. Louis, my adopted home.

Jesse Stoneking didn't belong in St. Louis. He belonged in the cesspool of East St.Louis. I was pumped and pissed and my partner realized it, and so did Jesse. Anybody could tell by looking at me.

"Get out," I ordered. He climbed out and we stood nose to nose. It would have been a good fight, Jesse and me, and I felt we were thinking the same thing. I could read him and he was reading me.

It could have been billed as the fight of the century; the crazed cop detective and the professional killer. We were identical in size, but he didn't wish to tread on me and I didn't know why. He was the killer. I was just a cop detective, and I could tell he was trying to be courteous.

He offered me his drivers' license. I didn't take it. "You think we don't know who you are?" I glared at him as I spoke. My partner searched his car and I patted Jesse down for a weapon. He was clean.

He stood and stared knowing that this unpleasant moment was soon going to pass and he would soon be driving down the streets of St. Louis, a free man, in his big Lincoln, and there was nothing I could do about it. It's called being an American.

There were only certain things I could say to Jesse Stoneking, so I said them. "You'd better carry your murdering ass back over to East St. Louis, Jesse, or you're going to get hurt real bad. You understand me?"

He nodded and was surly, like a convict, which he had been just months earlier.

"I know everything about you, Jesse. I know you beat up and robbed that old man and his lady friend over in Brussels and stole his ring. I know that about you, Jesse. You probably wonder how I know, don't you?"

"Maybe the FBI would like to know the way you're talking to me," he muttered.

"Hey," I loudly said, "fuck the FBI and fuck you. You get your ass back over to the Eastside where you belong. I don't want to see you again. Get out of here."

He climbed into the Lincoln and drove off of the lot, heading south, probably going back to utopia, Oakville. "Calm down," my partner said. I knew he was right. I quickly regained my composure. I detested overreacting, and I had just done it. The Eastside was haunting me and it probably would for the rest of my life.

We had a real good free lunch, took our time and had two desserts and glass after glass of iced tea, then climbed back into the little detective Chevy and rode around the streets of St. Louis for the remainder of the day. We had checked out the wealthy housewives who shop on Euclid and Maryland Plaza in the Central West end. We would see them parking their Jaguars, BMWs, Porsches, and Rolls Royces, and watch them enter and exit the exclusive shops, carrying bags without a care in the world.

Then we would go to the downtown area and watch the businesswomen scurrying from building to building, going in to shop on their breaks, power walking with dress clothing and athletic shoes, trying to make it a workout experience.

Then we would go down to the Landing area, restaurants and night clubs. These were working-class girls, hustling tables in the daytime and slinging booze in the evening. After the lunch crowd diminished, they would walk around the cobblestone streets for exercise and relaxation. Sometimes they would go to the Mississippi River, which was only a block away. We would always find the group we were searching for.

We would compare the three groups, and discuss what attracted us, as individuals, to each group. I liked the downtown group. I liked the traits they had; work ethic, but intelligence. Dressed well, but not snooty. Educated, but not overly sure of themselves.

My partner liked the Laclede Landing type of woman. Hard-working, hustling, working day and night to make a living, but caring enough to exercise when possible by walking, even though they would be on their feet until the early hours of the day.

Neither of us liked the snooty rich gals from the Central West End. My partner didn't even like their choice of cars. Porsches are high maintenance, Jaguars are too, and Rolls Royces are gaudy. I had to agree with him, but I had always wanted a Porsche. This was pre-vacation activity. If a cop gets caught up in an arrest or an investigation, he might not be going on vacation. He could be in court, or in the hospital, or in the morgue. Vacations were sacred; the only thing a cop has, except discretion, and a pension if he can hold on long enough.

We strolled into the office and I plopped at my desk waiting for the clock to turn to seventeen-hundred. I couldn't wait to get home to my family, drink a couple of beers, cook some burgers on the grill and forget about Jesse Stoneking and St. Louis, Missouri. It is what weekends were for.

My partner was cleaning off his desk, locking everything inside, preparing for the great American escape, vacation time. We tell ourselves when we're clearing our desks, locking everything up and saying goodbye, that we'll never come back, that we'll live the life of Reilly near the ocean and beach, and we won't even think about St. Louis and the police department. But we all come back.

Boob came out and stood at my desk, blowing cigar smoke at me. He was pale and shaky and he wore that damn gangster hat. "You guys make a car stop on Jesse Stoneking?"

"Yeah," my partner replied. I tried not to converse with Boob or Captain Bud, so I let my partner do the talking.

“You threaten him?” He aimed his question at me.

“Maybe,” I said in a Jesse Stoneking manner and stare.

Boob paused, drew on his cigar and blew a straight-line plume at me. I had disrespected him in front of my partner and I shouldn’t have. I felt like an East St. Louis thug, but I was still pumped over the car stop. Boob read me and calmed down. “Stay away from Jesse Stoneking,” he said. He walked back to his office.

I turned to my partner, “Jesse Stoneking the great criminal, murderer and robber of old folks went to the FBI on us? How ludicrous.” I was getting angry again.

“I’m out of here for a couple of weeks,” he said as he got up and walked out of the office. I had the weekend to calm down and figure what I was going to do on Monday. I would be alone, unencumbered, and I liked the feeling. I would leave the killer Jesse Stoneking alone, for now.

15

I was excited the way a professional would be when plying his trade. The race car driver sliding into his Formula one car. The championship boxer entering the ring, certain he was going to win. The sound of the bell was vibrating in my brain. I was chomping at the bit to do what I did best. I was the ultimate interviewer: the collector of innuendos, the walking talking lie detector, the KGB interrogator. The Brussels diamond was in St. Louis and I was going to recover it.

I was a man on a mission on this crisp, late fall Monday morning. I strolled into the office and ignored the stars and the rest of the crew. Lieutenant Boob was passing by my desk at regular intervals trying to figure out what I had planned for the day. I ignored him, too.

I dissected the robbery report on old Carl Wittmond given to me by Agent Mike Fair, Illinois Division of Investigation. I could visualize the crime, step by step because I knew the scene, the victim, and the perpetrators.

I placed myself at the scene. I was actually with the victims as they went about their nightly vigil of securing the hotel. Two men had hidden in a room adjacent to the kitchen. They had removed a window screen, raised the unlocked window and entered, undetected. They apparently sat there and smoked cigarettes until they figured Carl and Jane were closing the establishment. Cigarette butts littered the floor.

They crept out and waited for Carl and Jane in the gift shop, which is between the dining room and the bar. Jane Stewart, attractive, dressed to the nines, (she only shopped at the best stores in St. Louis and Chicago for her apparel) sporting her gold and diamonds, was gliding through the store area from the dining room, toward the bar to make certain everything was locked. What a looker she must have been when she was a young woman.

Carl had been turning off the lights in every room, making sure he didn't forget any of them, and checking the kitchen to make sure everything was off. They were cautious about the old building. It was the gift goose that had laid the golden egg for Carl Wittmond for his entire life.

Carl and Jane met up in the middle of the gift shop.

The two intruders rushed them, knocking Jane down and tussling with Carl. They beat Carl on the head with a pistol, kicked his feet out from under him. He fell hard. I was so close to the crime that I felt the pain in my head and body as I read.

Jane was pleading with them not to kill her. Carl tried to get back onto his feet; one of the gunmen pointed a pistol at him and told him to stay down or he would kill him and Jane. I was frightened for them, and angry that scumbag robbers of elderly people are allowed to be free on this earth.

I had a flashback of what one of the stars had told me when we talked about lying on search warrant affidavits. “We do this so one of these criminals doesn’t have a chance to rape your wife.”

I blushed as I sat at my desk. Maybe they were right and I was wrong. Had I been naïve? I thought I was street smart, but maybe I was ignorant to the way the judicial system works when it comes to career criminals. The stars and Captain Bud refer to their misinterpretation of the Constitution as dedication.

In the intelligence unit, adhering to the rules of life is hidden behind the skirts of dedication. Were the stars telling me the truth? Is it strictly dedication? At the time I thought they were lying because Captain Bud told them to.

Carl looked at the gunmen, they were wearing Batman Halloween masks. One of the intruders grabbed Carl’s big ugly diamond ring, ripping it from his finger, and they ran toward the kitchen area of the hotel. Carl and Jane got up and locked themselves in the Crystal Room. He telephoned his nephew, State’s Attorney Charles Burch. He couldn’t make contact with Charles, so he dialed the Sheriff’s office and told them he had been robbed.

I continued to read. These guys were small in stature, five-foot-seven or five-foot-eight. Jesse was about my size, five-eleven. Maybe he wasn’t inside, but he had to be somewhere around the scene.

The Sheriff, who should have been a factory worker instead of a cop investigating the robbery of the wealthiest person in the region, found the screen removed from the window near the set-up room. The window had obviously been left unlocked, he detected. Apparently, exit was gained at the same window. So, when the kitchen closed, they snuck into the rear dining room, hid out until the bar closed, then when Carl and Jane were securing the building for the night, they came out and attacked them.

The Illinois State Police had done a good investigation. A local had recovered one of the Halloween masks at the side of the road near the Hardin roadblock. A young lady had seen two suspicious vehicles parked across the street from the Wittmond Hotel. One of the vehicles had one person in it, the other had two.

I stopped and tried to gather a theory. Jesse would have stayed on the outside, maybe watching for the local deputy to come by for a late-night drink. Jesse would have killed him to save his compatriot.

The attackers of the elderly couple broke into the hotel, hid and then committed the robbery. They ran out, handed the ring to Jesse, and then they split up. But, Jesse wasn't stopped at the roadblock, which means he didn't leave the island. He stayed behind until things cooled off. It was well thought out.

But why just the ugly diamond of Carl? Why not cash? Or Jane's pure and perfect European cut stone and ring? Somebody had the fetish for Carl's stone and they hired Jesse to get it for them. That was the only plausible answer. But that didn't make sense. What could they do with it? It was a one-of-a-kind diamond. They couldn't wear it. Someone just wanted to deprive Carl of the pleasure of wearing it.

So, they have the stone stolen, place it in a safe and wait for Carl to die before they drag it out and have it placed in another setting. The stone was so unusual, somebody would recognize it, even though they couldn't prove to whom it belonged. State's Attorney Charles Burch would recognize it. He is the first in line to inherit everything Carl has.

What if, twenty years from now, Charlie Burch is at someone's cocktail party and the stone is there on someone's ring finger. He's a cocktail party kind of a guy; a politician, of sorts. He would know it was the stone. But could he do anything about it? Doubtful. He could try, but he would be spinning his wheels.

I had to revise my theory. The crook who paid to have Carl knocked over and his stone stolen, had two driving factors: to deprive Carl of his favorite diamond, and to someday sell the stone for a huge profit.

Most stolen gems go through the Paul Brown Building, Ninth and Olive in downtown St. Louis. Easily identifiable stones are usually shipped out by mail to New York City or Los Angeles. So, by now, some rich socialite in one of the wealthy cities in this country, or outside of this country, could be wearing Carl's diamond. But, it would go through the Paul Brown Building. That's where I should start. I was ordered to leave Jesse Stoneking alone. I would do that. I had hoped never to see him again. It was too upsetting to see him out and about.

But I was never told to leave the recovery of the stone alone. I pulled Jesse's file and read it from cover to cover. Guido had written a memorandum to Captain Bud that he had seen Jesse exiting a jewelry store in the Paul Brown Building. He stated Jesse is personal friends with the two brothers who own the store.

So, what if I find out that the stone came through the Paul Brown Building and had made its way to another state? What have I accomplished? Maybe I could get enough evidence to put a case on Jesse and the fence who shipped the stone out. Or, maybe I could go all the way back to the guy who hired Jesse to rob Carl Wittmond. He's probably a wealthy businessman with the fetish. He would deny it and tell me to prove it.

I was compelled to find the stone, pure and simple. I could call Carl and ask him who he thinks stole his ring, but he wouldn't tell me. That would be incriminating for him. The stone was stolen for a reason. Carl was part of the reason.

Boob slid by my desk, glancing over at me, blowing cigar smoke my way, still wanting to stop and ask me what I had going on, but he didn't. Captain Bud wasn't in yet. I had to make a move. I left my two-way radio in the charger on my desk. I didn't want to be encumbered by it. I was going to be incommunicado for the day, maybe for the next two weeks.

I strolled out of the office, right in front of the stars, who noted my departure for future conversations with Captain Bud. I was free.

I slid into the detective Chevy and headed for Ninth and Olive. The downtown buildings were tall, red brick and they blocked the sun in most parts. Walking on the sidewalks was like trekking through a canyon with predators walking about and lurking in the dark crevices, waiting to pounce on you. You had to be aware of your surroundings. Folks who worked downtown were alert.

I was there, parked and walking toward the Paul Brown Building in about five minutes. One good thing about St. Louis, you're never far away from anything. It was time to use my training as an interrogator and my cop intuition to find Carl's ugly diamond. It was recoverable. I just had to shake the right tree.

I milled around on the sidewalk near the entrance to the jewelry store. It had a street level entrance, unusual and no doubt expensive to lease. This was the spot where Guido had seen Jesse coming out of the building. It pays for a big-time jewelry thief to have friends in the business. It pays for both parties.

I was familiar with the building. I had frequented it often. It was a St. Louis landmark. Built at the turn of the century, it had all of the class St. Louis demanded at the time. Ornate coved ceilings with artwork painted into them. Arches, marble floors, brass elevators, and enterprise everywhere.

The economy in this burg might be flat, but the jewelry business was thriving. There was money in gold, precious metals and stones. The place was crawling with criminals, businessmen, diamond merchants, beggars and hustlers. It was the marketplace for items of intrinsic value in the City.

On the first floor there was an arcade; a mini-mall, featuring shops selling gold coins and jewelry, sterling, gold inlaid picture frames, household goods made of precious metals, and bulk gold, if you desired it for investment.

These shops were always packed with folks buying and selling. If the stock market had been strong they would have been at brokerage houses, but it wasn't, so the movers and shakers, the ones with money to invest were here, buying and speculating that items of intrinsic value, including gold, would go up drastically in value in a short amount of time.

This town was built on the fur trade, trappers coming to St. Louis to sell their wares. It is surviving on the diamond fencing business now. Same principal, except the Feds, the City and the State can't charge a sales tax on stolen gems. They're contraband and don't exist unless recovered.

One of the owners of the jewelry shop Jesse frequented had a big silver Mercedes four-door, the other one had a new Corvette. Both expensive rides were parked at the curb near the entrance to the shop, in a part of the canyon where the sun never touches the ground.

The place appeared small from my vantage point, maybe not larger than five-hundred square feet. I wondered how a guy could go to that small of a workplace every day of his working life and still maintain his sanity. Being a cop was a terrible and unrewarding job, but for most of the time I was out and about.

There wasn't much foot traffic coming and going in and around the store, so I walked in. The two brothers were there working on custom jewelry. They wore Plexiglas masks and were operating torches, forming gold into bracelets and rings and repairing necklaces in a cubby-hole at the rear of the shop.

They both looked up at about the same time, and they both had the same expression on their faces. They were in a state of panic. It was as if a poisonous snake had slithered into their store, one they had been expecting. I was a copperhead, a mildly poisonous species. Jesse was a spitting cobra. There was no chance of recovery from his bite, but they respected him and considered him their friend. It was all about perception.

The elder brother, he was probably thirty-five, walked to the counter and asked me the age-old question, "Can I help you?" He was a good-sized guy, full head of blonde hair, muscular, big boned, but soft in the waist from wrestling jewelry instead of weights. I could see how a guy like Jesse could intimidate him. I could see I had intimidated him with my presence.

It was obvious this guy had seen me before, and he knew I was a cop detective with the intelligence unit. It was the KGB syndrome. We were like the secret police, the ones the Constitution of the United States says can't exist. Crooks and citizens keep their eyes on us.

We exist in St. Louis, partly because this town is a police state within itself. It's just St. Louis. The cops are controlled by a state appointed Board of Police Commissioners. And if you wish to live or work here, you as a citizen of this police state must reconcile yourself to the fact that the KGB is, from time to time, going to pay you a visit. It was visit time for these brothers and they didn't like it.

"What's your name?" I began. It was an intimidating question, one that would be taken as an insult by an innocent person and not answered, except by a return question.

I was the grim reaper to him. He backed up, his back to the wall, "Frank," he replied. He feebly offered me his hand, I took it. It was soft, wet and shaky and he had a huge nugget and diamond ring on each hand. The guy was showing all of the signs of panic, so I smiled at him. It loosened him up a bit. I offered him my business card.

He read it and slid it into his jeans pocket, and continued to stare at me. I wasn't finished intimidating. "Has Jesse been in today?"

"No," he muttered. I stared as if his answer wasn't good enough. "He doesn't come in every day. Sometimes we don't see him for weeks." He was grasping at straws and he was angry at himself for copping a plea about Jesse Stoneking.

"But, you guys are friends, right?"

"Yes, sir," he meekly said.

"Did you hear about that robbery in Brussels, Illinois?"

"No, sir."

"An old man got knocked around, they beat him and his elderly girlfriend and they stole his sixteen-carat diamond ring. He got beat on the head, pistol whipped, his ankle and wrist broken, like fire kindling. That's what old folks' bones are like. Did you know that?"

"No," he meekly replied. I kept eyeing him, looking for signs of a chink in his armor, so I could attack him without mercy with my questions.

"You've probably heard about the stone. The guy was famous for it. It was in a platinum setting, it has a yellow cast to it, it is extremely large and very unusual. He runs a hotel and restaurant over in Brussels, and he takes it off and shows it to whomever wishes to see it. You know what I'm talking about?"

"Yes, sir."

"Oh," I said, then paused to allow my straight line questions time to sink in.

"You think Jesse did it?" Frank asked.

It was a direct question from a guy I had just tried to intimidate. It usually doesn't work that way. They just want it to be over with. "I don't know," I said with a smile. "I'm just looking for the stone. I need to recover it. The crime didn't happen in my jurisdiction, but I feel the stone is in this City. What do you think?"

"A good possibility, detective, but it didn't come through this store." I gave him a cold stare.

"I didn't think it did, but I thought maybe if you heard anything about it maybe you'd contact me and let me know. I'd keep your name out of it."

He was starting to loosen up, and I thought maybe I could like this guy. He told me a couple of stories about the jewelry business, how things are marked up, and how selling jewelry was akin to selling sports cars, or performance boats. The fetish had no boundaries. He told me he would sell me anything I wanted for my wife at his cost, or a little above it.

We talked about Jesse Stoneking, about how they met and what kind of business he did with him. "Jesse's a perfect gentleman in my store," he told me. "I've heard of the stories about him, but I've never witnessed anything but the gentleman side of him. I see him socially, my wife and I, and his wife and him. We've eaten dinner together on numerous occasions, and I like being around him."

"Which wife?" I asked with a laugh.

"Both of them," he came back with another laugh. We both paused and stared.

"Okay," I continued. "I'll let you get back to work." I shook hands with him. His hand was now dry and firm. The conversation was good between us. We were communicating, and now he knew I wasn't out to get him for being associated with my enemy. I started to walk out the door.

"There's a shop on the third floor, the owner might know something about it." He paused and scribbled a suite number on a pad then handed it to me. "I heard that a big stone recently passed through his shop.

"What's the guy's name?" It was too direct of a question and it spooked him.

"I don't know his name, I just heard he had a large stone come through his store recently."

He knew more. I could feel there was something he wanted to tell me. I waited and stared at him. He was pushing me off to one of his enemies, dispatching me to do his dirty work for him; to frighten a competitor.

He got set and started talking again. "There was another large, yellow-cast stone, that came through the building about thirteen or so months ago. I don't know which shop handled it, but it was immediately shipped out to California; Los Angeles, I think. The person who sold the stone to the jeweler in the building sold it on the condition that it be sold out-of-state and never come back to St. Louis. It was unusual, a strange request from a seller of diamonds. That's why I remembered. Usually the seller just wants the cash out of the stone; he or she doesn't care what happens after that. That's all I know."

"You said, he or she. Was it a woman?"

"I think maybe it was. I'm not certain."

I thanked him and exited onto the street. The interview went as I thought it would. I had gathered a little information, probably more than an average investigator would have gotten. But jewelers don't want to be perceived as being on the wrong side of the law. They want their customers to think they're honest, sincere and selling a pure and limited commodity.

Part of their sales pitch is the limited availability of gold, diamonds and other precious stones. But is there a limited availability? Gold and diamonds are mined for and found every day. And if the buyer can't find a newly mined stone, he can always purchase a stolen gem. Nobody knows the difference.

They are all on shaky ground, these unethical jewelers, buying off of the street and making a good living at it. But there are no ethics in the business world. It's about profit and nothing else. There are no ethics in the cop business, either. The Feds say they have ethics and standards, but it's a farce. They lie just like every other cop wanting to make a name for themselves.

These jewelers are artisans and hustlers, a scary combination of talent. When you hustle, you remove your heart and replace it with a twenty-dollar gold piece. You exchange your soul for a hundred-dollar bill. Profit is your God.

The game plan for an interviewed hustler is, "tell the cop something, anything as long as it's something he can verify, just to get him out of the shop and into somebody else's shop." That way he will be the cop interviewer's friend for giving him some information.

I visited twelve or fifteen shops in the building. I didn't gain anything, but I was met with the same response every time I walked through their doors. They were all terrified of me. Not because of me, but because of them and how they had made their living for so many years, buying stolen diamonds.

It had to be the largest fencing operation in the world, right here in sleepy old St. Louis, in the center of downtown. And it had gone undetected for generations. But, not being able to prove who the owners of diamonds are is the main reason for the fencing. These guys are in the diamond business. If somebody wants to sell them one, then why not buy it and re-sell it.

They're worse than used car dealers selling stolen re-tagged Corvettes.

It's the same principal. Who needs a sixteen-carat diamond? Who needs a Corvette or a Porsche? We perceive ourselves desiring these baubles and bangles and we will steal or kill to get them.

The problem arises though, if they continually buy diamonds from a guy who is a burglar, then the burden of returning the stone to the rightful owner, when the owner comes in and says, "that's my stone," should fall on the jeweler who purchased the stone off of the street. But it doesn't. But it would draw attention to them, so when the KGB comes calling, they get real weird.

I had shot the entire day at the Paul Brown. I headed for the office, plopped down at my desk and watched the clock, waiting for 1700 hundred to roll by. It did, and I was out and on my way home. Tomorrow will be better, I told myself. Something will pop.

16

Yesterday had been the beginning of the race. The first few rounds of the championship fight, and I was winning on points. I had calmed down. I wasn't anxious for another man's stone. I knew for certain I was in hot pursuit of it. I figured it was being moved around, now. The word was out that the KGB cop was seeking it. The bad guys were scrambling. They knew I would be coming for them.

It was a new investigative day, unencumbered, and I was as free as the wind. I breezed into the office and was seen by the stars, and Lieutenant Boob. Nobody questioned me about yesterday, maybe because I had not caused any trouble. They could rationalize my being absent. I hated being in the office, the place where the stars shined, their phony investigations always in your face and their bragging.

It was sickening to me. I hoped the lead star would be promoted soon and leave, so the ordinary folks in the unit could work without his aggressiveness. But he would leave his influential buddy behind for a while. I would still have to contend with him. Captain Bud wouldn't give the okay to promote both of them at the same time. Somebody had to be left behind to do the cheap search warrants.

I was in the office long enough to drink one cup of coffee and read the previous day's memorandums. It's how we learn what the other crews are doing. That way, two investigations don't overlap each other.

I had been seen, and I had seen enough office politics, so I got up, leaving my two-way radio in the charger again, and I escaped out into the crisp, late fall air of the City. I headed for downtown, again toward the Paul Brown, but hesitated. The word was out on me by now. Every jeweler in the building would be expecting me to come calling. I could hear the descriptions of me being given to all of them; KGB-looking guy, secret police, watch him, he's crafty. Give him something, but don't give him what he wants.

I turned away from the building and headed toward the shop of Boob's Jewish jeweler friend, Paul. I hadn't seen him in a while. I liked him and was looking forward to kibitzing with him. I parked at a meter and strolled into his store. It was too early for much foot traffic in the store. He was cleaning his wares, adjusting his cabinetry, making everything just perfect to the eye of the possible buyer. It was all about perception.

He gave me a big smile, and I waved as I approached him. I sat on a cushioned bar stool at the counter while he poured me a cup of coffee. He always had the best coffee, imported from where-ever expensive coffee is grown, ground to perfection and always fresh.

"How's life? What've you been working on?" he asked.

He loved the cop stories. The investigations, the conspiracies, just like I did, and he couldn't wait for me to fill him in. I ran the Brussels robbery down for him. "I know the stone," he said. "I went there to eat so I could see it. Carl Wittmond took it off of his finger and let me hold it. An unusual stone, unable to be cut again. You know that, don't you?"

"No, I didn't. Why can't it be cut?"

"It's a solitaire for one thing, cut to perfection, and the yellow cast makes it unstable for a cut. Whoever has it will sell it as it is, and whoever buys it will take it as it is, an identifiable, very large diamond. It will show up one day, maybe years from now, but it will show up."

I studied him as he refilled my cup. He was avoiding eye contact with me which was unusual for him. Part of his shtick was eye contact. It reinforced the perception of honesty. Every good salesman uses it. I got the feeling he knew something he wanted to tell me but was waiting for me to ask.

"Have you heard anything about the Brussels diamond? Is it around here?" He didn't answer immediately. I knew what he was thinking. Should I tell the cop detective what I know? I like him, but what can I gain by giving him this kind of information? I can tell an FBI friend or Lieutenant Boob and gain power from it.

So, Paul blew the question off. He talked about the jewelry business. He busied himself with his baubles and bangles while I intently watched him. He knew I was reading him. He had never blown off a question of mine before.

It didn't hurt my feelings. Information was power. It had to be used like a tool, at the right moment, with the right person. Paul was weighing his options, and weighing my demeanor at his actions, seeing how I would react to his tack. I was cool with it.

"Here's a diamond test for you, detective." I watched him without verbally responding. "How do you tell if a diamond is real?"

"You look at it through one of those magnifier things, a loop," I replied.

"No. The loop will only show you imperfections in the stone. You get two more tries." He was smiling at me, he loved the game. I looked at him like I had gone to grade school in the metro-east. "You check to see if it will cut glass," he said with a smile.

"No kidding," I exclaimed.

"Yes, it's the only way. There are a lot of phony stones out there being worn and passed off as real. The real stones are in a safe deposit box, gaining equity. It's the way wealthy folks have their cake and eat it too."

"Interesting," I mumbled. I wondered why he told me that. Why was it pertinent to our conversation? The guy was a computer on the diamond business. He had to know where Carl's stone was. I stayed cool and watched him.

"There's a diamond merchant at Ninth and Washington, Joe Collins. You ever heard of him?"

"No, Paul. Should I have?"

"He's friends with a bunch of cops. Most of them are high-ranking guys. I thought maybe you had met him at some point in time."

"No, I haven't."

"I heard he recently had a large diamond come through his shop. It was a sixteen-carat, yellow cast stone. It's just something I heard. Can you use it?"

"Yeah, I can use it, thanks."

"There's another guy in the business, an honest guy, Curt Parker. He's always got his ear to the ground, and he knows the business well. He's out in Clayton. It wouldn't hurt for you to talk to him."

Customers started coming in. I waved to Paul while he was pitching a guy on a Rolex, and walked out. I left the detective Chevy parked near

Paul's shop and calmly strolled down to the shop of Joe Collins, diamond merchant.

There was a young lady working the counter, bleached blonde, too much make-up, but good bones and a great body. She dressed the part for a gal who had always been in the limelight because of her looks, one with all of the tools to make a good living selling at the retail hustle. She did the right thing when I walked in. She gave me a big smile and stuck her breasts out so they'd be perky and interesting. "Joe," I said.

"Oh," she replied as she let the air out. She'd made me as a cop, I surmised. Why the let down? I could have been her best customer on this fine fall morning. "Joe," she said over her shoulder, "there's another cop here to see you."

A man in his sixties came out and greeted me. He was frazzled, white hair and pale with a paunch. I shook his hand and gave him my card. He read it and tucked it away, then seriously stared, probably thinking I wanted some kind of a super deal on a wristwatch or pinky ring.

He could tell by my business card I wasn't a ranking cop, and he showed his displeasure that I had asked for him personally. If I wanted something from him at a discount, I should have been escorted in by a high-ranking guy. Every important cop had his own personal jeweler friend. Sometimes they would introduce their most special friends to them. The introductions were usually saved for an attractive rookie female cop. It was the cop/jeweler pecking order in this town. I read him like a gold and diamond-encrusted Rolex at 1700-hundred hours.

I figured I would get directly to the point. I didn't care about the pecking order or about him and who he knows. I just wanted to recover the stone. This guy was a feeble old man, bent at the shoulders from worshiping diamonds and gold at the altar of his jewelry business. He glared at me as if he could read my thoughts. Maybe he could.

"A guy got beaten and robbed over in Brussels, Illinois. The stone taken from him was sixteen- carats, a solitaire in a platinum setting. I was told you've got it. I want it so I can return it to him. Give me the stone."

I stared, but he wasn't intimidated. He had an ace in the hole, several aces to play. He knew I was selling him wolf tickets and he wasn't buying.

"Do you know who I am?"

"Yeah, I know who you are. Now, give me the stolen stone so I can give it back to Carl Wittmond. We'll talk about how you got it some other time."

"I don't know what you're talking about, detective. I don't have such a stone. I'm a friend of the police officer. I've saved police officers lives before. I took a bullet for a police officer, right here in this store, right where you're standing. I shouldn't be accused in this manner."

"Good, Joe, now go and get the stone and give it to me. You've never saved my life. What about the life of the old man who got robbed, beaten up, and his girlfriend? Do their lives matter?"

"Who told you I had that stone? I demand to know who has been a false witness against me."

"Okay, Joe. You know what you know, and I know what I know. You can deny all you want, but I know you've got it, or you had it. It came through this shop. My informant is impeccable, my information sterling. I may not get it today, Joe, but I'll get it. You'll see." I turned and walked out. I had shaken the tree, now I had to wait for the apple to fall.

It was police-discount lunch time. I calmly strolled back to the detective Chevy, climbed in, cranked it and headed west toward my friend's buffet in the Central West End. I went through the line while the cashier, the chunky Russian, Svetna, was eyeballing me with fear. She could have been the poster girl for the Russian immigrant persona. The terrified look, the large features and the uncut hair, all bundled on top of her head. Huge rolling, untrusting eyes.

She couldn't leave the KGB association alone. I terrified her, even though I smiled and was polite to her. "KGB smile, too," she would begin. "KGB polite, too, until they get you into their office. Then, no more polite. Then they beat and torture you. You KGB!"

The owner came out, "You eat free today; I'm sorry for Svetna. She had a rough time in Russia."

I smiled and veered away from the cash register. Svetna's name-calling had saved me the cost of a half-price lunch. We KGB guys are cheap, and scary. I know that's what she was thinking. But, she was correct in her assumption about me and the other cops. I had seen dozens of suspects handcuffed and beaten. It's a police-state mentality, sickening and prevalent. It isn't my style, but lying on search warrant affidavits isn't either. I find joy in investigating conspiracies. That is my thing. I don't think the KGB guys do that. I think they intimidate, beat-up and torture their supposed suspects. Then, they toss them in the clink for life.

Svetna watched every bite I took as she attempted to force a smile as the customers handed her cash for their meals. For some reason I thought about my associate, Detective Frank Reed. He's killed before, robbery suspect, armed and dangerous. I wondered if Svetna would think Frank is KGB. I wondered if there were any black KGB agents? I made a mental note to bring Frank into the restaurant. I would study Svetna to see if she says KGB to him.

I finished the meal, said goodbye to the owner and made a humble attempt to be nice to Svetna, patting her on the back and smiling at her. "KGB pat on back, too," she mumbled. The woman really didn't like me.

I climbed back into the detective Chevy and headed for Clayton, Missouri, the economic center of the St. Louis region. It was skyscraper heaven, corporate headquarters to many large companies, the way downtown St. Louis once was. But, these buildings were new, glass and chrome, not old brick and wood like the downtown architecture.

I located Curt Parker's shop, modern and open, a storefront with appeal. I walked in and browsed while I waited for someone to approach me. An attractive woman came up to me, outgoing and sure of herself. She didn't give me the feeling she was attempting to pitch me. She was a professional salesperson, and I instantly liked her. We had something in common, but I didn't know what it was.

"I'm with City Intelligence," I said as I handed her my card. She read it and smiled, then gave me the opportunity to state my business before we continued with our conversation. I told her about the stone and the robbery. I went into detail about it, describing to her how the elderly Carl Wittmond and Jane Stewart had been beaten, had broken bones, and that it was all for the yellow-cast diamond.

She listened intently, and after I finished my spiel, a man came out from a partition and stood beside her. He had been listening at his work bench. They were a nice-looking couple, attractive and complementing to each other. He wore the gear of an artisan, glasses with magnifiers on swivels, vinyl bib, Plexiglas facemask, up and out of the way on his forehead. His hands were cut and burned, with scars. We shook hands as she introduced him to me as her husband, Curt Parker.

"He's the best jeweler in the Midwest," she said pointing at him. "Curt makes almost all of our jewelry, most of it custom ordered. He can't be beat. Maybe we can make something for you, someday."

"Maybe," I replied.

"I've seen that ring before," Curt began. "We went to the old hotel and had their fried chicken dinner. It was good. The old man, Carl, I think his name was, saw my interest in his ring. He took it off and let me look at it. Interesting stone. I'd know it if I ever saw it again."

"Will you call me if you ever do see it?"

"Yes, give me your home phone number." I wrote it on the back of my business card and handed it back to him.

"This is a strange investigation," I continued. "The robbery wasn't in my jurisdiction, but I know the old man, and I just wanted to help him. If I can get it back for him, then maybe we can figure out who knocked him around. Elderly folks aren't supposed to be beaten up like that."

"I know about strange investigations," Mrs. Parker said. "My dad was an Alcohol Tobacco and Firearms Special Agent. I grew up around investigations." I stared at her and realized what our common ground was. I was reassured that Boob's friend Paul was right in his assumption; these folks were honest jewelers.

I strolled back toward the detective Chevy, taking my time and watching the people hustling and bustling around Clayton. There was a business atmosphere here that was lacking in downtown St. Louis. I tried to figure out why. It took me a couple of minutes but I came upon one of the reasons.

There's no fear here. The sun hit the streets and sidewalks. There were no canyons and crevices. People were free to walk around the streets without having to watch over their shoulders for purse-snatchers, robbers, panhandlers, insane street people who live on the street and in alleys. People can leave things in their cars without having to replace the window every month.

I climbed into the Chevy, cranked it and tried to decide where I was going. I didn't want to go back to the office. I couldn't bear the scene there, the stars, Captain Bud, who for some strange reason was frequenting the office more often, and Boob. And, the lead star was starting to zero in on my friend Frank Reed.

Frank was trying to piece together an investigation on the Moorish Science Temple, a religious sect comprised of criminals. The lead star had decided that since these guys were black, and they were rumored to traffic in heroin, they were his quarry, not Frank's.

The lead star was complaining to Captain Bud about it, and Frank

Reed had overheard their conversation. Frank was an unstable and violent man. I didn't want to be there if and when the showdown happened. Both of them were gun-guys.

I dug into the glove compartment where I had placed the piece of paper that Frank, the jeweler friend of Jesse Stoneking, had given me. I never had visited the shop he had told me about. It seemed too pat at the time, like a set-up. But I had nowhere else to go in the investigation. I found it, tucked it into my pocket and headed back downtown to the Paul Brown.

I parked at a meter, entered from the front door and took the brass door elevator to the third floor. The aisle on three was wide, it seemed wider than the other floors, and there were several large, exclusive jewelry shops on the floor, the kind that required a buzzer to gain entry. They knew their clientele and only buzzed the door for them.

I found the suite I was searching for at the northeast corner of the building, overlooking the shop I had visited earlier in the day. I strolled in and waited for someone to greet me. The shop wasn't a retail store, but a place where jewelry was repaired, or custom made. There were no display cabinets or jewelry for sale. It was a workshop.

A man came out from behind a partition and stared at me as if he was trying to determine if he knew me. "I'm a cop," I reassured him. "I need to ask you a question." I figured I would get to the point. Either he will tell me something or he won't.

"What's the question, I'm real busy. I've got an order going out this evening and it isn't ready."

I took toll of him. About forty-five, unshaven, stooped over, dirty clothing and hands, and his face needed to be washed. His hair stuck up like it was spiked, but it was from perspiration and stress; he was always running his dirty hands through it. He wore a T-shirt, dingy and spotted. How could this guy help me? He's tucked away like a slave, repairing jewelry all day and into the night, a workaholic out of the public view.

"A guy got robbed, over in Illinois, a little farm community. His sixteen-carat diamond in a platinum setting was taken from him. It's got a yellow cast, a solitaire diamond. I'm trying to run it down. Heard of any stones like that being set around here?"

He paused and studied me. I got the impression he liked my candor. He was a busy man and he didn't appreciate any frivolous conversation. "There's a shop in Frontenac, Le Chateau, it's on the ground floor, north section of the building. There's a diamond setter who works in there, much like I do, in the back out of the view of the public. I heard he just set a stone like that into a brooch. It was a difficult job and those type of jobs get conversation in the trade. His name is James." He walked away from me. I left his shop.

I took the elevator down, walked out onto the street and clamored into the Chevy. I was moving like a zombie, my mind whirling. I was becoming anxious again to get the stone in-hand, but cautious about how I was going to do it. In reality, I had gotten farther than I ever expected. I presumed the stone was in this jurisdiction, but it was just a hunch.

I figured I would stir the pot, cause a big riff between some enemy jewelers and maybe, if I was real lucky, I would hear about what happened to it. But this information seemed too good to be true.

It is why I love conspiracies, there are so many people involved. In the jewelry business, it's all one huge conspiracy. They have all got something to hide, and for the most part, they individually feel guilty about it. That is why they talk to a lone cop who wanders into their cave and asks the question, "Will you help me find a stolen diamond?" It gives them purpose in life, and their response clears them of the crime and puts the blame on another crook.

I fired up the Chevy and jumped on the Daniel Boone Expressway, headed west. I would be out of my jurisdiction again, but I knew the Detective Sergeant in Frontenac, Ben Branch. He was an unrelenting cop, feared like the secret police in the City, and he didn't like conspiracies in his wealthy little town.

I parked in the police department parking lot and sat for a moment looking at the building. Everything was new in Frontenac. The little town was chock-full of millionaires, like Beverly Hills, California. The town had money, because of the tax base provided by Plaza Frontenac, a shopping mall much like Rodeo Drive, so the City government had money. It must be strange to work under those conditions.

St. Louis doesn't have money for anything, especially pay raises. We were about the lowest paid department in the area. It was an embarrassment, considering the workload we have. But they didn't balk at my youthful indiscretions when they hired me. I was an ex-Marine from the Eastside, a street kid. I was lucky to get the job. I would have never gotten hired in Frontenac, or any other town with money. I got out and walked inside the modern, split-level building.

"Ben Branch," I told the desk person as I handed her my business card. She talked to Ben on the phone and told him I was waiting. He came out immediately, shook my hand, slapped me on the back, and escorted me into his office.

He was a man ahead of his time, or he was reincarnated from Randolph Scott. He was country-western with a cheap suit, long light-colored hair, combed back, sideburns and a mustache. Cops shouldn't be required to wear suits. It is demeaning to us. We can't afford well-fitting suits; cop life is hard on good clothing, so we buy cheap and wear it until it shreds. He could have shed the suit, tugged on some western garb, hung a star and a low-slung gun belt on, and played the leading role in any Hollywood western. He was surly, but intense, and he studied the person he was talking to.

He was studying me, now, the way I study folks who I come into contact with. We all want something from the person we're talking to. Ben wanted to know what I wanted from him, but he didn't ask. He was too crafty for that, he just waited until the subject came out. He was loyal to the wealthy folks in the City who wanted his loyalty, and feared by the ones who didn't.

If I came calling so I could get close to him to obtain information about one of his wealthy friends, then the conversation would be over. That's why he was the Detective Sergeant in one of the wealthiest cities in the state.

I ran my case down to him, and went into detail about Carl Wittmond and his girlfriend, Jane Stewart. We talked about the diamond and how I ended up in his jurisdiction searching for it. I mentioned the location of the shop, and his eyebrows raised. "James," I said. "A diamond setter in Le Chauteau. Do you know him?"

"Come with me," he said. I followed him to the parking lot. We climbed into his Ford detective car and headed for Le Chateau, which is about four minutes from police headquarters. To say Le Chateau is exclusive is like saying Ben Branch is surly. It is a shopping locale for only the wealthy, built to resemble a Swiss Chateau. The shops are quaint and expensive, and the sales folks act as snooty as their clientele.

The restaurants are so snooty they only serve half-portions, but they charge full-price for the grub. There are lines to get into them for lunch, with only the wealthiest of clients getting pulled to the front of the line by the snooty maitre de.

We entered at the ground level and I followed Ben like a little brother into the jewelry shop. "Where's James?" Ben asked the young counter kid. James came out from behind a partition, obviously frightened by Ben's presence. "Come with us," Ben said, and we walked out of the mall building and to his car.

James was typical of the other diamond mechanics. He was a laborer, a grease monkey working on diamonds instead of cars. If the stolen items were Porsches instead of diamonds, James would be the guy in the back of the shop changing the serial number on the engines and frames.

James didn't ask any questions, he just sat in the back and looked out the window. He was smug, like he had been through this routine before. He probably had, many times. Ben knew him well, I could tell, and James knew how to play the game. The word was out. James knew I was coming.

We parked in front of headquarters and we all got out and filed in. Ben led us into an interrogation room, pointed to a chair, slammed the door and stood over James with me behind him.

"This gentleman," Ben began motioning with his thumb, like he was hitch hiking, "is a detective from City Intelligence. He thinks you know something about a sixteen-carat, solitaire yellow diamond. He wants it back, and I want you to give it to him. I told you the last time I had you in here. I won't stand for any contraband being in my City. You understood me then, didn't you?"

"Yes, sir," James muttered.

"I just want the stone back, that's all," I began. "We can clear up the matter of where it came from at some other time. Tell me where the stone is."

James froze up. He knew if he lied to us we would catch him in it. He was smart enough to know we had been trained to spot liars, so he just sat there and bided his time. It infuriated me. Ben walked out of the room and closed the door. I figured the room was soundproof.

I placed my hands on the table and got my face close to James face. "Hey you thieving asshole I don't think you know who you're talking with. I'm with the City, and in the City we don't take kindly to assholes who refuse to cooperate with us." I slammed my fist down on the table for effect. I want that stone, and I want it now. You'd better start talking. You understand me?"

Ben came walking back in and this time he left the door open. The office personnel were staring into the room from the doorway, smiling and acting embarrassed. The room wasn't soundproof. All of police headquarters had heard my threat. They weren't privy to City police tactics. I was embarrassed.

"Are you going to tell him what he wants to know?" Ben asked.

James wouldn't comment. He knew he would be out of there in five minutes and that nothing would happen to him. I was beside myself with anger. He was the one who could tell me what I wanted to know, and he was refusing to cooperate.

The realization of what I was doing crept upon me like a lioness approaching a baby antelope. I was doing what I despised. I was overreacting. I had the fetish for someone else's stone. The old man, Carl Wittmond, had projected his fetish onto me, and I had taken it, hook, line and sinker.

I shook Ben's hand, thanked him, walked out of the room, and made it to the parking lot without anybody calling out to me.

I climbed into the Chevy and slowly drove to the office, parked, climbed out like an old man and slowly walked into headquarters. I milled around the lobby for a couple of minutes, watching the show of weirdos coming and going, then took the elevator up to the fourth floor.

I walked past the unit secretary's desk, "Message," she said as she handed me a piece of paper. It was an order for me to go to Internal Affairs to see Major George, one of the deputy commanders of the unit. I looked into Boob's office. He was on the phone, but didn't motion to me or give me any indication he wished to speak to me, so I walked out and took the stairs up to the sixth floor.

I walked in and told the receptionist I was supposed to see Major George. She pointed to his office and I went in. I had known the Major for years. He was one of my lieutenants in uniform patrol, and I always liked him. He was a politician, and he jokingly admitted it. He was cousins with the controlling political Syrian faction, the same ones related to the controlling Syrian killing faction.

He was serious on this fine day. He stared at me with a straight Arab face and said, "Leave Joe Collins alone." I didn't react. I just stared back at him. It was like being scolded by the company commander while being in the Marine Corps. I knew there was nothing I could do but to just take the abuse.

In fact, Major George reminded me of a Marine Commander. He was crisply dressed in his white shirt, oak leaves shining, and he was in tip-top shape for a guy his age. He had always been real cool with me, almost friendly, which is unusual for a police commander as high up the ladder as he was. But I could see he was all about business this afternoon. I had treaded on one of his influential friends, another sacrilege in the City of St. Louis and its police department. There are some things a cop just shouldn't do.

"Joe Collins doesn't have that damn diamond," the Major said.

"I was told he did, Major."

"Well, I'm telling you he doesn't." He stared at me with hatred. "You have gall and contempt, detective. Joe Collins is a friend to the cop. He loves cops. He took a bullet for a cop working secondary at his store. He's an honest man, and he'd do anything for you. He is a friend of mine. Leave my friends alone. Stop with this diamond caper and stay away from Joe Collins. Understand?"

"Yes, sir," I quietly said. "Can I go, now?" The Major waved me off, disgustedly, and looked down at his desk at some paperwork. I turned and walked out of the office and strolled back down to the fourth floor, wandered into intelligence and plopped at my desk.

Boob came out and stood in front of my desk. "What have you been investigating?" He was in a foul mood, his cigar was reverberating between his teeth. His hat was off, and I inadvertently fixated on his scabby, scarred head.

"I've been trying to find that diamond stolen over in Brussels. I've gotten some good information, and I've been following leads that I've come up with."

"You were told to stay away from anything concerning Jesse Stoneking. You disobeyed a direct order. You can be suspended for that. It is conduct unbecoming a police officer, or insubordination, or something." Boob was stammering. His heart wasn't in the suspension of me, or anybody else.

"I wasn't investigating Jesse Stoneking. I was just trying to help the Illinois guys recover the ring. I was going to leave it up to them to find out who committed the assault and robbery. The stone's over here. It's in Frontenac, or it was. No telling where it is now."

"Okay," Boob said. He was sucking on his cigar and blowing straight shots at me. "I'm going to give you another order. Don't assist the

Illinois guys with their investigation. Do you think they'd assist you? They wouldn't. They've never given this unit anything. Let those fucking farmers do their own investigating. Any questions?"

"No, Lieutenant." I could hear the stars giggling in the next room. They loved it when I screwed up. My compatriot, Frank Reed, was standing at the doorway listening to my problems. He hated authority about as much as I did. I knew all of this unit turmoil was taking a toll on him. He didn't have the disposition for this type of office political dissension.

Frank was the type of cop who, when confronted with a problem, was compelled to solve the problem, immediately. If that means with violence, then he takes that tack. He's prone to it, and good at it.

These long drawn-out conflicts between Boob, Captain Bud, the stars, and me, were damaging to him. He was a part of it, mainly because of his loyalty to me. I didn't ask for his loyalty, it just happened. He was holding anger inside of him, and that's not healthy.

He was going to break someday, and I didn't want to see it. It would be violent. He gave me the look of brotherhood, showing me his support, and then went back to his little office overlooking the alley to resume typing the Moorish Science Temple fiasco. He typed all day, never coming up for air, except to research some oblivious clue. It was fruitless. The lead star was going to take it all away from him. It was only a matter of time.

17

The vision of Frank Reed standing and watching me take Boob's reprimand tortured me. He was there to assist. I could sense it. I could see it. He wanted to retaliate. He was prepared to go to war with the stars and the bosses. He wanted me to give him the sign to attack. I wasn't going to do it. It would have been political suicide for both of us. Not only would we be terminated, we would most likely be criminally prosecuted. I was frightened for him.

I had seen it in the Marine Corps. Two guys who are in shape, and know how to fight, can wreak havoc on a large group of people. Punching and moving, kicking and gouging. Two good fighters can punish ten people. Most are knocked unconscious within seconds of the attack. It's what Frank wanted. He was waiting for me to give the okay. He wanted me to lead him.

I drove home slightly depressed, and by the time I got home I was totally depressed. My wife, who constantly monitored me, popped a beer for me and stuck it in my hand. She didn't use alcohol but she was aware I was highly stressed. She constantly monitored my mental stability. At this point in the cop detective/crook game, it was all she could do for me. I slugged several down and was feeling numb while pork steaks were being seasoned and the Weber was being fired up. She didn't ask me what the problem was, and I didn't offer any information to her. It was all a part of the job.

The beer thing was a crutch for me, and I knew it was an East St. Louis, Marine Corps thing that someday I would have to get a handle on. But people in high-stress occupations do worse to their bodies and minds, seeking refuge from the pain. It was a band-aid for a slashed throat.

The telephone rang and I picked up on the second ring. It was Curt

Parker, the honest jeweler from Clayton. "I just saw the diamond," he began. "I saw the stone you asked me about."

"Where?" My heart was racing.

"It's in the window of the Regency Jewelers in Plaza Frontenac. It's been set into a brooch. It's right in the window."

"Are you certain it's the same stone?"

"Yes, that's it. I know stones, and I've seen the stone before. I've held it in my hand. That's the stone. It's so unusual, with the yellow color, and its size. That's the stone."

"Okay, Curt, thanks for the information. I'll get right on it." We hung up while my head was reeling. I knew I couldn't pursue the stone any further. I was on thin ice in the unit, and in the police department. I didn't want to look for a new job, not with two young children, a mortgage and a stay-at-home wife.

I was the nonconformist who had become institutionalized. My past lifestyle wasn't going to work for me anymore. I was going to have to change, start bending to the rules and regulations. I needed to conform, just to survive. I hated the feeling. The detective job in intelligence had gotten me. It was something I liked, and that was being used against me.

It is why my East St. Louis relatives never succeeded in any venture. They detested the ultimatum, the carrot on a stick, probably offered to them by one of Buster Wortman's henchman, so they said, "Screw you, and screw Buster Wortman, too."

That spelled unemployment for those poor souls. They all thought they could make a living on their own, and maybe they could have in another town, a town with economic development, but not in East St. Louis, Illinois. And, I knew I couldn't make a living in St. Louis, Missouri, except doing what I was doing (sharecropper syndrome). It was a further depressing dilemma.

I called old Carl Wittmond at the hotel. Jane Stewart answered for him. Carl was still hobbling around on crutches. She asked who I was, and I told her. Carl was on the phone immediately.

"I found your stone," I began.

"Where is it?" He didn't act surprised. He was a gambler, and he had probably placed a bet with some country/western bookie that I would find it.

"It's in the window of the Regency Jewelers in Plaza Frontenac, in a brooch. I didn't personally view it, but I've got an informant who knows the stone, and he's seen it. He just telephoned me."

"We'll be over there tomorrow morning, about eleven. Will you be there?"

"Maybe, but if I'm not there, I'll have an associate meet with you."

"Okay, thanks." He hung up.

I slugged down some more brews, had a pork steak dinner and was staring at the tube, but not assimilating it. My mind was on the yellow stone in the window in fashionable Plaza Frontenac. I had an epiphany. I wondered if my partner was still in town. The guy could afford to go on vacation to any locale, but he usually opted to stay at home and save money. I dialed him at his residence.

We started out with small talk, office politics, gossip, and I hit him with the question. "Would you go out to Plaza Frontenac tomorrow and meet someone for me?"

Boob didn't tell him to lay off of the investigation. Major George didn't give him the third degree about the stone. He was new to the investigation. He was a fresh face. It might work. I explained everything to him. He said he would meet them for me.

"Okay," I continued. "Call me at the office after you meet with the victims. If the stars hear us talking about it they'll snitch to Captain Bud or Boob, so don't come in."

"Okay," he replied.

"When I hear from you, I'll make arrangements to leave the office and meet up with you. Carl Wittmond is the victim's name, and he'll probably have his nephew with him. He's the State's Attorney for Calhoun County, Illinois. Charles Burch is his name. Take notes and get me the names of those who show up, and what happens to the stone. Okay?"

"Right, I've got it." He was a good partner, after all.

It all happened as scripted. My partner called me at the office at about ten-thirty and told me he was on his way to Plaza Frontenac. The stars didn't see him, they didn't know what was going on, and they couldn't snitch. I hung out with Frank Reed, trying to help him piece his humongous investigation together. It wasn't working. Frank had a year's worth of paperwork ahead of him. I read some of what he'd done. They were the ramblings of a madman. But it gave him something to do.

I tried to think about what had sent Frank off the deep end. I felt he was suffering from combat fatigue. I had seen it before, but not in the intelligence unit. He came from the same district I had come from. It was a busy place, but you could manage it with discretion. Discretion governs our lives. It's what keeps us sane. Frank didn't have discretion. Everything was a challenge to him; a kill or be killed attitude.

My partner called me at about thirteen-hundred. He asked me to meet up with him, and I strolled out of the office without any fanfare. I headed for the Missouri Athletic Club for a free lunch, something that always brightened our day. He was there waiting for me in the parking lot. A free lunch on a vacation day. It fit his criteria as a good thing.

We were on our third dessert when he began the story. "They all showed up."

I listened without asking any questions.

"Carl Wittmond, the victim. Charles Burch, the State's Attorney. A guy from the FBI, Special Agent Julian Stackhouse. And, the guy who says he owns the diamond, an influential newspaperman. He showed up later at police headquarters and told Chief Blazer he owned the stone. That's where we all ended up. He claims he bought the stone from jeweler Joe Collins, from the shop in downtown St. Louis, about thirteen months ago. He's got the paperwork proving that fact."

"Joe Collins?" I exclaimed. "I was told he had the stone. I paid him a visit. He denied having it. I knew he was lying. He put his attack dog, Major George, on me."

"Yeah. Detective Sergeant Ben Branch was there, and the Chief of Police of Frontenac, David Blazer. It was a big deal. The FBI Agent seized the brooch with the stone in it. I don't know what they're going to do with it."

"So Carl Wittmond didn't get his stone back?"

"Nope. FBI's got it."

"Damn," I mumbled. "I wonder what's up with that." It wasn't a victory for me. I felt empty inside, although I could rationalize I had found the stolen diamond. Big deal. Carl probably wouldn't get it back.

It was the diamond thief's creed. You can say it's yours, but you can't prove it, unless it's in the setting, and you've got pictures of it in the setting. The diamond was in a brooch. Someone should ask Joe Collins where he got the stone, but nobody will.

No wonder Boob told me not to screw with Illinois' crime problems. It was a waste of time. Carl can collect his insurance money, but that's all. He got beat up by some gangsters, terrorized by union thugs, humiliated in front of his girlfriend, and they got away with it. Ludicrous!

We went back to the office and I called Carl Wittmond's nephew, Charles Burch, State's Attorney for Calhoun County, Illinois. It was usually a two-man office, sometimes there was a secretary. Charlie answered on the first ring.

"You didn't get the stone back?" I asked without identifying myself.

"No, the FBI seized it."

"A big-shot newspaperman has paperwork saying he purchased it from Joe Collins, diamond merchant. What's up with that? I interviewed Joe Collins. I had an informant who told me Joe Collins was in possession of the stone. I got chastised by some brass for questioning Joe Collins about the stone. And, who the hell is this influential newspaperman?"

"He's a personal friend of Carl's. He comes to the hotel regularly. Last New Years's Eve, he had a big party over here, rented rooms in the hotel and spent the night. I don't know why he would come forward and say the stone is his. Carl isn't talking about it. But someone thought Carl was going to sell the business here and relocate to Arizona with Jane Stewart. He was angry with me because I wasn't helping him enough around the restaurant. I was busy trying to get elected to the state legislature and he blurted out one day that he was going to sell the place."

"Oh, okay," I said, confused.

"That was just eight or nine days before Carl got beaten and robbed. Someone wanted Carl's ring but they knew if Carl was still around he would recognize it when he saw it. So when they heard he was leaving the area, they acted, and contracted with someone to come over and rob Carl. If he relocated with the ring, this person could never have it.

"But how would that person know about Carl blurting out that he was leaving?"

"It was in the St. Louis newspaper. A gossip reporter was here dining when Carl said it." I paused to mull on the information.

"How's Jane doing?"

"Not well. She's on Ativan, an anti-depressant drug. She eats the stuff like candy. She's scared to death."

"Okay, Charlie, let me know if you find out anything more." I hung up.

I couldn't stop thinking about the scenario. It was too pat. I didn't have all of the information when I started the investigation. I was used, but I knew that. But I thought I was being used as an investigator. Maybe it was more than that. Maybe I was being used as a patsy.

The same type of stone had come through the Paul Brown approximately a year ago, Jesse's jeweler friend told me. But he was probably lying to send me in the wrong direction. Thieves try to alter your thinking with poison information. It is a devious plan to confuse and distress the investigator. The influential newspaperman told the FBI, Ben Branch, and Chief David Blazer he had purchased the stone thirteen months ago.

There aren't two stones like Carl's, solitaires, yellow in color, sixteen carats. Somebody's lying. I'd have to let it play out, but I'm dealing with another group of super-criminals. Businessmen with the fetish. Wealthy, treacherous, and as dangerous as the union thugs. And these guys aren't just cunning like the union thugs. These guys are smart.

Guido passed by my desk, paused and then came back. "Jesse Stoneking and Art Berne were subpoenaed before a federal grand jury in the Eastern District of Missouri." I looked up and didn't comment.

"That's on the west side, across the river from East St. Louis, Illinois, your hometown."

"Yeah, Guido. I know where it is. What's the grand jury investigating?"

"I'm not certain," he muttered. Grand jury investigations are super-secret, but cops and agents investigating the crime know what the story is. I didn't believe him so I gave him an incredulous look. "Okay," he said, "it's got something to do with the John Paul Spica murder. Apparently the prosecutors on this side of the river thought they knew something that the grand jury could get out of them."

"So, did they honor the subpoenas?"

"Hell, yeah, they had no choice. Both of them invoked their 5th-Amendment protection against self-incrimination. Jesse was in there for thirty minutes. I heard Art Berne's big-time upset. These guys don't like being investigated by grand juries. It means the government's got something on them. They feel the end's near for them."

"Neat, Guido." He sauntered off as I continued to worry and ponder over my mistakes on the Brussels diamond robbery. It was time for me to lay low.

18

I pondered the Jesse Stoneking, Art Berne grand jury testimony. What did the Feds think those guys were going to tell them? It seemed an exercise in futility. A waste of time. It was done as some sort of subterfuge. The 5th-Amendment was made for guys like them.

But I had other problems to ponder. I had to survive the inner office political game. I was now a sitting duck. I was a prize fighter who had been dinged in the tenth round and was wobbly and confused. I retreated into my corner and held my gloves over my jaw and temple as my opponents thumped me about the head and shoulders with vicious rights and lefts.

But unlike a real prize fighter, I had no seconds, no one to tell me I had done the right thing, no one to rub my neck, put water to my lips, ice to the back of my neck or to stop the bleeding of the cuts over my eyes. I was on my own, except for moral support from Frank Reed.

I was devastated and embarrassed to the extent I even said "yes, sir" and "no, sir," to Boob, but not to Captain Bud. The diamond caper made a believer out of me. I now knew I shouldn't venture into other jurisdictions' investigations, no matter what.

But there was a problem. The little conspiracy had turned into a complex conspiracy. There were questions which demanded answers. I called FBI Special Agent Julian Stackhouse to ask him one little question. Why had the FBI gotten involved in a little assault and robbery caper of a stupid, and ugly sixteen-carat diamond? It wasn't a federal crime. But I never got to ask him the question. He never returned my call.

I called my friend, Special Agent Sam Thompson to ask him the same question. I never received a return call. There are two kinds of people in law enforcement: those who return your calls and those who don't. Sam Thompson was the type of guy who would return your calls. I couldn't figure why he didn't return mine. But he was in a different office now. He was in Belleville, Illinois, not St. Louis, Missouri. He had no reason to confer with me, on anything. He was a Fed. I was a local. The Feds control the ebb and tide of information; not the locals.

The only other reason I could conjure up was he knew I wanted information on the Brussels robbery, and that it was none of my business. He was right. I was snooping for information. I couldn't help myself.

I knew a cop in the little town of Jerseyville, Illinois, which is about twenty miles from Brussels. I called him and engaged him in small talk. I casually brought up the diamond robbery just to see what he had to say about it. He had heard that Carl Wittmond was hosting a poker game at the hotel, after hours, and he'd lost a great deal of cash, probably an unusual occurrence for him.

The cop said he refused to pay the two or three guys he had gambled with and that he told them to get out of his establishment. Supposedly, they beat Carl, and pistol-whipped him. Jane Stewart came to Carl's defense. They beat her up too, took Carl's diamond and kept it as collateral.

That made sense, since Carl is a gambler. I had heard he hosted high-stakes poker games in his hotel, and it explained why the robbers didn't take the hotel receipts, or Jane's flawless, European-cut diamond ring. The window screen in the back dining room where the robbers allegedly entered the hotel could have been out of the window for months. It also meant Carl knew who beat him and took his ring.

I also wanted to know why the FBI seized and retained the diamond. If the folks who had the diamond say it belonged to the influential newspaperman, and if he had paperwork and receipts showing he purchased the stone thirteen months previously from Joe Collins, then said diamond should be returned to the influential newspaperman.

It was one conundrum after another, and I was beside myself for the answers. I heard from another cop friend in a neighboring community, Jesse Stoneking was indeed the robber, and the reason he wasn't stopped at the roadblock was because he was spending the night with one of Carl's employees. Supposedly, Jesse befriended this homely girl who had been divorced and lived alone, and she had been giving Jesse information on Carl and the diamond so he could knock Carl off.

Jesse went to this homely girl's house in Golden Eagle and spent the night. In the morning, he woke up fresh, showered, had a good country breakfast and took the ferry over the Illinois River into Grafton. No roadblock. No search. He had the diamond and was home free.

I called Carl and asked him about this information. He verified it and said he had fired the girl, even though he couldn't substantiate the rumor. Carl was certain Jesse Stoneking and his associates robbed and beat him and Jane Stewart.

Before our telephone conversation ended, he said, "Can you get me my diamond back? The FBI's got it and I want it back." He was baiting me again, I knew it, but I couldn't figure out why. It was some kind of a game he was playing with me. He took great pleasure in it. It had to be a control thing. He was seeing how far he could go with me before I refused to do his bidding and told him to screw off.

But for some reason I didn't tell him to screw off. In a strange East St. Louis kind of way, I respected the guy. He was crusty and bold, but he was powerful and in control of everything pertaining to his life. He knew how to survive and prosper, and I had to respect that.

I was never in the presence of anyone who had gotten down and dirty with the world and came out on top, the winner, and a wealthy winner at that. Carl was a winner who enjoyed me and my family and enjoyed teasing me with a hollow friendship.

The weirdest part of the situation was that I really, truly, wanted to get his stone back for him, still. And that was real weird. I had found it once. Wasn't that enough? Didn't that prove that I was a cracker-jack cop investigator? I had damn near done the impossible. I tentatively identified who had stolen it, and I had found it. It was hidden in a maze of guilt and deceit.

I sniffed it out like a good little Labrador retriever. It wasn't my fault Carl and his State's Attorney nephew couldn't finagle it away from the greed in St. Louis, so it could go back to the greed in the peninsula of Brussels, Illinois. Greed is greed, no matter where it festers.

"Carl," I began, "You're a wealthy man. You've got the law of the State of Illinois behind you. There's no need for me to tell you the rules of the law. You could get a grand jury to indict Jesse Stoneking, and the folks who claim to own the stone you say is yours. I'm a cop with no rank in a neighboring state. I can't help you."

"You could get it back for me," Carl countered. "You work with the FBI. I don't work with them. Charles doesn't work with them. You know them; we don't."

"Okay, Carl, I'll see what I can do," I wearily replied. But I wasn't going to over-extend myself on the caper. I would react if I heard of anything substantial, but the chances of getting the stone back from the FBI were slim. I still couldn't figure for the life of me why they seized it. It didn't make sense.

The unit was changing for the better. The lead star had gotten promoted and he was leaving to go to a uniform district. It was good for me, Frank Reed, and almost everybody involved. Everybody congratulated him and paid him homage. He was now a sergeant. Cops from across the hall from vice and narcotics came into the unit and shook his hand.

His influential buddy followed him around the unit offices, praising him to the visiting cops. The lead star had dressed for the part; shiny brown suit pants, and a white dress shirt. He had apparently chain-smoked all night in anticipation of the pending promotion. His lips were yellow with nicotine. His right hand was stained all the way up to his wrist.

He had the smile of a boa constrictor preparing to eat a rabbit, and his eyes were darting about. He glanced at me several times. I just stared. I couldn't get into the spirit of the event. What was the big deal of being a sergeant? Who cares?

I sat at my desk watching the absurd theater of the damned; the cops begging for someone to lead them. I catalogued their body language; they were shouting to the lead star, "Please lead me, I want to follow someone. I need to be led." I was a foreigner in a strange land.

The lead star was reveling in the light of his stardom. He acted as if he had won the lotto, or he had inherited a lot of money. But the pay increase was minimal. Then it dawned on me. To guys like him, it wasn't money they were scratching and digging for. It was power over other cops.

It is the way the system is set up for cops. We've got the power, if we seek it religiously, but we don't get the money, ever. That's reserved for the crooks and the crafty businessman. If I realized this little-known fact, then why didn't the other cops?

Frank Reed was standing to my right, and my partner was standing to my left. My partner broke ranks and went to the lead star, smiling and offering his hand, bent at the waist as if he was subservient, undeserving to be in the presence of such a great man. I tried to detach myself from this scene and move up to the ceiling and observe the happenings below me.

Captain Bud wasn't in attendance, but Boob was. He had a strange look on his face, as if he was scared, but he had reason to be. His days in the unit were numbered. He would be going back to the blue army, a fate we had all been programmed to despise. We in the unit were deemed important. The uniformed guys were thought to be below us in stature. But that was a ruse, a method to make us prostitute ourselves to stay in the unit, to make unit crime statistics available to the commander. We were supposed to be great. Captain Bud and Lieutenant Boob were even greater.

The cops were flittering around the lead star. Me, sitting at my desk, the unrepentant non-conformist from the east side. The madman Frank Reed standing beside me, Bo Diddley look-alike cop, holding his madman notations in his right hand like a security blanket, wearing his leather-brimmed Bo Diddley hat. It was a Norman Rockwell painting, had Norman been on crack.

I gave my partner a strange look. "He got his sergeancy," my partner exclaimed. He was trying to justify his actions. He had gone to the dark side without attempting to hide his disloyalty. He was begging the star to lead him, too. I knew there was no such word describing the rank of sergeant. It was something someone made up to trick the cops striving for power.

The lead star had entered into cop nirvana, as far as he was concerned. He was going to lead cops. But that seems to be the American way. Do what you have to do to please the bosses and don't get caught. He twisted the rules to uphold the law. Is that the way it's supposed to be? It was interesting to me that the system needs to be tweaked on the local level in order to attain success, and that the tweaking is rewarded by the bosses and ignored by prosecutors.

It's the way criminals end up in prison. It is blind dedication. I wondered if I was viewing unit events in their proper perspective or if my jaundiced Eastside attitude was governing me.

"He's management now," my partner added. "He will have the ear of other managers in the department. He'll be gunning for his enemies."

I was surprised by his insight. "Thanks for the warning," I replied. Frank didn't respond but I could tell he was prepared to go into combat. It's what he was about; the only way he knew to resolve unpleasant situations.

The two smart guys of the unit, Guido and Stretch, were conveniently out of the office during the promotion performance. I was grateful for that. I would have lost it if they had worshiped the lead star.

A couple of days zoomed by and Captain Bud was transferred out of the unit. Another good thing for all parties involved. The new Captain, a professional Irishman, was a good guy, a thinker, which is what the unit needed, and what it was intended to be: intelligent. An intelligence unit should develop and assimilate criminal information. It is what he told us to do, and we did it.

The problem arose when Boob started asserting his knowledge. He had been there for so long he could do the deputy commander job in his sleep. It didn't sit well with the new commander. It was another ego thing, so the new guy kept a short leash on Boob. In fact, they shared an office. Everything Boob did was monitored by the new guy.

We continued doing our thing on the Eastside, snooping around the massage parlors. And we had our dignitary-protection details. Bob Hope came back into town. I hadn't seen him in about a year, or more.

My partner and I were to escort Bob and his wife, Dolores and their little French poodle, to an outdoor fair at the Gateway Arch. It's a federal park and is governed by federal laws, and patrolled by United States Park Rangers. But City Intelligence cops do the protection details there.

I met Bob and Dolores at the airport and drove them to the Chase-Park Plaza Hotel in the Central West End. It was like old home week. Bob had apparently told Dolores about me. She treated me as an equal, not a servant, just like Bob, and I enjoyed being around her.

They had the day to themselves, and my partner and I picked them up in a limousine at the Chase and drove them to the stage, which was at the east end of the park with the back of it to the Mississippi River. There were hundreds of thousands of people in attendance.

We were back stage with Bob, standing stage right. The little star asked me to get his new girlfriend close to the stage so she could watch the Linda Ronstadt performance. The girlfriend was a looker who worked in the chief's office.

I got her in a great position to observe, close up while Linda sang, and eventually ended the act with Blue Bayou. We were so close to Linda her voice made the hair stand up on my neck and arms. I wondered where the little star's wife and kid were. The crowd was pumped and primed with cold beer.

Before Bob went onstage, my partner told him there were a million fans out there. I had to admit, although it looked like a million people, it was a St. Louis cop exaggeration.

It was a magical night, and Bob could feel the magic, I could see it in his body language. It was old St. Louis, turn of the century, with the smell of the Mississippi, the St. Louis skyline, and a million or so adoring fans. Everything Bob loved.

He went out and did his routine, and the fans loved it. They cheered and howled and clapped, and they loved Bob Hope as much as Bob loved old St. Louis. He bonded with the drunk, shirtless, stinking working-class fans. If he could have, I think he would have shaken each one of their hands and kissed each one of their wives. The guy had heart.

We got Bob back into the limo and we started the trek back through the adoring fans toward Interstate 70. We were taking Bob and Dolores directly to the airport for their flight back to Hollywood.

The mounted patrol was waiting for us as we entered the wide walkway leading out of the park. "Is everybody's door locked?" I asked.

"They're all locked," the limo driver replied. Dolores hit the button to make certain everything was locked up. We felt safe and secure in the back of the big limo, with tinted windows, locked doors and the almost soundproof quality of the vehicle.

The mounted patrol had their horses in front of the limo, swinging the hind-quarters of the horses outward so the limo could get by the crowd. It was an interesting maneuver and I was impressed by the intelligence of the horses, and their riders.

The fans were trying to look into the windows of the limo, wanting to see Bob Hope close up. Some of them would put their tongues on the windows, but mostly they were trying to peer into the darkness and catch a glimpse of him. They were climbing all over the limo, lying on the hood and the trunk lid, trying to look inside.

We finally made it to Interstate 70, but we were still on the walkway, and still in the park. The crowd had subsided, but some stragglers were still following us trying to look in. The limo driver stopped the car, and was preparing to find the right location to jump the curb to get onto the interstate.

The back door of the limo suddenly opened, and a shirtless, intoxicated and stinking St. Louis beer-head jumped into the back seat with us. Dolores screamed, and the poodle screamed, but Bob was cool with the program. He showed no fear. The intruder was on my partner's side of the car. I was going to stand in a bent position and toss him out, but my partner got to him before I did.

He pushed the guy out of the car and then the guy seemed like he wanted to fight. It was bad- choice night for the drunk, curious beer-head. My partner quickly knocked him into submission, left him lying on his back and climbed back into the car. It was normal procedure for St. Louis cops. It's what we do. The public expects over-reactions from St. Louis cops. It's acceptable.

But Bob was unnerved by the violence of the act. There was dead silence by everyone in the car on the way to the airport. Even the poodle didn't growl or bark. Dolores was staring down at the floor for the rest of the trip. She had inadvertently unlocked the doors after the limo driver had locked them.

I felt as if I needed to clear the air. I glanced at Bob. "When these guys are drunk, Bob, they can't be trusted. He could've had a gun or a knife. There's no telling what he intended to do. He was out of his mind."

"He wasn't going to hurt anybody," Bob said. "He just wanted to see me. You didn't have to beat him up for wanting to see me. I could have shaken his hand and you guys could have gotten him out of the car without violence."

I was embarrassed, but I shouldn't have been. It was our job to protect Bob and Dolores. We were trained attack dogs; we would have done anything to keep them from being harmed. But I knew Bob, and I knew he was a non-violent person. If he wasn't a wealthy and powerful entertainer, and didn't have bodyguards at his disposal, he would be a victim, a statistic for some federal flowchart.

We dropped them at the tarmac of their private jet. It was a cool departure for me. I really enjoyed Bob and his wife, but I never saw them again. They never came back to St. Louis.

19

With the new boss, my partner and I had carte blanche to do whatever we wanted. I started investigating Jesse Stoneking again. We drove by his Oakville house, but the place was vacant. I asked some neighbors about the house, but nobody knew Jesse, or where he had gone.

I called an ex-cop friend who worked security at the brewery and asked him if Jesse was still employed there. He wasn't. He had resigned without giving two-weeks' notice. But that was no big deal. Local 562 will send another gangster down there to replace him. It's the way it works, kind of like the police department.

Somebody was throwing Molotov cocktails onto the roofs of the massage parlors on the Eastside. I suspected Jesse Stoneking. The brunt of the organized criminal activity apparently was staying on the Eastside. A good thing, but the crimes still had Jesse Stoneking's autograph on them. He was back at doing his thing over there. I still wanted to place handcuffs on him. It wouldn't be long before he was back over here on the west side terrorizing folks.

I had gotten a call from Agent Mike Fair, Illinois Division of Criminal Investigation, lead investigator for the Wittmond diamond caper. He told me he had been contacted by FBI Agent Sam Thompson, my friend, and another agent, concerning the stolen ring and stone.

They told him they had recovered the ring and stone, they had it tested by an independent jeweler and that it was a fake diamond. It was a zircon. I thought he meant the stone I had located in the brooch in Frontenac, so I was silently pondering how that could have been, since several diamond merchants had been in possession of the stone. There was no way that stone could have been phony.

"It wasn't the stone in the brooch," he continued. "Apparently the stone you found wasn't the same stone stolen from Carl Wittmond. The FBI showed me the ring and the stone, and it looked like the described stone and setting stolen from Carl Wittmond."

He had taken the wind out of my sails, and I could do nothing but remain silent and blush. "We went to the hotel in Brussels, me and the FBI guys," Mike Fair continued. "We showed him the ring with the phony stone, but we didn't tell him it was phony at the beginning. Carl said the setting appeared to be his, but that he wasn't certain about the stone. He said the stone he had lost had a more yellowish color than this stone."

"Oh," I muttered.

"Carl called his State's Attorney nephew, and when he showed up, they both examined the stone and both said the mounting looked like Carl's but the stone did not. So neither Carl nor his nephew took the bait, and we're back to square one."

"Did Sam Thompson say where he got the stone, or ring?"

"No, he didn't say. I just wanted you to know what the outcome of the case was. It's over with as far as this office is concerned. But Chief Blazer, Sergeant Ben Branch, FBI Agent Stackhouse and the alleged owner of the ring met with the St. Louis County Prosecutor. The stone was remanded to the custody of the influential newspaperman. He had the paperwork stating he purchased it from Joe Collins."

"When was the stone given to the alleged owner?"

"About ten days ago."

"Okay, thanks." I slowly hung the receiver up, in deep thought.

My mind was going a hundred miles per hour. I had questions only I could answer. Nobody else was going to tell me the truth, so it was up to me to decipher the information I had and come to a conclusion.

I was sure Jane Stewart knew Carl well enough that she was resigned to the fact that he roamed, when given the opportunity. I wondered if she felt betrayed by his unfaithfulness.

He had treated her well during the years they had been together. He bought her expensive jewelry, gotten her a job with the State of Illinois, and kept her housed and living in the lap of luxury. She should have known the type of man he was, and expected cheating.

But women don't forget infidelity. They silently hold grudges, and they usually get even for it. I wondered if somehow, somebody got the ring away from Carl, and had an exact replica on hand to replace it.

A shower after a romp in the hay would have given someone an opportunity to photograph the ring and stone, in order to have an exact replica made, if Carl haphazardly laid it onto a night stand while he showered.

Then after another romp and shower, somewhere down the line, the casual lover could exchange the ring with the phony and be in possession of a hundred-thousand-dollar gift from a wealthy landowner, ex-politician and banker.

It would be the perfect crime for someone. A crime they had gotten away with. So, Carl the egomaniac with the stone fetish, was sporting a glass diamond on his finger and showing it off, without knowing it was trash. How embarrassing to him. But, I doubt he could become embarrassed by anything.

Scenario number two was that Carl had made arrangements to sell the stone, probably to a jeweler in the Paul Brown, and he had enlisted the assistance of a lady friend to deliver the stone for him.

Jesse's jeweler friend told me he thought it was a woman who had sold the ring and stone to an unknown jeweler in the Paul Brown. He said it was a similar stone. There are no similar stones. It was unique. But that didn't make any sense. Carl didn't need money, and he loved the stone. It was his moniker, his shtick, what he was identified with. The draw to make people come to his chicken restaurant and spend money so they could see it and fondle it.

Boob's Jewish jeweler friend, Paul, had asked me some pertinent questions when I was talking with him at the start of the investigation; questions like, "How do you tell if a stone is real?" Was he prepping me? He was acting surreal at the time, like he knew something I didn't, but that I would have to find out on my own. It was a game of hide and seek, a cloak and dagger ruse and I felt he was aware of something I wasn't privy to. I was naive.

He knew the diamond game so well. He had made reference to the wealthy having their cake and eating it, too: Having fake stones made so they could keep their real ones hidden and safe.

Is that what Carl had done? Had he sold the ring with the condition the stone be sent out of the Midwest? Well, it didn't work that way. The jeweler sold it to Joe Collins, who sold it to the influential newspaperman, who was trying to sell it to someone else, in a brooch.

But Carl dogged me into finding it for him. Why would he do that if he had sold it? Did he want to score twice on the stone? Sell it for a hundred-thousand, wear a fake, and get knocked over for the fake? His plan would have been, the phony stone and ring is stolen, but I've got a trained cop-dog who will find the real stone for me, and I will get it back. His rationale would have been, the jeweler lied to me. I told him to ship it out. He didn't. Now, I'll victimize him.

But, I had forgotten the creed of the wealthy. It's all about money, and then power. If you get enough money, then you'll naturally acquire power. Carl had both. Maybe he wanted more.

I was getting confused. My main question was: how did Sam Thompson acquire the zircon in what appeared to be Carl's setting? If he wouldn't tell Agent Mike Fair, then I was sure he wouldn't tell me. Why the big secret? Why the FBI's involvement? It wasn't a federal crime. Simple assault and robbery isn't covered under federal statutes.

Bringing a stolen Corvette across state lines to sell is a federal crime. You can identify a stolen Corvette. It has hidden numbers all over it, identifying it. You can't positively identify a stolen diamond. The Feds would never waste their time with such a case. But they did.

I accepted the realization I had recovered a stolen diamond that hadn't been stolen. I didn't like being duped, but it was what the rich and powerful do to cops. They use us in any way they wish. We are paid to do their bidding. I was doing what I had been trained to do; satisfy the wealthy. Another sickening set of circumstances.

I kept thinking. Wealthy businessmen are always looking for new ways, preferably tax-free ways of making money. They barter with each other, buy stolen merchandise from each other, loan each other money, bankroll devious and illegal schemes. Carl was right in there with them, scheming, plotting, looking for the next sucker to come his or his cronies' way.

They are treacherous, but each one of them knows there is no loyalty between them. It's all about money, that's what makes them work with each other. It's a game to see who can cheat whom. There's no honor amongst thieves.

Carl knew the person who had set him up for a beating and a robbery. His next step in this game of money and intrigue would be to call the friend who got him, and talk to him. "Okay, you got me, now give me my stone back or I'm going to retaliate and do worse to you than you did to me. You thought I was relocating and you thought you'd get away with it. But I had a cop I could trick into finding the stone. He found it and I want it back. You can bring it over this afternoon. I will be waiting."

So, Carl and Jane took an ass-kicking from an indiscreet business associate. It happens every day in the business world. Let your guard down and there's always somebody waiting to pounce on you. Usually it's somebody you know.

His business friend brings the stone back, they have a couple of hard stares, a friendly drink and discuss some of their old crime crusades, some old victims, have another drink and some more laughs, and all is forgiven.

"You would have done the same thing to me, wouldn't you?" Carl would look around with his shifty eyes and smile, and they would be buddies again. If that's the case, and I felt it was, then I had recovered the Brussels diamond, twice. I didn't even get a pat on the head for my toils.

Who was the victim? Jane Stewart. Now she's a basket case, dependent on anti-depressant drugs. The stone is probably in a safe-deposit box in the bank across the street from the hotel. Carl owns the bank, and it is close by so he can go and fondle it when he gets the desire.

But, why didn't Carl, my friend, tell me he'd gotten it back? I thought I knew the answer. I had already answered it. He didn't want me to know he had put one over on me, made me do his bidding, successfully imposed his will upon me. I felt foolish for forgetting the golden rule. Never give a sucker an even break.

20

I made a vow to myself, I was going to hold my cards close to my chest from now on. I was embarrassed I had danced like a monkey on a chain for the wealthy old man over in Brussels. I did it for him, but in reality it was to satisfy my fetish for conspiracies. All he did was make a small but complicated conspiracy available to me for solving. It was fun and I solved it. It was time to move forward.

Our new commander was a visual guy. He didn't mind us going to the Eastside to investigate the organized criminal scum, but he wanted photographs during surveillance. The unit had expensive, heavy-duty cameras, Canons and Nikons, with telescopic lenses. I talked the new guy into sending me to an FBI surveillance-photo class being held at the police academy. In two weeks, I was a competent photographer.

We spent hours on the Eastside conducting surveillance on the sex clubs, taking pictures and following any organized crook we could find. The problem was that we didn't see many of them. I was obsessed with interviewing Dennis Sonnenschien, the massage parlor guy. I didn't know why, I knew he wouldn't tell us anything, but I felt it would be interesting.

My partner figured my interest was sparked by the gorgeous prostitutes he had at his disposal. And I admitted he was probably right. What could make a person do that kind of work? Sonnenschien was no more than a pimp, a wealthy, successful pimp. I hated pimps almost as much as I hated a structured working environment.

But Sonnenschien came from a working-class family from southeast Missouri, and he wasn't an old guy, not like the other organized criminals I had been dealing with. He didn't drive a fancy car, he drove a van. He was a wealthy young pimp from a good family background. I couldn't figure it. I couldn't believe that having money was that big of a deal. But it was.

The closest we had ever gotten to Sonnenschien was at one of his Jefferson County, Missouri, massage parlors, Afternoon Delight, on Gravois Road. It was a flukey kind of rolling surveillance.

We had been working the night-watch for a week and we were tired of the Eastside. It was so sleazy and lucrative, and it was depressing to think there were so many desperate people in the metropolitan area squandering their money on prostitutes. It made you leery of whom you met on a daily basis. We had documented bankers, doctors, school teachers, judges, lawyers, and cops.

We had our free lunch at the Missouri Athletic Club and were just riding, trying to eat up time so we could go home. I made a pass by the Your Way and Classy Lady, on Highway 141, Fantasy Land and Relaxation Station, on Highway 30; then passed by Afternoon Delight.

We both saw Sonnenschien's van parked in front of Afternoon Delight and commented about it at the same time. We decided to set up on it and we settled on a closed service station lot about five-hundred-feet from the front door.

It was after 2200-hundred hours, dark as coal, and the place was doing a good business. The lot was packed. It didn't take long before Sonnenschien came out and climbed into the van. He headed toward St. Louis County, not speeding or breaking any traffic laws.

But even if he did, we couldn't stop him. We were out of our jurisdiction, as always, investigating, snooping, playing cloak-and-dagger cop, which I loved. He went directly to a sports bar in West County, parked and met another guy in the parking lot who he was apparently friends with. They shook hands and walked into the bar.

"We should go in and snoop," I told my partner. He agreed. We went in and observed the pimp, Sonnenschien, and his friend sitting at a table near the bar. We plopped at the bar, ordered a beer and tried to eavesdrop on the conversation the two were having.

I glanced around the place, using the bar back-mirror as a surveillance tool. It was a neat place, packed with young, wealthy-looking West County types; professional people, or going to be professional people. It was the BMW and Porsche crowd. None of these folks would be caught dead in a Corvette. I observed a guy at the end of the bar glaring at me. He looked familiar to me, but everyone does at this point in my cop life. I had come into contact with so many people, I couldn't keep them all catalogued.

I wondered if I had arrested him at one time, or if he was a teamster I had dealt with or interviewed. He didn't look like a West County young professional. He was older, maybe forty-five, dressed down, not stylish, short haircut, open collar, khakis, thickly built. He was still glaring through the mirror and chugging his beer while I sipped mine.

By the use of the bar mirror, the glaring stranger also had a vantage point to the table where Sonnenschien and his friend were sitting and talking. I felt strange we were doing the same thing, gleaning information and watching every move in the bar mirror.

But the guy was slugging beers down like they were free. He had chugged three since we sat down. I figured he was just a drunk, they stare at folks at times, not meaning anything by it, they just stare.

I was amused at the contrast between Sonnenschien and the guy he had met up with in the parking lot. Sonnenschien was business-like, almost West County BMW yuppie. He had money and it showed in his demeanor.

The guy he was talking with looked like a street pimp; young, like Sonnenschien, and reeking of new and quick cash, but trashy and dangerous looking and acting. I expected him to come to the bar and try to sell us a stolen wristwatch.

I was on my second beer and feeling no pain. I started looking at the patrons of the bar, mostly the female patrons. They were all gorgeous, athletic bodies, fresh looking and satisfied. Too young for me, if I had been interested, which I wasn't. They looked as if their daddies had big-time corporate jobs and had sent them to college in Florida or California, and they were just home visiting, and torturing mom and dad, and their old boyfriends, before going back to the beach.

But these gorgeous creatures were all smoking, drinking, and cursing like drunken sailors. I couldn't figure it. I was starting to stare, wondering how long it would take for the booze and bar lifestyle to destroy these perfect chicks' skin, faces and bodies.

Sonnenschien and his friend started arguing, apparently over money. The friend apparently owed Sonnenschien some cash and he was reluctant to pay him. The argument grew into an altercation; they stood at the table and shoved each other, like kids in a high school cafeteria.

The bartender, who looked like a professional football player, loudly told them, "Take it outside, or take it home. We don't allow it in here."

They measured the bartender, the way pimps would do, gauging him on a physical level, wondering if they should heed his advice. Sonnenschien, using his thumb said, "Let's go outside."

They quickly exited the bar, and the stranger at the bar who had been staring at me walked out behind them. My partner and I chugged our beer and slowly followed them out. They were shoving and cursing by the time we got out to the parking lot. Sonnenschien shouted, "You got your gun, Jay?"

We backed off, preparing to leave. If there was gun-play, we didn't want to be a part of it. If one of them got shot, we would be compelled to intervene, and maybe we would be expected to shoot the last man standing.

We were supposed to be covert, investigating, collecting information, playing James Bond. Being involved in a shooting outside of our jurisdiction was not in our job description. Sonnenschien started patting down the guy, Jay, looking for a weapon. The guy was trying to fend him off, but it was to no avail.

Sonnenschien didn't come up with a gun, but he did come up with a neat little tape recorder, and it was on and recording. "You've been taping our conversation, you dirty snitch fuck," Sonnenschien shouted.

"No, man, it wasn't for you, I had it to tape a conversation with one of my whores, I swear."

Sonnenschien examined the recorder, then stuck it into his front pocket. "I'm keeping the recorder. You had better get the money together that you owe me, or there's going to be trouble." He walked toward his van and climbed in.

We hung around the parking lot, in the shadows, to see what was going to happen next. The staring bar stranger came up to the pimp, Jay, and whisked him away from the scene. We went to the detective Chevy and left the area. It was time to go home.

We showed up for work the next evening and Boob was waiting for us. He hovered around our desk, blowing cigar smoke at us like a dragon, not saying what he wanted but acting as if he was preparing himself to speak.

"You guys get on Dennis Sonnenschien last night?"

"Yes, sir," my partner replied.

"You follow him to a bar in West County?"

"Yes, sir."

"The guy he met with was undercover for the FBI. Did you guys know that?"

"I suspected it," I muttered. "How did you know we were there?"

"The guy at the bar sitting near you was an FBI agent."

I didn't comment, but I was embarrassed. Boob looked at me as if he wanted a response. I didn't give him one.

Boob wanted to preach to us, I could see it in his face as he drew, blew and stared. "Why were you guys on Sonnenschien?"

My partner didn't cop a plea, he just looked at me to answer the question. "He's an interesting guy," I replied. "It was my decision to place surveillance on him. You never know what you're going to find out on surveillance. I thought maybe we could get something we could use at a later date."

Boob studied on that answer. "You know," his preaching began, "when you've been in a unit like this one for as long as I have, you get stale on the crimes, but you get sharp on the criminals. I'm sharp on criminals, but I'm also sharp on cops and other alleged square folks. You enjoy getting inside on these criminal types, don't you?"

"Yes," I replied.

"I think I know you fairly well, having been your deputy commander for as long as it's been. I think you're fascinated by Dennis Sonnenschien, mainly because he's got lots of nasty, but attractive ladies working for him, doing unthinkable things to paying customers. You're intrigued by that, right?"

"Probably," I muttered.

"You're wondering how a guy like him could be so villainous. He wasn't a street kid, he came from a good background, and you can't help wondering what led him to this lifestyle. Right?"

"Yes."

"Well, to quell your curiosity, I'll tell you. He isn't a good kid gone bad. He's always been a bad kid. When he was young he aligned himself with Paul and Anthony Leisure. They were pimps. Did you guys know that?"

"Yes," I said.

"And now he's aligned with Mike Trupiano, through Nando Bartolotta. They're in business together. He's been targeted by the FBI, and eventually, they'll get him. He'll do federal prison time, you can make book on it. This undercover guy last night was a prime example of how he'll go down. He's a marked man. You're wasting your time being interested in him. He's too hot."

He looked at us to see if we had any questions or comments. I did. "Aren't there any sincere criminals anymore? Everybody's an FBI snitch. It's disheartening, and no fun for us local guys with no informant money; we suck hind tit, always."

"If you are a criminal, and you're not incarcerated, then you're snitching to someone. It's just the way the game's played. These big criminals aren't going to snitch to us. We can't do anything for them. We're whores for the FBI, plain and simple. Everybody is."

"Tell us something we don't already know, Boob," I muttered to myself.

Boob walked away from us. He had made his speech and he was a happy man. I had to admit I enjoyed his knowledge about the career criminal, and I was almost feeling sorry for him for being transferred back to the blue army, although it hadn't happened yet, and with his luck it might not happen.

I was pining for another Jesse Stoneking investigation. He's the only one who's got criminal integrity. I was sure I would get him, someday. I had been reading the southern Illinois and metro-east newspapers, and I read an article about Jesse being stopped in some little burg over in Illinois, searched and found to be in possession of a large amount of diamonds. Some large, some small, but more than fifty assorted diamonds, without settings.

The article went on to describe how the patrolman handcuffed this career criminal and conveyed him to jail, where he would stay until an investigation revealed the ownership of the diamonds. Jesse finally told the cop the stones were fakes. They took them to the town jeweler and he verified Jesse's claim. He was released, with the fake stones.

It was relevant to the Wittmond case. But it would be difficult to have a fake stone made to look like Carl's yellow diamond, unless you had a picture of it and the exact dimensions. And why would Jesse want to do that? Another puzzle to contend with.

There was a big bank robbery in Bartelso, Illinois, out in the sticks, and there was also one in Irvington, Illinois. Two guys with machine guns hit the banks right at closing and got away with a lot of cash. I figured Jesse was behind them. They were successful crimes with large amounts of loot; his modus operandi.

Guido cruised by my desk and gave me the once-over, which meant he had some information for me. "Art Berne's building onto his estate over in Carlyle, Illinois. It's on the lake over there. You know where it is?"

"Yeah," I replied.

"We got word Art didn't want to pop for the building materials so he told Jesse to go out and steal them for him. Jesse didn't particularly want to rip off a working stiff, so he went out and paid for the materials for Art. It caused a bad feeling with Jesse. He hates anybody who's cheap, and Art Berne's apparently cheap."

"How are you getting this information?"

"Confidential informant," Guido replied.

"What confidential informant is that close to Jesse Stoneking and Art Berne?"

"I can't tell you right now, maybe in a couple of weeks, but not now."

"Got any other information?"

"Yeah. Remember those fake stones Jesse had in his possession when he got stopped by the cop in sticksville?"

"Yeah."

"Well, he gave those to Art Berne, told him they were real and to hold onto them for him for a while. Berne said okay, but instead of holding them for Jesse, he drives up to Chicago and gives them to Joey Aiuppa. He was kissing ass with the boss."

"You're kidding," I exclaimed.

"Nope. Joey gets them appraised and they come back worthless. He jumped all over Art Berne, and Art jumped all over Jesse. They're in a strained relationship right now."

"Incredible," I replied. "Jesse didn't want to rip off a working man, so he buys the building materials for Art? More incredible. A crook with scruples. I can't believe it. I'd love to know who the informant is."

"You will, someday soon. Are you sure your parents were white? I never heard of any white folks living in East St. Louis, Illinois."

"Screw you, Guido." He walked away laughing.

21

The promotion bug was infesting the unit again. Boob had put the word out that some guys in the unit were going to get made. That caused a feeding frenzy like a school of Great White Sharks in a group of baby seals. It was sport for Boob. The starved for recognition detectives would get on the unit phones and contact their aces.

All of the phones in the unit were bugged. Boob and Captain Bud, when he was still in the unit, would sit in the captain's office, listen to the conversations and laugh. They would tape the conversations as the cops begged and pleaded for political support. They would play the tapes over and over again for anyone who might be interested.

The lead star had access to the bugged telephones. Before he had gotten promoted and left the unit, he taped a conversation between the Irish Prince and his girlfriend, talking sex and cooing at each other. The lead star had been having discipline problems with the Irish Prince, even though they were the same in rank, detectives.

But the Irish Prince had pursued the stars and he advised them he wanted to be one of them, so that made him a subordinate. Kind of like a high school girl wanting to be a member of a sorority. Everybody who wishes to elevate themselves socially or professionally has to pledge. The Irish Prince pledged, but now was becoming surly to the lead star.

The lead star took insubordination seriously. He played the sex tape over the office intercom. The two detectives came nose to nose but nobody threw a punch. Boob loved it when there was dissension within the ranks. He was safe when the troops were fighting amongst themselves. Boob's jeweler friend Paul, told me the pawn brokers who regularly paid a visit to the unit offices, after hours, bragged about listening to the telephone tapes of the unit detectives.

My partner was making noises about getting promoted and leaving the unit. He had made the calls to his high-ranking black friends, and I was sure they were making calls to their influential friends in his behalf. I loved working for the new Irish captain, and I loved investigating organized criminal groups. It was my thing in life.

I was already at the pinnacle of my law enforcement experience. Being a cop was bad enough, but being cop management was alien to me. I couldn't see myself babysitting a bunch of pilfering, lying cops. And having to act like I cared for their well-being? It wasn't me.

I didn't care what other cops did, as long as they left me alone and let me investigate the real crooks of the world. I wouldn't have made a good supervisor. But, I knew I was in a lower management position already. It's why the cops in the unit snitch on each other. It is management. Managers are company men, whether it's in a factory or a specialized police unit.

Managers bend the rules to appease their bosses. I wasn't emotionally equipped to do it. At least I realized it, because if I had gotten promoted by the good commander, I would have never stayed in the police department to get my pension. I would have been the square peg in the round hole, unhappy and looking for a way out.

My partner was making himself scarce, campaigning for the big promotion to sergeant. I will never figure out what the attraction was to the promotion craze, but it is a disease and it takes over the patient and destroys him. So, I was alone a lot again, and straining to enjoy it.

I was on the Eastside continually, cruising and snooping, looking for crooks, but finding sex-fiends from the west side. I was curious about the bank robberies in the sticks communities, so I drove to them. I did rolling surveillance on both little town banks, and I couldn't figure how the robbers could commit these daytime robberies and get away with them.

The banks were in the center of town, both of them, and there were people all over the streets; restaurants, gas stations, shoppers walking to shops. These were country folks who know everybody on the street. They didn't trust strangers, and they note them as they do their daily routines. I snapped some quick pictures to show the new boss and headed out of town.

The locals noted me in the detective Chevy. I was out of my element, out of my jurisdiction, and I was feeling like I was going out of my mind. Nothing was working. I was the Wichita Lineman. I was still on the line. The big crooks were hiding, or they were dead or incarcerated. They had chumps like Dennis Sonnenschien and Nando Bartolotta to run their sex-for-cash ventures in East St. Louis. They just sat back and raked in the cash.

I was riding, and it was a nice day, so I headed southeast, toward Carlyle, Illinois. It has a neat lake, a reservoir for all of the little towns in the area, and the water is clean. The land is flat as a pool table, and there is acre after acre of farmland, as far as the eye could see, for farming wheat, corn and beans.

But, there had been no water. The farmers had to rely on wells and rainwater runoff to sustain life. So, the State of Illinois built this huge reservoir, named it Carlyle Lake, and deemed it a recreation area. It was a success, and folks came from all over to fish, camp, boat and swim in the clean lake. It is great for sailboats because the land is so flat the wind is always blowing. It's prairie land with a lake. There are big-time, ocean-going sailboats there.

I had been coming to the lake for my entire life, enjoying all of the things it was meant to provide. I didn't know there were any organized criminals living there, especially one of the most hated criminals, Art Berne. He was the guy who took Buster Wortman's job, the head of organized crime in southern Illinois. And he was cheap, just like Buster Wortman. It gave me cause to hate him even more.

I cruised by his compound, for that's what it was. There were several buildings, a barn, a machine shed, and a gigantic yard before you got to the house. I slowed and took picture after picture of the place from the car on the blacktop two-lane road.

I figured I was probably the hundredth guy who had taken these pictures. Every FBI, ATF, and IRS guy in the region probably had the same pictures, taken to appease some grumpy federal boss. It's the reason I took them. A waste of time and money, but I didn't make the rules.

I had heard from Guido that Art Berne's wife was a normal human being, and she cared for the yard and kept everything spruced up. I wondered if she knew Art was a slime-ball, organized crook.

She would almost have to know. Art worked out of his compound. He always had people calling on him who were obvious criminals. Jesse was there a lot, but he wasn't there now. At least his Lincoln Town car wasn't parked anywhere near the residence. Could be hidden at the rear, or in the barn.

Guido said Art's wife liked Jesse, and that she was an astrologer and she predicted Jesse would go straight, someday. Going straight in the crime business usually means going straight to the FBI and telling everything you know about your friends. Jesse wouldn't do that. He had criminal integrity. Guido said the reason Art Berne's wife liked Jesse was because he killed Don Ellington, Art's right-hand man, which was never substantiated, but was speculated.

Allegedly, Don asked Art to recommend to him a young lady he could take out for an evening, just to make an impression on someone for some kind of a deal that was going to make them rich.

Art, with his wife picked out some local girl who they had met and was single, and arranged the date. Don Ellington beat the woman and raped her, disfiguring her face and breaking her arm. It was fright night for the Carlyle lady, and Art and his wife were pissed.

Don Ellington had been acting disrespectful to Art, even threatening him physically, so Art enlisted Jesse to remove the problem. That's all it took for Jesse. He was still carrying a grudge over the Fairmont Race Track caper Don Ellington wouldn't allow him to do. Jesse killed Don Ellington, and Art's wife liked Jesse ever since. If you have knowledge of a murder, you're involved in it, and you're happy about it, then you've got to know your dear husband is involved in organized crime. The lady of the house was privy to what her husband did for a living.

I headed back toward St. Louis. I had been chasing ghosts, grasping at straws and accomplishing nothing. I enjoyed bopping around in Illinois, but it was fruitless. I had no guidance. I was always fishing where the fish weren't. I was starting to get depressed at the whole operation: cops, FBI agents and crooks.

I knew deep down in my soul the reason I hadn't seen any big-time crooks was because they were all going to drugs for a living instead of corrupting labor unions. They were in Florida living the good life, making contacts and getting tans. They had probably purchased boats, and fished and cruised every day. The smuggling of cocaine was lucrative, better than home invasions, diamond stealing, burglaries, armed robberies and union thuggery.

It was the thing for criminals, and they were all dabbling in it. The Italians had the heroin trade all sewn up. They had hooked the black inner City population on the junk eight decades ago, and they just sat back and watched them kill each other and steal anything and everything that wasn't welded down, to get the cash for their habits.

They reinforced the popularity of heroin by getting entertainers, musicians and celebrities hooked on it. They did what the film industry did to tobacco; they made it sexy and attractive to folks who thought they had the gift of creativity; music, writing, acting. It was the biggest sham in show business.

But cocaine was different. All you have to do is drive down to Florida, haphazardly make a connection with some South American dude in a bar, and you're in business. And after a couple of small deals, where you pay cash, they'll give you the stuff on consignment, if you can take a large amount at one time. For gutsy career criminals, it is better than any other crime, even being a pimp.

If the Leisures hadn't been so violent to their union-thug friends, they could be free now, smuggling cocaine and marijuana, making millions of tax-free dollars and living the good life. Instead, they're either dead or incarcerated for life.

The Leisure crime family was just a couple of years shy of lucrative careers in drug smuggling. They chose the crime category available to them in St. Louis. Murder and union thuggery was the thing, then. Just two short years later, it's old hat. I was amazed at how the crime picture had changed. And I was flabbergasted at how the career criminals were able to adapt to new ways to make a crooked dollar.

The leaders of the crime families wouldn't be snitching to the FBI now. It would be the Drug Enforcement Administration who gets the big-time criminal snitches. I could do that kind of work, mainly because I knew who the career criminals were in the St. Louis region.

I hated working drugs, but if I wanted to stay in the crime business I would have to adapt, just like the crooks. There was a federal task force in operation. The Drug Enforcement Administration ran it, and it consisted of local cops and DEA Agents, who acted as supervisors. They swear you in, federally, give you DEA federal credentials and you do the same job, work out of the same office, and have the same powers as a regular Fed.

They have offices out in Clayton, in a modern high-rise office building. It's a class operation, I had been told. I had seen the detached cops driving Corvettes and Jaguars, all seized vehicles. They dressed the part, just like I did; jeans and Polos.

I wondered if I could get that job. It paid more money, and I would enjoy the cool seized sports cars. But I had to do something different. This game had changed. Dope had ruined the crime business.

22

I sat at my desk and pondered over how I was going to get into the narcotics investigation business. I had to gear myself to think outside of the box. It is what big business does. When one plan burns itself out they devise another one. I hadn't done any dope work since T.J. and I had tried to be search warrant stars. It was not a satisfying experience. The little star referred to them as investigative search warrants. Your lie on the affidavit is the investigative part. Your search determines if you can make a case, and continue lying.

I figured it was the same in every police department. It was why the local judges make you swear the information you have in the affidavit is the truth, the whole truth and nothing but the truth. Folks don't relish having local cops kicking their doors in and searching their possessions for sport. I guess the judges figure that if they make a cop swear to the truth it will stop investigative warrants. It worked for me.

I had the pictures of Art Berne's compound spread out on my desk, with pictures of the bank robbery locales I had taken, as Guido cruised by. He stopped and looked at them, then picked up the bank pictures of the country towns.

"These the banks in sticksville?"

"Yeah."

"You investigating this?"

"No, not really, I was curious and I was in the vicinity so I rolled by to look at them. It took balls to rob these banks in broad daylight. They're in the middle of town."

"Yeah," he muttered, "but don't waste any time on it. Feds know who did it. The bad guys will be arrested soon."

"You sure? Where did you get that information?

"Sam Thompson," he smugly replied.

"Sam Thompson? Is he back in the picture? I haven't seen or heard from him in months. I figured he got lost in Belleville."

"He's alive and well. He's been on a big case, kind of like undercover, but you'll be seeing more of him soon."

Guido acted like he wanted to talk, he didn't saunter away from my desk; he stayed and waited for me to ask him a question, so I did. "What other news do you have for me, Guido?"

"Going to be some big indictments coming down, real soon."

"Yeah? Like who?'

"Like Nando Bartolotta. You remember him, don't you? You and your partner interviewed him at Golden Girls. He gave you guys a stand-up comic routine."

I smiled as I thought about it. "The guy was funny. The gangster comic. What's he being indicted for?"

"Well, you know he had the reputation that he'd do anything for a dollar, right?"

"Yeah."

"He somehow got connected up with the manager of a Venture department store in St. Peters. He talked the store manager into faking a robbery on Christmas day, with the help of Nando, and stealing the store cash which was kept in a safe. There was three-hundred-thousand in it. It's a federal indictment. Nando's going to jail for a while."

"Federally? Why federal? Burglary isn't a federal crime."

"They had this elaborate plan, orchestrated by Nando. They were going to take the cash over into Illinois and divide it. It's a conspiracy charge, but what the hell? Nando's going away for it."

"How did the Feds find out about that? Was he bragging about it at a bar, or something?"

"No, an informant."

"Damn," I muttered. "Is everybody an informant for the FBI?"

"Like Boob says, if you're a crook and not incarcerated, then you're a confidential informant. It seems like the whole world's a C/I. " Guido walked away leaving me to stew on his information, then came back to my desk. He had a serious look and I figured he was soul searching, wondering if he should tell the outsider the news.

"The Feds had a wire in Jesse Stoneking's Lincoln Town car while Jesse was driving Art Berne to Chicago," he began. "Art Berne explained to Jesse about the pecking order of the mob in St. Louis and Southern Illinois."

I looked while Guido paused, then I said, "Oh, yeah?"

"Yeah, Art Berne confirmed that Joey (Doves) Aiuppa is the head of all of the rackets in Chicago, Southern Illinois, and St. Louis. He gave the okay for Mike Trupiano to lead the St. Louis mob. Anybody who comes over here to work has to go through Chicago before they can do it. That means Detroit, Denver, New York. They can't come to East St. Louis and start a sex business without Chicago approval."

"Didn't we already know that, Guido?"

"Yeah, but it's interesting it's now verified. Anyway, Nando's going to be going away." Guido walked out.

It was good that Nando Bartolotta was going away. He was an up and coming criminal who needed to be stopped now, before he became powerful. I wanted to know who the informant was so I wandered into Guido's office and listened while he was on the telephone.

The little star was in there studying me. My philosophy on law enforcement differed from his and he was intrigued at my openness. It was simple, I didn't wish to lie. I gave him the once-over, and studied him back. He had lost some of his punch since the lead star had gotten promoted and left, but he was still venomous. He had been coached and cribbed on how to get ahead in the cop business in a political system like the one in St. Louis. Once he got the political ball rolling there was no stopping it.

But I've got to admit, most of the people he arrested were deserving criminals, and it took big-time guts to do what he did. But they weren't gangsters. He and the lead star concentrated on black dope dealers or small time burglars.

The juries in the City of St. Louis were skeptical about cop detectives giving testimony on dope cases. So many black folks had been "cased" in the past. It was fodder for conversation in the black neighborhoods, and I know the little star, who had a big reputation in the black neighborhoods, had been discussed at many a barbecue.

I knew he would probably be a high ranking guy, someday. He had the pull, Local 562 state representatives. And he had what the political leaders of the City and State wanted; he was unconscionable and he would do anything for the power he craved. There was no difference between him and the union thugs.

Guido got off of the phone. "That goofy Nando Bartolotta. He had another scheme he's going to be arrested for. He was going to target area bankers and trick them into thinking their wives had been kidnapped. He'd pick out a banker and watch him for several days. Then, one day when the banker goes to work, he'd cut the telephone lines to the banker's house and then call him at the bank from a pay phone. He'd tell him the guy's wife's being held for ransom, and that he wants a hundred-thousand or he's going to kill her."

"You're kidding," I muttered.

"No, apparently a crook in the area had been doing the scheme outstate, and it worked a bunch of times. One banker told them to keep her. One of the bankers had a heart attack. Anyway, Nando says the trick is to not give the banker time to think. Tell him he's got five minutes, or she's dead. The banker calls home and the phone lines are cut, so he gets panicky and then Nando calls him back and they set up a drop point and the cash gets dropped off."

"That came off of a federal wire?" I asked.

"No, wired informant," Guido said. The little star was gloating as he watched me. He wore rose-colored glasses and he looked over them as he smugly stared. I had heard he had been having trouble getting promoted, even though he had lots of outside political steam. He was positioning himself for help within the chief's office.

He had left his wife and kid so he could move in with the secretary to the chief's aide. The same cute girl I had stood next to on stage while Linda Ronstadt sang Blue Bayou. He would no doubt be promoted, soon. The aide liked his secretary and respected her and would probably do her bidding.

The chief tries to hand-pick his promotion candidates, with the recommendation of his aide and the unit commander, but sometimes the state legislators override him. It's the way the system works.

The secretary had been through too many cops. She was beaten down by failed romance. The little star would do the same thing to her. Use her and dump her.

The little star forfeited his family for a promotion to sergeant. Now he's staring at me with curiosity because I don't want to swear to a lie. But he only needed this one little promotion and he would acquire cop royalty status. I hoped it was worth it to him. It was evil and I personally wouldn't have anything to do with the process.

"Another informant?" I muttered. "Feds seemed to be wired in on organized crime these days."

Guido's phone rang and he picked up. He was smiling and talking quietly, "That's great, that's very interesting, okay, I'll talk to you later."

"What now?" I muttered.

"Art Berne and Mike Trupiano got indicted in the Southern District of Illinois. Nando's in trouble big-time over there, too. He's an unindicted coconspirator."

"Wow," I exclaimed. "What's the charge?"

"Extortion, and Trupiano was charged with three counts of interstate travel in aid of racketeering. They were extorting Dennis Sonnenschien, the guy who owns Rub-A-Dub-Dub and Golden Girls. The pimp guy."

"Another wired informant?" I stared and Guido stared back.

The little star was beside himself with glee, he stood and pranced around the office saying, "You don't know what we know, you don't know what we know," like a grade school

cheer leader. I chuckled at his charade.

I glanced at Guido, my friend and confidant. I couldn't believe he had confided in the local 562 search warrant guy with any confidential information, and left me out in the cold. Guido read me, he was pondering his choices.

"You want to know who the snitch is, don't you?"

"Yeah."

"It's Jesse Stoneking. He's the snitch. He's been undercover for two years. He's going to get all of the organized crime guys locked up. He's got taped information on all of the big-time crooks."

"You mean he's been wired since he got out of prison?"

"Yeah."

"He was wired when I pulled a Mississippi State Trooper car-stop on him?"

"Yeah. The FBI's got you on tape saying fuck the FBI."

I must have looked like I had been hit in the face with a banana cream pie. The little star jumped to his feet and pranced around the room saying, "Fuck the FBI, fuck the FBI," in his little girl voice, laughing and slapping his knee. It was the comic relief I needed. I tried to stifle a laugh but couldn't. The guy could put a bag on his head and double for the Unknown Comic.

"Is that why Sam Thompson won't to talk to me?"

"I don't know, maybe," Guido said.

"What about the grand jury subpoenas that Jesse and Art Berne got served with? Was that a ploy?"

"Yep," Guido said. "Just some fodder to make Art Berne think Jesse was still okay."

"You mean there was doubt?"

"Yeah, Ray Flynn had been telling Art he felt Jesse was a federal snitch. Sam Thompson dreamed up the grand jury scheme. It worked, too."

I thought for a minute as the little star gloated. "That means Jesse was working for the FBI when he had his buddies beat and rob Carl Wittmond in Brussels and steal his ring. Right?"

"I don't know," Guido said. "Why don't you ask Sam Thompson?" He dialed the phone and handed it to me.

Sam answered, I identified myself and he was cordial. I asked him the question, and he stalled. "No," he finally said. "Jesse was still in prison when that went down."

"Okay," I replied. It was obvious Sam was prepared to lie to keep Jesse out of the Wittmond diamond caper. But Sam had other evidence and my curiosity was eating at me. He had gone to the hotel and showed Carl Wittmond and State's Attorney Charles Burch the setting that the diamond had been in, with a phony stone. I wondered if he would tell me where he got it. He could only tell me a lie, or tell me to mind my own business. It wasn't my crime.

"That setting and fake stone you guys took to Brussels, where did you get them?"

He gave me the pause, then said, "From Jesse."

"Then he knocked off the old man and took his ring," I said.

"No, we told Jesse to get the stone back for us so we could take the heat off of him. We knew this case was hot and somebody was going to keep stirring the pot, and we didn't want Jesse compromised. He was doing stellar work, something this region's needed for centuries. We couldn't chance him being taken down for something like this."

"So, where did he say he got the setting and stone?"

"From a friend. He and another guy beat and robbed the old man and his lady friend. Jesse went to him and retrieved the setting and stone. We had it appraised and it was fake, so we took it to Brussels and tried to pass it off for real to see what the old man would do. He said it wasn't his stone, but it was his ring."

"I need to interview the friend," I said. "Where is he?"

"Witness protection program. Nobody's going to interview him. He's got a new identity."

"Jesse too?" I muttered.

"Yeah."

"Okay, Sam, thanks," I said and handed the receiver back to Guido. Jesse wasn't in prison when Carl Wittmond got robbed. Guido and I saw him at Augustine's Restaurant, two weeks before the Brusssels robbery. Sam Thompson was covering for him.

That's why the FBI was involved. That's why the FBI seized the stone and eventually gave it to the prominent newspaperman who had claimed to own it. Jesse did the robbery, for sure, in my mind. Is that the way the FBI works? Anything for a case? No holds barred for a confidential informant placed in the right spot?

What if Jane Stewart had died, or Carl Wittmond? Would the FBI have come forward and given Jesse up for the robbery and murder? Probably not. It's a different game on the federal level. I was feeling nauseous, again. The embarrassment of being taped by Jesse Stoneking while making disparaging remarks about the FBI haunted me. I was playing Eastside thug with an Eastside thug.

I respected the FBI and I enjoyed working with them. It had been the highlight of my investigative experience. But I had lowered myself to the level of a murdering gangster, thinking we could communicate, since we were both east siders. It was so easy for me to do. I came to it naturally.

The little star pranced out of the room leaving Guido and me alone. "When did you confide in the little star? When did you tell him about Jesse Stoneking being a snitch?" It was a stare down.

"Just before you found out," he coldly replied. "I wouldn't trust him, you can rest assured."

Jesse was in hiding, but he was the darling of the press, especially Post-Dispatch writer Ron Lawrence. He courted Jesse and was granted special interviews. Ron wrote feature articles on how Jesse achieved the incredible, snitching feats of courage in order to rid the region of its criminal vermin.

Jesse talked about his life, his code name, Scorpion, and his government-owned Lincoln Town car which was wired for sound. He had recorded over one-hundred and fifty conversations with career criminals in that Town car, and some with a bulky tape recorder taped to his ankle outside of the Lincoln.

He bragged to Ron Lawrence about his criminal exploits, the criminals he had set up, and how close he got to being discovered, which would have led to his instant death. He was a snitch's snitch, and admired by cops, agents, and Ron Lawrence. But snitching is an acceptable trait of cops and robbers in this City. Those who don't brag and snitch want to.

I had to admit, I was impressed with his results. There was hardly a crook left standing by the time Jesse was finished. He turned out to be more of a cop than anybody I ever knew.

Dedication comes in strange packages. Jesse wanted revenge. He had believed in the code of the underworld. He was told by Art Berne his two families would be cared for while he was in prison, but they weren't.

Jesse was infuriated. His wives would come to visit him in jail and tell him they were destitute, and that no one had helped them. Jesse's vengeance overrode his loyalty to Art Berne. He telephoned Sam Thompson from prison, and Sam and his partner paid him a visit.

The plan was hatched, and the FBI guys went to a federal judge to get Jesse released. The judge set him free, and even told him that if he didn't wish to cooperate with the government, there was nothing the government could do about it. He was a free agent. He didn't let the FBI down.

Jesse was the hero of Ron Lawrence. After writing about organized criminals for twenty years, getting his scoops from Boob and Captain Bud, and other cops, he finally had a real-life hero-mobster who would talk to him. Ron was star-struck and Jesse knew it. It's what he was about, he knew how to read and play people to benefit his needs and desires. It's the creed of the criminal-hustler.

Jesse was a con-man and he had the ear of the press. He knew how to milk a mark, and he fed Ron Lawrence stories about himself and his exploits. Ron wanted stories about Matthew (Mike) Trupiano, the reputed head of the St. Louis Mafia. Jesse gave him what he wanted.

Trupiano had offered Jesse a job as an undercover enforcer, a sneak man, a guy who would kill or maim on command. Jesse talked it over with his FBI handlers and he was given the green light to go forward with the plan.

Trupiano gave Jesse a contract to break the legs of a doctor in Franklin County, for reasons unknown. Jesse went to the doctor's home and made surveillance, just so he could tell Mike Trupiano what the place looked like.

The FBI agents told the doctor he was in danger, so the doctor made plans to place two fake casts on his legs when the FBI told him to do so. For some reason, Trupiano cancelled the contract.

Jesse didn't want Art Berne to know about his agreement with Trupiano. He was a freelance hustler, doing anything for cash, but his loyalties were supposed to be with Art Berne. Art would have had Jesse killed if he found out. I figured Jesse and Mike Trupiano were talking over the plan to hire Jesse as a "killer-in-waiting" when my partner and I did a Mississippi State Highway Patrol car-stop on Jesse, (the one taped by the FBI). In this game you never know who you're talking to, or who is listening.

Jesse bragged about his biggest score, the robbery of a jewelry salesman in the salesman's home, in front of the salesman's daughter and wife. Jesse described how he had watched the guy for several days, and followed him to his house. Jesse and his associates did a home invasion, wearing masks, armed with pistols.

They made the jeweler and his wife and daughter lie on the floor. They took the jeweler's ring, then took his car which had jewelry in the trunk. It was a million-dollar score. Later Jesse learned the jewelry belonged to organized crime boss Nick Civella of the Kansas City, Missouri, mob.

Apparently the jewelry salesman "had laid down with dogs" somewhere down the line.

Jesse disclosed a murder plot against a state representative, Patrick J. Hickey. He was an officer in Pipefitters Local 562. Representative Hickey allegedly had not been following the orders of Joey (Doves) Aiuppa in Chicago.

An officer in the local, and an alleged overseer for the Chicago mob, was one of the guys giving orders in the local. Representative Hickey had apparently had a falling-out with the gangster official and the crook went to Art Berne with the problem. There was always a power struggle going on within the union.

The hard-working craftsmen were always at odds with the organized criminals who ran the local with fear. Representative Hickey apparently had had enough, and voiced his rebellious thoughts to someone close to the thug union official.

Union officers were in constant peril. Tommy Callanan, a business representative whose father helped form the union, had gotten himself blown up by a car bomb. The bomber detonated it as Callanan was driving past a schoolyard full of children. His Lincoln rolled into the schoolyard and Tommy fell out of it, legless. A pistol fell out of his pocket. He lived, but was confined to a wheelchair until he died.

A personal friend of Art Berne's and a 562 union official found a bomb attached to his pickup truck. He called Jesse and told him. Jesse came over to the west side and removed the bomb for him. He figured Tom Callanan had the bomb placed on his truck because Tommy blamed the union crook for the bombing of his Lincoln when he lost his legs.

The contract to murder Hickey had been given to Don Ellington by Art Berne. Ellington and Jesse had attended a meeting at the pipe fitters compound on Larimore Road in North County.

When Hickey left the meeting, Jesse, driving the car, and Ellington riding shotgun, followed him to Bellefontaine Road and Larimore. Jesse pulled up alongside the car and the trigger-man, Don Ellington, opened the window preparing to shoot Hickey with a 45-automatic, point-blank, but he froze at the last instant.

Jesse asked him what happened. Ellington said, "He saw me."

Jesse allegedly replied, "So what? You're going to kill him aren't you?" That was the end of the conversation. Art Berne was pissed. Don

Ellington turned up dead, shot with a forty-five in Jefferson County shortly thereafter. The botched assassination was just another reason for Art Berne to order the demise of Ellington.

Jesse said he was then ordered to kill Tommy Callanan, the business agent for Local 562, who had been maimed by a car bombing and was in a wheelchair. Allegedly, Tommy also was defiant of the control coming from Chicago mob boss Joey (Doves) Aiuppa, as was state representative Patrick Hickey.

Jesse and Mark Stram went to the pipe-fitter's compound where Callanan had an apartment, armed and prepared to kill him. The grounds were spacious, about three square miles, and there was a ten-foot fence and a guard shack manned twenty-four hours a day.

The local was wealthy, even though they were repeatedly raped financially by Art Berne and Joey Aiuppa. They built condominiums for retired pipe fitters to live in. They were state-of-the-art, modern and expensive. Tommy Callanan and his family lived in one of them.

Jesse and Mark Stram climbed the fence and found the apartment, looked in the window and observed Callanan with his wife and kids, so they gave it up, temporarily.

Later, Jesse was told by Art Berne Callanan was in a restaurant in Granite City. Mark Stram and Jesse went there, had dinner and on the way out, Jesse told Callanan that there was a contract on him. Jesse told Ron Lawrence that he couldn't kill a man in a wheelchair.

Jesse the con had bragged himself into celebrity status, with the help of Ron Lawrence. Every story was self-serving, making Jesse look like the Robin Hood of organized crime. Jesse didn't speak of the home invasion and robbery of senior citizens Carl Wittmond and Jane Stewart.

He and associates couldn't shoot another criminal who was in a wheelchair, but they could beat and rob two old folks for a diamond. It didn't make sense.

23

Jesse was the hero of federal prosecutors. They are like any other lawyer. Give them a good case and they'll be your friend for a while. When you're no longer useful to them, they will shun you. Jesse was still useful. There were big time jury trials coming up. He was the government's star witness. I wondered how that was going to fly. Jesse was a contract killer. If I were a juror I would not have much faith in anything Jesse Stoneking had to say. I couldn't separate Jesse the famous gangster investigator, from Jesse the stone cold killer. I could never figure what mindset these killer gangsters get themselves into to shoot an unassuming victim. Or to blow one up. It was inhuman.

Ron Lawrence wasn't the only fan of Jesse. Everybody with connections to the judicial system had stories about Jesse's undercover work. Assistant United States Attorney Clifford Proud, the lead federal prosecutor in the Southern District of Illinois, and an ex-City of St. Louis cop, admired Jesse's heroic work. He prosecuted the cases Jesse made for the government. Cliff's star shined brighter when Jesse came into his life.

Proud looked like a professional baseball player. He was tall, large-shouldered, square jaw, full head of dark hair, and moved like a professional athlete. Had he been a pro athlete, he would have been an MVP. In the United States Attorney's office, Southern District of Illinois, he was the most valuable player. Jesse the criminal was a hero to him. Jesse was getting the bad guys who had been untouched for decades.

Proud knew how to shmooze, a trait one is born with, not acquirable in its pure form, and Proud had the purest of form when applying the shmooze. He had federal judges, the United States Attorney, and even the sleazy defense lawyers as his fans. And he was a damn good lawyer.

Another federal prosecutor related to me how when Jesse was at a

Super Bowl gathering at Mike Trupiano's South County home with a group of other gangsters, the conversation became incriminating. Mike feared his home was bugged, so he told everybody to shut up and follow him out to the back yard.

The six or seven crooks walked into the back yard and got into a football huddle to talk over criminal enterprises. Jesse was wired and the crooks were speaking into a microphone Jesse had under his shirt.

During the huddle, Jesse brought up the fact that the FBI only bugged telephones, not houses, for some unknown reason. Of course, that was a lie, but Mike Trupiano bought into it. Jesse suggested Mike get rid of his old telephones and Jesse would provide him with new ones, which he conveniently had in the trunk of his Lincoln.

He told Mike he had just scored them from a thief friend of his and they were still in the boxes. Mike liked it, the huddle broke up and they went back inside. Jesse went to his car and obtained the boxes of telephones. He went inside and gave them to Mike, who unplugged the old phones and installed the new ones immediately.

Jesse took the old ones, which had old FBI listening devices in them and were not working properly, to his car. The new phones had been provided by the FBI and had new state-of-the-art listening devices in them. They would pick up conversation from anywhere in the house. Mike the inept had signed his own incarceration papers. Most gangsters do.

Jesse was trusted by every criminal and most prosecutors. The criminals trusted him because he lived by a code; he never thought twice about cracking a guy. At least that's what he told everybody. But he wouldn't crack Tommy Callanan because he was in a wheelchair. His code included snippets such as, "It is how you make your bones, cracking somebody. It makes a man of you."

Jesse knew how to sell himself. Give the crooks, the press and the cops anything they want, so long as you make them believe it. They were all sold on Jesse. He had landed them hook, line and sinker.

Jesse was in need of cash. He had been a guy who had made a million a year by his wits, and it was tax-free. He always had 200,000 dollars in the floor of his kitchen, for emergencies, but his crime cash was quickly being depleted. Supporting two families was expensive.

He knew his criminal life was over. No more quick cash. He would be dead if any crook saw him. There was a $100,000 bounty on his head. So

Jesse, the super salesman, thief and murderer, had his back against the wall.

He had borrowed thousands of dollars from Mike, the inept, Trupiano, but it was running out. Mike would never see that money. He burglarized Art Berne's house, trying to crack the safe where he knew there was $200,000 , but he couldn't get it open. He ultimately stole $100,000 dollars in jewelry, which he couldn't fence because of the bounty on him.

He was back where he was when he was in prison. He had to rely on the federal government for cash and protection. Both of his families were under federal witness protection. They were being cared for, but his legal wife, Carolee, his childhood sweetheart, had disappeared into the witness protection program and she wouldn't have anything to do with Jesse. She had become a Christian. The likes of Jesse sickened her. But, Jesse had a spare.

The threat of having Jesse Stoneking testifying against him in federal court apparently terrified the notorious east side gangster Art Berne. I wondered if Buster Wortman would have been intimidated. In his day, he would have gone to court in East St. Louis and probably beaten the rap. He had beaten federal prosecutions before. Even one for assaulting a federal agent.

Art Berne, the scourge of the Southern Illinois rackets, and security consultant to Pipefitters Local 562 in north St. Louis County, admitted he had used intimidation and threats of violence to extort large sums of money from owners of topless night clubs and massage parlors.

He pleaded guilty in Judge James L. Foreman's court to a charge of extortion and interstate travel in aid of racketeering. He pled just two days before he was to have gone to trial before Foreman.

He stood before the God-like judge and verbally gave his occupation as a security consultant for Pipefitters Local 562, and told him he only had a sixth-grade education. He looked like what he was; a slime-ball country gangster who took orders from another slime-ball from Chicago.

Judge Foreman wasn't impressed. The judge was an east side guy. He knew Buster Wortman and Art Berne, and Jesse Stoneking. He had seen the devastation those gangsters had wreaked on this little region.

It was Dennis Sonnenschien and Jesse Stoneking who had brought Art Berne down. Art admitted in front of the judge to extorting Sonnenschien. Jesse's tapes of Art discussing the extortion put the final nail in the coffin.

The United States Attorney, Frederick Hess, who was as tall as Cliff

Proud, but not as athletic, yet as good a lawyer, recommended the fourteen-year sentence. Art's attorney and Art agreed to the sentence. It was a part of the plea agreement. It's what big-time crooks with competent lawyers do. They make deals with the United States Attorney's office just like they've made deals with union thugs. It was the same.

Foreman wasn't bound by the United States Attorney's recommendation. Sentencing was set for a later date. But, one thing was sure. Art Berne was going to a federal penitentiary. His gangster and security consulting days were over.

Mike Trupiano was Art Berne's co-defendant. United States Attorney Hess told the judge that Art Berne and Mike Trupiano extorted twenty-five percent of Sonnenschien's profits from Golden Girls, which was about one-thousand dollars a week.

In conversations with Stoneking, which were taped, Berne and Trupiano discussed that Sonnenschien should pay them $4000.00 a week, just for their cut on the massage parlor, Rub-A-Dub-Dub, United States Attorney Hess told Judge Foreman. Mike Trupiano wouldn't plead guilty. His case was set for trial. He had the best attorney money could buy in this area, Irl Baris.

The prosecution played the Stoneking/Trupiano tapes. They discussed a $2000.00 payment to them from Sonnenschien to prevent the Golden Girls Nightclub from being fire-bombed.

They discussed a $500.00 per-week extortion from Sonnenschien for protection of his Rub-A-Dub-Dub massage parlor, and for his massage parlors in south St. Louis County.

The final tape was between Stoneking and Bartolotta. Bartolotta told Jesse Trupiano wanted him, Bartolotta, to physically threaten Sonnenschien for being late on payments. "He wants me to choke this guy, or strangle him or something," Bartolotta said. Bartolotta said he feared the whole scheme would fall apart if he applied too much pressure.

During cross examination by Irl Baris, Stoneking was asked about his description of himself as a "hood." "What is a hood, Mister Stoneking?"

"That's a guy who's capable of anything against the law," Jesse replied.

Jesse was asked if the crimes he had committed after being released from federal prison didn't violate terms of his parole on a state conviction of voluntary manslaughter.

"Yes," Jesse replied. "But when the federal government's got you, you don't worry about what the states have. When you work for the FBI, with the law, you don't worry about the law."

In closing arguments Baris said Mike Trupiano was the real victim in the case. He said Mike had been incriminated by Jesse and by Mike's fear of Art Berne.

In the prosecution's closing, United States Attorney Rick Hess said calling Trupiano a victim is to say the chicken is taking advantage of the wolf.

Baris then countered, saying Jesse was a master manipulator of people, who had led Trupiano toward trouble to ensure that Jesse would continue to be paid by the government. "Stoneking was trying to maneuver Trupiano into a position where he could stab him in the back, where he could give him the scorpion's sting."

Jesse's government code name was Scorpion.

"He missed the boat here," Irl Baris said. "He didn't get the evidence on Mike Trupiano."

The trial was a big deal and watched like the outcome of the final game of the World Series the Cardinals were winning. Everybody in the intelligence unit was straining to hear the blow- by- blow from Sam Thompson, who kept Guido informed of the contest. Guido was out of the office when somebody called to tell us that the case had been given to the jury and that the United States Attorney expected a quick deliberation.

It appeared to be a slam dunk. Jesse Stoneking's tape recordings. Dennis Sonnenschien's testimony. The guilty plea of co-defendant Art Berne. It was textbook, get-the-bad-guy day. It was a day of reckoning for the organized criminals who had been raping this region for a hundred years. Buster Wortman was dead. Art Berne was going to prison, and now Mike Trupiano, president for Laborer's Local 110, and the head of the Italian faction of organized crime in sleepy old St. Louis, was going to prison.

I left the office and slowly drove over to the courthouse in East St. Louis. There was going to be a huge victory party after the verdict and I wanted to be a part of it. AUSA Cliff Proud was a friend of mine. Sam Thompson, Rick Hess, Guido and Stretch would probably be there. It was a time for rejoicing. I wondered if Jesse Stoneking would be at the party. I didn't know if I could look him in the eye and smile. I still felt he was a snake waiting to bite any unsuspecting victim.

But, I couldn't hate him for the Carl Wittmond caper. Are you a victim if you go to a bad neighborhood to buy drugs, get followed home by the crook you did business with, and then you get robbed? You're looking for trouble. It's what most victims are, they are their own worst enemies. The solution? Don't lie down with dogs.

I parked and walked into the old courthouse, which was connected to a modern federal courthouse and the United States Attorney's office. I took the elevator up. The old building stunk, just like most courthouses: musty, smell of books, pencils, trouble. Sam Thompson was in the hallway looking worried.

"What's up?" I asked.

"I'm leery of these Eastside juries. You never know which side they are going to identify with. One bad juror can poison the lot of them. There is always a standoff." We walked in together.

I pondered the standoff between the jurors. These were Southern Illinois folks. Most of them probably were born in East St. Louis, and had become refugees like my family. Leaving East St. Louis to them was like leaving hell for heaven.

Most of my relatives wouldn't even tell their children that they once lived in East St. Louis. Mike Trupiano wasn't Art Berne. Art Berne was the bad guy in the Southern District of Illinois. Mike Trupiano was the alleged bad guy in St. Louis. Why should they care about his greed?

In their minds, the bad guys are Dennis Sonnenschien, pimp and sex merchant, disgracing an already disgraced City with his filthy sex clubs. Jesse Stoneking was Art Berne's right-hand man. He was no better than Art Berne, who had already pled guilty.

So when the jury weighed the credibility of the witnesses against the labor man, Mike Trupiano, and the fact the labor juror wasn't going to change his mind, they figured screw it. They wanted to leave East St. Louis and never come back. It's why they had left to begin with and they no doubt resented being called down to hell for a federal visit.

The courtroom was packed; reporters, labor folks, working men and gangsters. And there were Italians in attendance; family members, friends of the family of Mike Trupiano, friends of friends, neighbors, covertly eating salami sandwiches and slapping their kids. Everybody wanted to witness the verdict. The judge went through the ritual of "Has the jury reached a verdict?" and the jury foreman went through his spiel. The end result was they found Mike Trupiano not guilty.

The United States Attorney, Frederick Hess, and the Assistant United States Attorney, Clifford Proud, couldn't hide their shock. The slam dunk didn't go into the basket. I figured Art Berne was shocked, too. He no doubt wished he would have gone to trial instead of copping a plea.

Mike Trupiano's family wept, and Mike was red-eyed as he left the courthouse. The system worked for him, for once. Mike the inept got a break. But he was already guilty on the other side of the river, in the Eastern District of Missouri, for running a bookmaking operation. Jesse had gotten him for that one, too.

The tapes were too damning for the jury on the Missouri side. Mike went away for four years for the bookmaking charge, thanks to Jesse, the man he wanted to hire, his personal killing machine.

The United States Attorney's office on the Eastside made a statement to the press about the jury's decision. They had voted eight to two for conviction, with two undecided. But all twelve jurors signed not-guilty ballots, thinking it was the proper procedure.

The jury was confused, and that's a fact. A lone juror had convinced them to sign the not-guilty ballots. The system appeared to be flawed; not everywhere in this country, but just in East St. Louis, Illinois.

24

I was amazed that my old home town, East St. Louis, Illinois had been the focal point of this gangster side show. There was nothing there but scummy sex clubs. There hadn't been anything valuable in East St. Louis in fifty years. The Holiday Inn even closed up and moved on, leaving the building to rot. But it was where the action was, and Jesse Stoneking was right in there making the Eastside, again, an infamous noticed part of the world, temporarily.

When it was all said and done, Jesse had tricked dozens of career criminals into the slammer. He was the kind of crook other crooks wanted to talk to, brag to, and trust. He was the king of the crooks, but in reality he was the king-snitch.

The bank robberies in the Illinois country towns I had been interested in were prime examples of Jesse's prowess as a snitch/cop. Sam Thompson asked him to try and find out something about the robberies. He bopped around and eventually met a guy who wanted to brag to him about crime. Jesse went to the guy's farm and they shot machine guns together, the same machine guns used in the robberies.

The guy even bragged to Jesse about how they made their getaways from the broad daylight robberies. They had a County Deputy Sheriff, on duty, who would pick them up and drive them out of town with the lights and sirens going on the police car. No mere undercover cop could accomplish that investigative superiority.

Nando Bartolotta bragged to Jesse about all of his criminal dealings. The tapes revealed his bank robbery/kidnapping scheme, and the scheme to fake the robbery at the Venture store with the manager. They both went to prison.

The unsolved million-dollar robbery of Lordo's, the exclusive downtown jewelry store, the one where the owner gave handouts to the high-ranking cops; Jesse got the guys fencing the jewelry. One of the guys was Ray Flynn, the hard-core business agent from Local 42. The other guys: George Eidson, master thief, safe cracker, burglar and home invader, on a national level, and his right-hand man, Lefty Miller. They all went to prison. George Eidson advised me that the score for the Lordo's job was five million dollars, and that after he and Ray Flynn fenced the diamonds, their cut was a cool million.

George Eidson bragged to me that he pulled two-large diamond burglaries in the same day: Famous & Barr stores in South Town, on South Kingshighway, and the one at Crestwood Mall.

He bypassed the alarm on both stores, after some surveillance he had seen the small safe the stores kept their diamonds in. It was the size and weight that made it easily moveable on a regular sized dolly.

After rigging the alarm he pulled in front of the store in a van with a janitorial sign stuck to the sides. He got out with a working man's suit, twisted the door handle of with a large tool, entered with his dolly, located the safe and walked it out to his van. He used the same procedure for the Crestwood store.

These were Sunday afternoon burglaries, bold and successful. He told me he drove the safes to his residence on Ellenwood in the City and was cracking the safes when the FBI showed up.

George was at the back of the house and he had a worker doing some carpentry work at the front of the house. Two FBI agents approached the worker and said, "George, is that you?"

The worker said, "No, I'm not George, I'm just doing some work on his house. He's not here." One of the agents gave the worker a business card and told him to advise George to contact them. The agents left and never returned. George advised me it was a two-million dollar burglary.

There were other fences involved in the Lordo's Jeweler's robbery, but it was Ray Flynn, George Eidson and Lefty Miller who did the actual robbery. In the early 80s anybody with a good cash flow was involved in fencing diamonds. Doctors, lawyers, dentists, business owners, all were fencing and dealing in loose stones.

Interest rates were out of sight, ten-percent for a home loan. Money for business expansion wasn't available. People with cash dealt with the scummy burglars. There was always a fence. Vernon Hoerr, a north

County businessman, was murdered by a North County dentist, Charles Nowotny. An argument escalated into a fight on the parking lot of the Bristol, an exclusive restaurant in Creve Coeur. Vernon Hoerr lost the battle, and his life. The dentist went to prison. The argument was over a large diamond given to one of them on consignment from the other.

Clarence Decker, a wealthy jeweler doing business out of his residence in Rosewood Heights, a community on the Eastside, was murdered in his home. The crime was never solved.

The cop groupie owner of Lordo's collected his insurance money and relocated his store to the County. The cops out in the County didn't expect gratitude.

Jesse didn't like the federal witness protection program. He walked out on it and moved to Paducah, Kentucky, with his remaining family. Sam Thompson and his partner were against the move, it was too close to Southern Illinois. But Jesse wouldn't listen. We live where we feel comfortable, like animals always returning to their birthplace when they are relocated. Jesse could not be far away from East St. Louis.

There was no work for Jesse in Paducah. He excelled at being a criminal. He could have been a great salesman, but he had no past to show a future employer. Nobody would touch a guy who could not account for the first forty years of his life.

He was sick, and he had no health insurance. People were coming by his house and making surveillance, stupidly parking and gawking. Two guys walked to his house and looked through the window. It was hit-time for Jesse. He had to move.

A woman called the Belleville office of the FBI and told an agent she had overheard her husband and another man talking about going to Paducah and killing Jesse. Jesse moved to a small town in Southern Illinois.

He was betrayed by his best friend, Mark Stram. Stram got picked up by the local cops, in the same small town, and told them his old partner was living nearby. The cops hassled Jesse, dragging him in and trying to make him confess to recent crimes.

He finally disappeared, alone, to live out his life. He was far away from the Eastside, and that was a good thing. But his greatest fan, reporter Ron Lawrence, kept in touch with him. Ron was supposed to meet with Jesse in the sticks, in Illinois.

Somebody told Ron the bad guys were going to try and find Jesse through him. The meeting between Ron and his hero, Jesse, was cancelled. Ron contacted City Intelligence and two detectives were assigned to follow Ron around. The surveillance turned up nothing, so Ron and Jesse planned another meeting. Ron began getting strange telephone calls at his residence. He moved his daughter and granddaughter, who lived with him, to a friend's house. The theory was the bad guys were going to kidnap Ron's family and force Ron to tell them where Jesse was hiding.

He didn't know where Jesse was. Jesse probably made the phone calls, for the sake of theatrics, and to give Ron some excitement in his life. The reporter was a mark, a square, somebody to be manipulated and used. Jesse had already gotten all of the good publiCity he could ever get from the association. There was nothing left to siphon from him. Ron cancelled this meeting. Paranoia runs deep. It's the black mold of the mind, always there, growing and nagging at you.

But the alleged change in Jesse Stoneking was interesting to me. How can you be a cold- blooded killer one day, and then be a respected friend to a hard-working, square news reporter the next?

The quick change isn't feasible. Jesse had told his new friends he had gotten right with God, and was now non-violent, and a good guy. I was skeptical of him. I wouldn't have invited him to my house for Sunday dinner.

Activity in the gangster/cop game was dwindling. I wondered how long it would be before I got transferred back to a uniform district. I hoped it would be the Central West End district, if I went. I was scrambling for things to do. Most of the time I had no mission and the uncertainty was disturbing to me. For a unit like this, a detective needs an investigation to hide in. Long drawn out investigations were preferred, with long hours of surveillance. Something, anything to get out of the office. I had gotten stale and as much as I hated to admit it, I needed some guidance.

Things were starting to change in the intelligence unit. There were big-time rumblings a bunch of new guys were being transferred in. I had heard their names and I knew some of them. They were narcotics detectives.

Boob got transferred out. The new Captain, my Irish friend, was trying to change the unit for the better, he thought. With the union thugs gone, there wasn't much going on in organized crime.

The unit could have been disbanded very easily. Manpower was short and the guys in the uniformed districts were doing nothing but going from call to call. The radio ruled them; people in the City were calling the police for everything. The chief of police didn't want to jeopardize the unit, so he told the Irish Captain to get some investigations going so he could justify having his group of cops, loyal to him only, at his disposal.

My partner got promoted and he was elated. He went to a district and was leader of cops. The little star got promoted, too. He got his wish. He was now going to make his upward push for power. He strutted around the office like General Patton, staring at his imaginary enemies. It was a sick spectacle.

To my chagrin, the Irish Captain got promoted to Major and he left the unit. The lead star returned. The captain had made arrangements for some of his Irish friends to come into the unit. A new deputy commander, and a sergeant who was a friend of the captain arrived, but the Irish Captain was gone.

The lead star got a lot of his buddies into the unit and it basically became a drug intelligence unit. He took my detective Chevy away from me and gave it to one of his cronies, then told me I was not to leave the office without checking with him first. My world had come to an end. Freedom was what kept me going in this uncertain environment. But he gave me a plausible explanation. "You are driving around looking for organized criminals. The ones who are still alive are gone from St. Louis. You need a new direction."

I knew the lead star was correct in his assumption. I didn't buck him. He had trained himself mentally to be a great leader. He was on his way. He told Frank Reed to finish the Moorish Science Temple investigation, which was another good leadership decision. The investigation had helped push Frank toward the edge.

The lead star moved Frank's desk to the reception area, near his office door. It infuriated Frank, but he held it in. Had he objected he would set himself up for a transfer. Leaving the unit meant failure. We had been indoctrinated in this mind-set; cops don't wish to fail just because they don't like their bosses, or because their bosses don't like them; or because they are from the Eastside and are trained to be ignorant from birth.

The lead star had what he wanted. He was in complete control of the unit. He had every one accounted for and under his control, except Guido and Stretch. They were still the outside surveillance guys, and the lead star didn't like it. Organized criminals, in the traditional sense, were old hat to him. They always had been. The union thugs, what was left of them, turned out to be a benign group to investigate. Everything was dope.

Guido and Stretch knew sooner than later the lead star would zero in on them. He had the backing of the new regime in the unit. All he had to say was, "I think those guys are wasting time following the ghosts of organized crime guys around. There aren't any of them left to investigate, just distant associates. I need them in the office to process telephone numbers." Their good gig would be over. They would be with me, and Frank Reed, trapped on the prison ship going to nowhere, with a crazed egomaniac at the helm. But it took an ego freak to run the unit. Crime was now dope, and the lead star was good at catching dope dealers. He would save the unit from disbandment. The unit was his church. It was a sacred place for him. He would do anything to save it.

The lead star did his homework. He had seen state legislation allowing some electronic surveillance. An intelligence unit within the state could legally use something called a pin-register. In most states only a federal judge would allow any type of electronic surveillance, even a bug. A pin-register is a machine that records telephone numbers called and received from a certain telephone number. It basically shows an investigator the association between suspected criminals. In the intelligence community, you are guilty by association. KGB philosophy.

The machines required an affidavit, signed by a state judge, allowing the unit to install the pin-register for a prescribed period of time, if there was probable cause the person using the telephone was involved in a criminal enterprise. A confidential informant's word was good enough, one who had proved his reliability in the past and had given information that had led to arrest and conviction of a person, or persons, for a felony. Like a search-warrant affidavit.

The lead star typed up an affidavit, took it to a judge and gained permission to install a pin- register on a dope dealer in the County. The court order is basically a wire-tap, but without the listening-in part.

A problem arose; the unit didn't have any pin-registers. They were an expensive item, intricate and complicated to operate. The people installing the wire had to be trained in how to install it. The lead star got permission from the chief's office to send two guys to a wire-tap school.

The unit still didn't have any pin-register machines, so the lead star borrowed two from the local federal Alcohol, Tobacco and Firearms unit in the City. They were up and running in no time.

There is tons of paperwork involved in deciphering and documenting the telephone numbers that come off of pin-registers. The telephone numbers are recorded on a cash-register type receipt with the time and date and the number. The investigator then has to get an issue on the caller, or the number called, from the telephone company. Then the person is identified and investigated. The information included in the investigation includes the subject the number is issued to, his family, or other persons with access to the telephone, friends, neighbors, and tons of other documentation.

Many of these callers were out-of-town calls, so the investigator has to correspond with other intelligence units in the country. It's tedious, time-consuming, and worthless. The lead star had Frank Reed and me doing these paper investigations.

As a unit we always had to borrow a surveillance van from the bureau of investigation. It was a neat van, state-of-the art in surveillance and photography, but it didn't fit our purpose in narcotics investigations.

The lead star got funds to buy a van we could use for our own surveillance purposes. It wasn't new, but his cronies fixed it up and made it look like a telephone company van. It had Southwestern Bell placards, barricades, cones, and the wire team wore Bell hard-hats when installing a wire.

I inspected it out of curiosity, and it was super covert. I was beginning to think the lead star had been correct in his investigative theories after all, and I had been wrong. He was laying the groundwork for the unit to be the premier dope investigative unit in the region. It wasn't a bad thing. I had always been pro-Intelligence Unit. I loved it there. I was just mainly my usual self, a cursed non-conformist from the Eastside, and I felt guilty about it.

I didn't enjoy doing the paperwork for the lead star's goofy machines, but I figured if Frank Reed could stand the confines of the office, and be the lead star's house mouse, then I didn't have any reason to bitch about it. I still got paid the same. I still got a ride to and from work, and lately, I had been getting out of the office with one of the wire installers, standing guard for him while he climbed the telephone pole to install the wire equipment.

The guy had been in narcotics, working undercover for years. He had been in some tough situations, shootouts, killings, investigations involving wealthy folks and poor folks. I enjoyed talking to him.

I took him to my favorite half-price restaurants and he was impressed. He was short, stocky, and he combed his hair straight back. He was a scary looking fellow, so scary Svetna the Russian didn't even call us KGB or other derogatory names. Narcotics officers don't eat half-price. They never want to blow their cover. He told me dope dealer stories and I enjoyed them.

He bragged about killing a dope dealer who was preparing to murder an elderly couple. He had pictures of the scene, the dead bad guy lying in a pool of blood, blown apart with the pistol still in his hand. But, my buddy went one better. He had a scrapbook of the autopsy of the bad guy, in color. He kept it with him like a family album. It was documentation of his trophy, a dead dope dealer.

I was having dedication issues again. How dedicated do you have to be in this game? How far must you go to feel like you've done your part? Most of the new guys in the unit were as dedicated as my new buddy. They had all shot and killed the bad guy at least once. They would do anything to catch a dope dealer, and that's what has to be done to put dope dealers in jail.

The dope dealers were wired up, had lots of money and were, in most cases, smart. It's why there were so many of them. They will kill anybody they think is snitching on them, but so would organized union thugs. But they are the same people, just different fields of endeavor. A crook is a crook.

But so far, with the new regime, nobody had gone to jail, and the office was always full of cops. The narcotics cops roamed around the office and smoked cigarettes. The lead star chain-smoked and hammered cup after cup of coffee, and Frank Reed and I kept toiling away at the pin-register information like secretaries to a madman. I had a smokers cough, and I didn't smoke.

The windows were kept closed and most of them in the back office where my desk was were painted with black paint so you couldn't see outside. The lead star felt that the crooks were going to somehow glean information through the windows and use it against him. Just like Captain Bud. I noticed the Oldsmobile spoke hubcaps were missing from my detective Chevy. I rationalized it. I didn't pay for them, they were a gift, a gratuity because I was a St. Louis cop detective.

The country-bumpkin cop who had been the recipient of my clean little Chevy had trashed it. He used it as his own personal car, even took it deer hunting. He shot a big deer and tossed it in the trunk and it bled out all over the interior of it. He showed everybody the pictures of the dead deer in the trunk, and the gigantic pool of blood. He laughed about it and all of his buddies congratulated him for the killing, but nobody said anything about the car.

I was in need of rescue. I had been office-bound for about a year, and things weren't getting any better. I wasn't a paper investigator. I was an eye to eye, hands-on cop detective, trained in detecting organized criminals, nationwide.

I was a long way off from my pension and starting to feel like my back was against the wall, again. The pension seemed so important. It was another way to control and manipulate us. The thought of it keeps us toiling, no matter what the circumstances. Frank Reed kept staring at me, like the eyes of the dead deer in the trunk of my neat little Chevy detective car. I wondered if he would ever see a pension check.

I felt sorry for him, and he felt sorry for me. We were trapped rats on a prison ship and the only way out for either of us was if the ship sunk. I could tell by Frank's body language he was about to break. I wondered if any of the bosses could tell, or if they cared. The man needed some help. He was totally depressed.

The new political captain, who was a good man and friend to the underdog cop had become completely ineffective as a leader because of his association with the lead star. He was being brash to Frank. It wasn't the captain's past demeanor. He faced the realization that he was there as a figurehead and that the lead star was actually running the unit and he didn't like it. He didn't make any decisions, nor did he lead in any of the investigations. But his attitude toward Frank got worse as the days went by. Frank was the weak link in the manpower chain. The captain was being cribbed by the lead star who wanted to deplete the unit of the old guard and get his buddies in with him.

But this was a local police department, political, not professional, but probably as professional as any local cop unit could be. Frank Reed and I weren't Feds, we were local cops, nothing more. We had to take what came our way. Our problem was we were outsiders, and the insiders were running the show. Once you realize this fact, things go smoother.

I wondered if I could make a conspiracy case on drug dealers. The lead star who I felt was trying to be friendly to me made some names available to me. I researched the files and came up with several associate names, criminals who had been associated since grade school, jocks, tough guys, and ironically, they all had grown up in north St. Louis County and lived in close proximity to the Pipe-Fitters complex. The lead star had given me a clue. Boob never did. Captain Bud never did. But the lead star had. I was feeling embarrassed again.

I did a complete background on them right from my little pigeon poop cubbyhole. These guys lived like millionaires, mostly because they were, and none of them were gainfully employed. They had started out their careers early in life, right out of high school, by driving down to Florida and bringing back trunk loads of marijuana. It was, and still is the drug of choice by most of the losers in the world.

They were instantly successful, trusting only in each other, moving their drug to friends of friends, and relatives. They would bring a load in, wait for a couple of months, and then drive down and get another one. The loads got bigger, and eventually, they were moving tons of weed around the St. Louis area.

They had contacts within all of the police departments; folks they had known as youngsters, and relatives. When the heat got on them, they were informed, and they would back off, sometimes for a couple of years, or until they needed more cash to live their flamboyant lifestyle.

I documented all of the facts, listed their assets, and identified all of their friends and associates. It was a neat little package on six wealthy dope dealers who had been cheating the system for decades and were never caught. I turned the packet over to the lead star, and one day I got a call from a DEA agent.

He wanted to interview me, so I said I'd love to talk to him. We met at a bar, and he told me I had done stellar work on making a case on this group of bad guys. He clued me in on the procedure. "We go after their assets, houses, boats, cars, bank accounts," he said. "If these guys haven't gotten caught yet with dope, the chances are slim they will ever be caught. They're too insulated."

I was flattered, and I asked him about the DEA Task Force. "Those guys kick in doors all over the country," he said. "It's different from what I do. They strike at once. I sometimes take years to make seizures of assets."

I was intrigued. I wanted to go to DEA. I wanted to be a Fed. I was amazed at how controversy and trouble at one's job can change his outlook on other things in life. Eight years ago I would have never wanted to go to a federal agency. When I went to intelligence I was happy that I had been one of the chosen ones. Now I wanted a change. I was turning into a conformist. A disgusting and frightening thought.

I had been having conscience problems. What if Captain Bud and the stars were just trying to change me for the better; make a better cop out of me from their viewpoint, and I had balked and rebelled against them just because I was Eastside ignorant? It was a scary thought, scarier than conformation. It was frightening because Frank Reed had followed my lead. Perhaps I had dragged him down with me, mostly because he wanted to follow me and not the lead star. I kept trying to get the thought out of my head. I didn't want to be followed. I didn't want to lead. I wanted to investigate organized criminals. Why was it so complex?

I kept telling myself Frank Reed was responsible for his own actions and I was responsible for mine. I didn't try to implicate him in my foreign attitude. It apparently just happened. I couldn't figure why he saw things the way I saw them. What if Frank did something insane, like beat up the lead star, or the captain? Would I be at fault? I wouldn't be, but I would probably feel like I was. It was the conscious thing. I had one. Frank had one. No one else in the unit did.

It was a usual Friday morning. I was in the cubbyhole office overlooking the alley, one of the few windows that wasn't painted black. Pigeons were roosting on my windowsill, diseased and dying, living in pigeon poop and hatching chicks. It was entertaining, considering the alternative, dancing to the tune of the lead star.

I walked out of the cubbyhole to glance at Frank Reed. It made me feel better. He was the only guy I knew who was more miserable than I was. He wasn't at his house-mouse desk so I wandered back into my cubbyhole.

I had been upset lately, living on plain yogurt; it was the only food I could keep down. My wife wanted to know what was going on at work, but I couldn't tell her about this disaster. I was embarrassed to admit I had been had by the establishment. I told her it was the smoke in the office, but she didn't believe me. She knew something was terribly amiss. My desk was near the toilet if I needed to take a quick detour.

Frank walked into my office. He had the look of a convicted killer who had just been advised by the judge he was going to be the recipient of a lethal injection. Nothing mattered to him. He nodded to me and then walked out of the offices, click clacking down the hall toward the elevators. I figured he was going for a walk in the fresh air and cool down before coming back to the office. It's what I would have done had the walls started coming in on me.

I heard the lead star shouting for his flying crew, the narcotics investigators. They ran into his office like a swat team training maneuver. I crept out and listened at the door. There was some banter, and the lead star said, "We're looking for an armed robber today. This guy's robbed stores all over this City, and this morning he robbed a bank. He's going to call his momma, so go to his momma's house, find his pole and get on it. I want to know where the bastard is. Do it for the unit."

"The unit," the cops said in unison, then headed out the door. My narcotics wire-guy buddy was with the group. He was the last one out the door so I stopped him and asked him what was up.

"Surveillance," he told me. "We're going to try and find a guy who's been robbing banks in the area. Lead star's got information on who it is and were going to bring him in." He followed the group leaving me in curiosity.

Frank returned to the offices and stiffly walked in. "What's with the pole thing?" I shouted to my wire buddy. He didn't answer me. I strolled back into my cubbyhole, sat down and watched a pigeon roost in a pile of dung. Frank followed me. I turned in my chair and studied him. He was a scary guy. He was about to explode.

"I'm going to kill the lead star," Frank announced. He had his hand on the butt of his magnum, stroking the polished pearl grips and looking at the pigeon show on the windowsill. He had a look of peace, like he had made a decision and that nothing else mattered, only pride and revenge, two of the more serious sins.

He turned and started to walk out of the office. "Wait, Frank," I said. He looked at me with his peaceful, determined eyes. I knew he was going to do it, he had finally seen peace at the end of the tunnel and he was going for it. "Don't do it, Frank. He's not worth it, man. Come on over here and sit down and lets you and me talk this out. We can come to a better solution. You'd be ending his life, but you'd be ending yours also."

"I've heard all of their secrets. They're evil. They hate the black man. I should kill them all, but I'll just settle for the lead star for now."

I was intrigued by Frank's statement about secrets. To me, secrets equate to conspiracies. "What secrets, Frank?" He stared at me like I was stupid; the way a black man stares at an untalented white guy who's trying to sing, or dance, or dunk a basketball.

"You mean you don't know?"

"Nope."

"Those damn pin-registers you and I've been deciphering, that's a ruse. The lead star's just trying to keep us busy so we don't find out what's really going on."

"What is really going on, Frank?"

"The levers on the machines, you don't know about the levers?"

"Levers, Frank? What levers?"

"You don't know? Man, I thought you were hip. Just forget it," he said as he waved me off and watched a baby pigeon take a suicidal dive off of the fourth floor windowsill.

The lead star apparently had some new investigative tool I didn't know about. The guy's brilliance never stops. It's wrong, I guess, but, it is a good way to catch dope dealers. I had been in the office for too long. I was starting to get star mentality; anything for a big case.

"And another thing," Frank continued. "They mostly target black guys. There's plenty of white dope dealers in this region. It's racist."

I thought about what he said.. "There is a white guy," I replied. "It's that bone-popping doctor who lives on McCausland. But I never see any arrests. What do they do with all of this information?"

Frank stared before answering "The arrests are pending. It's all just investigating for now. They're getting the cases ready and they're building probable cause."

"Huh?" I muttered

"There's a bunch of cases, just no arrests, yet. When they do, the City will get most of the seized drug proceeds. That includes money, cars, houses, jewelry. The seizures are legal. The City allegedly uses the cash for buying more law enforcement toys so we can do it again and again. Somebody's going to get rich off of this."

"So we get more money, and then we give the two machines back to ATF and we buy new ones for the unit. I get it."

"No, you don't get it. I'm talking real money, millions of dollars. And those machines we borrowed from ATF? There were three, not two."

"Where's the third one?" I asked.

"It's in the surveillance van. I'm killing the lead star!" Frank stood.

"No wait," I said. I looked at my wristwatch, it was nearing lunch.

"Let's go to lunch, I'll buy. We can talk about this, okay?" I didn't want to set him off. I had to handle him with kid gloves, but I knew I had to get him out of the office. Calmer heads would prevail; I just had to get some food in him.

He was fighting with himself. He was in kill-mode, and I was asking him to get into food-mode. His face was scrunched up as if he was in pain. "Come on, Frank, it'll do us both some good to get out of this damn smoke-filled cave."

"Okay, man," he thought for a couple of seconds, "let's go."

We walked out without telling anybody where we were going. Frank had his personal car, a Pontiac four-door with a big-block engine, big tires and fancy wheels. It was a part of his Bo Diddley facade. We walked to it and climbed in.

"Where to?" he asked.

"Central West End, on Euclid," I replied. "A buddy of mine owns a restaurant there, it's half- price."

We drove and parked at a meter. We didn't plug it; Frank had his cop parking pass hanging on the mirror. We strolled in, got trays and utensils and crept through the line. Svetna was eye-balling us, fearful as usual, eyes rolling, prepared to bolt. She had fixated on Frank's hat. I figured she had never seen anything like that in Russia.

I hoped that she didn't start calling us names. Frank was in no mood to take any abuse from her or anyone else. Frank went through the line first. Svetna rang up his bill and started to hand it to him.

"I'll take it, Svetna." She rang up my bill and I gave her the cash and she gave me the change and I started to head for a table. Frank was standing just within earshot. "KGB," Svetna muttered to me as if she just had to say something snide, or she would burst.

I ignored her and walked toward Frank. "What did she say to you?" Frank asked.

"It was nothing, Frank, just a joke between us."

"Didn't sound like a damn joke. She wasn't smiling." Frank's intense eyes were darting toward Svetna and then back to me.

"Trust me, it was. She's a friend of mine." Frank blew it off and we ate a leisurely meal. I was hoping I could keep it down.

My mind went back to the organized investigations. There was a place in Granite City, Charlie's Restaurant, where the organized thugs hung out and ate for free. I wondered how the owners of these restaurants could justify feeding for free, or even half-price.

It is difficult to make a living in the restaurant business. Most of them don't survive the first year in business, and the hours are worse than being a cop. Between the gangsters and the cops, I wondered how they survived.

But the more I pondered the situation, the more I realized the similarities to the cop-and-crook syndrome. We're the same, and it's damn scary. Two identical factions battling with each other with the same mindset, do anything to achieve your objective. If you have to lie, then do it. If you have to kill, then do it. If you have to steal, then do it. You have to be a crook to catch a crook.

But crime goes on, in fact it flourishes. And the cop lifers go on, but they don't flourish, they just survive with their imaginary power over other cops. They've got their self-serving dedication to a self-perceived cause, and they keep treading along.

But it's better than being on the thug side. Those guys go to prison, an unthinkable end of life for a cop.

Frank and I left the Central West End and drove around the City, looking at the downtown office-worker ladies who walk for exercise on their lunch hours. There were always dozens to gawk at, and they were all attractive. We had killed about two hours and I figured that if we went back into the office we would only have about two hours of the torture left, and then we could go home.

Frank had cooled down a bit, and he hadn't brought up the subject of killing anybody. I felt like I had done a good deed. I had saved the life of the unit leader, the lead star. All I had to do was agree with Frank, give him some encouragement, side with him, and the lead star would have been history.

But this goofy job in this strange unit wasn't worth killing for. I could have never lived with myself if I hadn't tried to stop it. The lead star would be promoted again, soon, and he would take another hiatus to a district and lead uniformed guys for a while, and then he would come back. Maybe by then Frank and I could find another unit to hide in.

I had puked all night after my lunch with Frank Reed. First I dreamt Frank had cracked the lead star and the ineffective captain, in the office.

And when homicide asked him why he did it, he told them he did it for me. I was beginning to worry about my future in this business. Nothing is worth the nightmare/puke experience. I got up, ate some plain yogurt and headed for the office. I drove my personal car, a Ford Probe G T, parked at a meter and crammed coins into it. I didn't know how long I was going to remain at work.

I walked into the lobby at headquarters with the other office workers, like a cow joining the herd going to the feed bin. It was depressing, like going to school in the seventh grade, same sounds, same people and smell. It went against everything I had ever been taught. Never join the herd. I was having problems.

I went up with the other cows, smoke-filled elevator, smoke-filled halls, and walked to the smoke-filled office. I went directly to my cubbyhole, started studying files and was preparing to write a memorandum pertaining to a dozen or so telephone numbers I had investigated for the lead star's pin-registers.

My desk phone rang and I answered it like a man on his death bed. My old friend, the Major, the one who had been a captain when he commanded this unit, was the caller. He asked me how things were going. I knew he was aware of the drama playing out up here. Everybody knew about it, even the guys in the uniform districts. There aren't many secrets in the cop business.

I told him things were okay, but I sensed he was laughing at my answer. "They don't want you up there anymore," he said.

"I know it," I replied. I figured this was my chance to re-group. Why else would the major call me? He wanted to help.

"Where do you want to go?" he asked.

"DEA task force," I replied.

"Hang in there." He hung up.

I spent the remainder of the day typing. Frank was still doing his house-mouse duties. I wondered how long it would take before he snapped. I had stopped his manic killing mode, but I knew it was temporary. The day went quickly, kind of like I was in a time warp. Time meant nothing to me, for a change.

One of the unit's sergeants stuck his head in my office, looking for something. He was a nice little fellow, political and frightened by the lead star. I figured he was looking to see if I was at my post. I looked up at him and he rolled his eyes at me as he turned and walked out. My body-language training told me something was wrong, but I was so nauseous I didn't wish to pursue it, so I just sat and stared at my typewriter and the diseased pigeons on my windowsill.

An hour went by, and I had accomplished absolutely nothing. I leaned back and heard some hustling and bustling outside in the main office, the lead star was talking loudly on the telephone. I heard my name bantered about. He was giving someone a recommendation about me. The guy never stopped. His dedication to the unit was all consuming.

About an hour passed when the little political sarge came back into my cubbyhole. "I've got some good news for you," he said juggling his cigarette and blowing smoke my way. I didn't ask him what. I just watched and listened. "You've been transferred to DEA."

"When do I report?" I quickly asked.

"Monday morning," he replied. The nausea was gone. I felt like a human again. I telephoned my wife and advised her of the transfer. She was wary of any gift transfers coming from the department. She had been through the same ordeals I had gone through. She wasn't there in person, but it was absorbed by her, and my children. It was a pity. I assured her it was going to be okay.

This was my last hour as an intelligence unit detective, a job I thought I would retire from. I obtained an evidence bag from the supply closet and loaded the junk out of my desk into it. Frank Reed wandered in.

"You out of here, man?"

"Yeah, Frank." He was down. I was his only friend in these hallowed walls. In his mind he was losing his best friend. I could see the despair in his face and body language. I felt badly for leaving him to fend for himself. We were brother warriors against the beast, fighting it from within, but I felt deeply that we were wrong in our actions. I was leaving him behind and I was stressing over it. I had violated the Marine Corps creed.

But it was the way the department was. Black commanders, at the request of black community leaders and politicians, promote and transfer black cops. White guys get helped by white commanders. The major no doubt figured I was friends with Dick Gephardt. It's strange how things happen. Politics control everything. "Your turn's coming, Frank," I quietly said. "You're well liked in the community and the department. You'll get out of here just like I did."

"Maybe," he said, as he walked out of the cubbyhole office.

25

I was to report to Special Agent Steve Casteel on Monday, but I had to telephone him first. I made the call, and identified myself, and as usual, I emphasized City Intelligence.

"Not anymore," he replied. "You're working for me now. I'll see you on Monday.

The transfer to the DEA Task Force had meaning to me. It meant I was now a made guy, something I never intended to be. The thought was alienating to me. I didn't like made guys, in organized crime or the police department, except for Guido and Stretch.

But that was a foolish Eastside attitude. The major who had rescued me was my friend. My thinking that made guys are management, snitches, and company men had to change. It was a belief damaging to me. Something I had to outgrow and I intended to do it.

Jesse Stoneking was a "made" guy, and he worked the outside, and he was his own man. Guido and Stretch were "made" guys, and they always worked the outside. Maybe I could keep my identity, my character and my sanity by playing my own game.

I could tell the DEA thing was going to be a good gig. I was given a Mazda RX-7 as soon as I walked through the door. It was seized, dirty and the interior stunk, but I took it home and cleaned it and used it as my own personal ride. Just like my little Chevy detective car.

There was a small problem. The Chief of Staff for Dick Gephardt routinely telephoned me at the DEA offices. He would leave messages using the congressman's name, and the DEA folks didn't like it. They hated Dick Gephardt. He was a liberal, and that made him their enemy. I figured I would have to work my way through this little problem. I didn't have the time or the inclination to guard dignitaries for Dick Gephardt.

I felt certain the congressman's chief of staff figured he was doing me a huge favor, since Dick was preparing to run for president, but it had opposite results. An agent, or someone, wrote a scathing letter, anonymously, to Dick, stating they, at DEA, were appalled a United States Congressman would telephone a City cop detached to DEA. My friend in Dick's office showed it to me. It was critical of my alleged friendship with Dick Gephardt.

Again, someone who didn't know the system figured I was friends with the politician. And again, I felt strange about the alleged association. Dick Gephardt was about Dick Gephardt, nobody else.

The government sent me to DEA drug school, and it was enjoyable.

Frank Reed telephoned me at my DEA desk. He wanted to know how I was. I told him everything was cool and it was time for him come out to DEA and be my partner. He paused and didn't seem interested in DEA.

I told him to do me a favor and work to get out of the unit. It should be deemed cruel and unusual treatment for any outcast cop to be there. It was now a place for unrepentant followers. "Promise me you'll do that, Frank," I pleaded with him.

"Okay," he replied.

I stayed in touch with Guido. He called me one morning to tell me Jesse Stoneking had shot himself in the head. Jesse had relocated to a little burg in Arizona. He had started a car-repossessing business. He was alone in life. His other wife had left him. Life hadn't been good to Jesse. But you reap what you sow.

I needed details on the suicide. It was too conspiratorial, too pat. I dug and found out what had transpired. Jesse was the passenger in a car being driven by one of his new friends in Arizona. The friend was speeding and he got pulled over by the local cops. The driver got out of the car to talk with the cop, and Jesse, without fanfare, shot himself in the head while sitting in the car. I had flashbacks of Jesse and me being nose to nose. The murdering mobster and the crazed west side cop detective from the Eastside. Jesse had probably always had a death wish. Why else would he have turned into a mobster killer who had ended his own life, violently?

Ron Lawrence, the Post-Dispatch reporter, had written that Jesse had a $100,000 contract on his head. I asked Guido if the pressure of the contract finally took its toll on him. He told me Jesse was sick, some kind of terminal disease, and that shooting himself was the easy way out.

He didn't leave a suicide note. He just shot himself. Probably an impulse thing. Impulsive. Angry. Depressed. I thought about Jesse's accomplishments in the cop business. Because that's what he was. He was a cop. Maybe the best cop ever to work the streets.

It takes a conscience to commit suicide. No gangster has a conscience, and very few cops have one. It's why they're what they are. It is better, easier if you don't carry a conscience around with you.

The cops who have one seem to hurt themselves, either by drinking themselves into oblivion, dying in a car accident, getting killed on-duty by some crazed suspect, or by shooting themselves. I had one, but I had the Eastside upbringing insulating my persona. I was quick on my feet, and trained by the best at survival. I never wanted to harm myself. It didn't make sense. It was the opposite of survival, what people living on the edge strive for.

And Jesse had a conscience, too; that's a good thing for his moral being, even though it came late in his murdering life. It was bad for his chosen profession. He cared and it was too much for him. It wasn't being weak, he just got blind-sided by his confusion.

I dug out an old newspaper article about Jesse listing the cases he was involved with: Guys he talked to with a wire on him. Tapes he had made that incriminated the most dangerous of the dangerous. I shook my head as I read. I was in awe of him. He got the ones nobody else in law enforcement could get.

He got the goods on Ray Flynn. He pleaded guilty in the case involving the downtown jewelry store robbery. He was sentenced to ten years in prison. There was also a charge of buying a stolen appliance. In the State of Missouri, it is against the law to purchase a stolen appliance, and it's a felony.

Jesse had set him up, sold him a stolen washing machine, and taped the transaction. Just another felony charge to add to the list of crimes Ray Flynn was going to prison for. Sergeant Steve Sorocko, always investigating, heard through some source that Ray Flynn was dying. He went to the federal penitentiary in Terre Haute, Indiana, to interview him. There were unsolved bombings, most of them out of Sorocko's jurisdiction, but that didn't matter. They were bombings and he wanted to solve them.

Ray admitted to Steve that he was dying of heart disease. He wanted to get out of prison before he died. He wanted to die a free man, and he wanted to work a deal. He would tell Steve about all of the bombings in exchange for freedom.

This isn't an unusual request, and most of the time it's granted to a dying convict. Lady justice is blind and hard, but she's sometimes relenting. She knows this is a free-enterprise system, one that allows anybody to get rich in any way they choose. But if you choose crime as your way to fame and fortune, and you get caught, you must deal with her.

She controls your destiny. Cops and convicts are aware of this fact more than anybody else in this country. "Give me something to work with," Steve said. "Tell about some of your conversations with your gang members. Did you ever ask any of your associates about some of the crimes they committed?"

"We don't do that," Ray replied. "If somebody wanted to talk about their scores, then that was up to them. We never asked any questions. Questions meant you were a snitch. Even if you weren't, you'd be labeled as one. I knew Jesse Stoneking was a snitch. I had a gut feeling. I told Art Berne Jesse was a snitch, but Art wouldn't believe me. Jesse had them all snowed."

"Then why did you buy a stolen washing machine from him?"

"Greed," Ray replied.

Lady Justice wasn't relenting this time. Ray Flynn died in federal prison. Jesse Stoneking ultimately incarcerated ten high profile organized career criminals. His success was phenomenal. No cop or agent could have accomplished this feat.

The little star made rank like Pac-Man on steroids. He realized his cop royalty aspirations. I knew he would. The non-made guys stood back and watched as he knocked down rank after rank. He was loyal to the lead star but always kept him just a couple of promotions behind him.

I would see him from time to time, walking around the police districts with his sycophants tailing him. Sometimes he would stop to talk with someone lower on the totem pole than himself. After a brief joke, a knee slap and a wink, he would quickly walk away from the scene with big quick steps, forcing his followers to scurry after him like eunuchs. The guy was a laugh a minute.

But like all super cops and super politicians, the little star disgraced himself. He was forced to retire under a cloud of suspicion. The FBI and the United States Attorney were investigating him. It will be interesting to watch him wiggle out of this mess.

The lead star became the type of commander everyone in the ranks admired. He praised his rank and file cops and gave them what he could wherever he was assigned. He was used as the go to commander for the office of the chief of police. If there was a problem in a unit, investigative or patrol, they would send the lead star and he would solve it.

Boob retired. I heard he went to work as an investigator for B'nai B'rith Society. Paul or David got him a position. Captain Bud retired and died.

David, the wealthy power broker was federally indicted on bank fraud charges. He died before he could be prosecuted.

Carl Wittmond passed on. Charlie Burch is still the State's Attorney in Calhoun County, Illinois. He's still hustling fried chicken on his days off. He told me he wrote a one-million-dollar check to the IRS after inheriting Carl Wittmond's wealth. Carl was in his nineties and still making large sums of money. He was addicted to it; he couldn't control his desire for more wealth.

I wondered what went through Carl Witmond's mind when Charles Burch loaded him into his Lincoln Town Car and took him across the Brussels Ferry for the last time. Carl didn't die at his beloved hotel. He was taken to a nursing home in outstate Illinois.

I wondered if Carl looked at the moon, or the sun shining on the Illinois River and reflected about his life. He was the legislator who made the ferry a reality. He had always been in control, a powerful wealthy man. The only bump in the road of life for Carl was when some inbred criminals beat him and his girlfriend Jane, and stole his gaudy diamond ring.

Carl was the King of Calhoun County from birth. It was because he inherited a whistle stop hotel with tasty food and cold beer. Things came easy for him. I can imagine his shifty eyes taking inventory of his golden egg hotel while he was preparing to leave for the last time. Carl is buried behind the hotel. There is a large memorial jutting out of a corn field; a memorial to a winner. Now his nephew, Charles Burch, is the King of Calhoun County, Illinois.

Special Agent Sam Thompson took early retirement. He's a private investigator and works with his son. The stone fetish subsided and turned into a cocaine fetish (more lucrative and easier to market). The Paul Brown Building became a vacant historical landmark and was eventually rehabbed and turned into apartments.

They are building another bridge linking East St. Louis, Illinois, with St. Louis, Missouri. I wonder if any law enforcement professional can remember the union gangster infiltration connected with the last bridge. Probably not.

There aren't any more federal agents like Sam Thompson and his partner. No more intelligence unit detectives like Guido and Stretch shadowing the gangsters and sharing their information with the FBI. They recognized pure evil and they set out to destroy it. In this day and age FBI agents are chasing ghost terrorists. The intelligence unit guys are documenting black gang members in north St. Louis. They've never seen them; they just write memorandums on what they've been told.

It will be the same old rock and roll. The Chicago gangsters are probably planning their crusade into St. Louis, licking their lips over the possibilities of the new bridge.

I got a telephone call from my wire buddy in intelligence. He started out with small talk but I could tell he had called for a reason. I was screaming on the inside, "Tell me why you called."

"Frank Reed didn't show up for work this morning," he tossed into the conversation.

"Yeah?" I muttered.

"Yeah," he paused for about ten seconds. "The lead star made a big deal out of it, walking around the office acting like it was a federal case. Frank hadn't called in sick, and the lead star took it personal. He got the ineffective captain, and the little Irish sergeant involved in the affray, and pretty soon, the lead star is telephoning Frank's girlfriend asking her about him." He paused again.

"Yeah?" I said.

"The lead star asks her if she'd give him a key so they could go to her apartment. It's where Frank lived. Did you know that?"

"Yeah, I knew that," I muttered.

"So the lead star and the ineffective captain and the little Irish sarge storm out the door to go to Frank's apartment to confront him on why he didn't show up for work. It was overkill."

I was following him. Frank had lured the inept supervisors to his house so he could kill them. My stomach was churning and I was flushed. I didn't want it to go down like this. I had tried to stop it, but I wasn't there to control Frank anymore. He had already made up his mind. I was feeling guilty. The supervisors all had families, and I was sick. I should have told someone that Frank was intent on killing them.

The wire guy continued: "The supervisors were gone for a while, too long, and everyone wondered what had transpired. Finally, they show back up at the office. The lead star goes into his office with the little Irish sarge, and closes the door. The ineffective captain composes himself and heads out the door. He tells the secretary he's going to the chief's office."

"Yeah?" I quickly said.

"I started prying into what happened," the wire guy says. "The little Irish sarge comes out stressed and anxious looking and I cross-examine him. You know he can't keep a secret."

"Yeah."

"He tells me they go to the apartment and instead of knocking on the door, the lead star uses the key and they try to sneak into the apartment but there's a chain on the door. The captain kicks the door in and they waltz in. They find Frank and they confront him, asking him why he didn't show up for work. The ineffective captain's berating him, shouting and cursing." He pauses.

"Yeah? I said.

"Frank gets the drop on them with his revolver. It was as if he was deciding on which one to kill first, like he's confused. Then he nonchalantly puts the gun to his head and pulls the trigger. He blew his own brains out right in front of the lead star and his supervisor cronies."

I was silent. I wasn't expecting that. Frank hated the lead star so much he wanted to kill him. He turned the hatred inward and he did himself. For what? So he wouldn't fail? So he wouldn't be transferred? Frank blamed himself at the last minute for his failure in the stupid intelligence unit.

Brainwashed, it's what we all are, brainwashed by our circumstances. We're better than the other cops, it's what is instilled in you from the minute you walk through the doorway. If you go back to the uniform, then you've failed. The only way out is promotion, but in order to gain promotion you must blindly follow the leaders and do exactly what they say and do. It's the only way out.

It happens all of the time in Japan. If someone fails in the business world, or in any endeavor, they kill themselves. It shouldn't happen in

America. This is the free enterprise system. If you fail at one thing, you can jump to another way to make a living.

"You think he thought he failed?" I asked. "There were rumors he was going to be transferred."

"I'd heard the rumors," the wire guy said. "I'm certain Frank had heard them, too. Maybe he did fail."

"He didn't get transferred back to a uniform, so he didn't fail," I quickly replied.

"That's one way to look at it," he said.

"That's the only way to look at it," I said.

"But he's dead, by his own hand, in front of witnesses. It's as if he had the whole thing planned," the wire guy exclaimed.

"I'm sure he did," I muttered. But I knew Frank had intended on killing the lead star first, then killing himself. He was just too righteous to do it. "I wonder, did Frank have his hat on when he killed himself?"

"I don't know, the little sarge didn't say."

"Do you know what gun he used?" I asked.

"Yeah, department issue thirty-eight, the one they gave us in the academy."

I had an emotional rush with memories of my time in the unit. I pined for Frank, my lost warrior friend. I wished I'd had another chance to help him, but it was too late, probably from the time he advised me he was going to kill the lead star. He needed psychiatric help. I should have told somebody. But who? His girlfriend was closer to him than me. She should have told someone he needed help.

Frank's supervisors knew he was stressed and angry, and they knew he was a shooter, a gun guy and a cop with his back against the wall. They were too busy leading and following. There weren't any other options. It was a social experiment within the closed society of police work.

Frank and I were expendable. We didn't wish to lead and we refused to follow. Frank's violent death wasn't solely my fault. But I accepted part of the blame, and in doing so, the entire eight years I was there, playing big-time organized crime detective, were tarnished.

I could see the whole picture, the beginning and the end of Frank's life.

The other guys in the unit couldn't. The lead star couldn't, and the captain couldn't. They didn't wish to recognize the problem. They were in pursuit of more promotions. That is all that mattered.

I drove downtown to police headquarters to obtain a copy of the suicide report for Frank. I was told I couldn't have a copy, that it had a lock on it, an order from the chief's office. I had other means and I obtained a copy. It didn't read like the description given to me by the wire guy. It said the Captain and his crew were at the door and heard a shot, then, they kicked the door open and found Frank dead.

I rationalized the incident. What did it matter? A dead cop, one who was an individual instead of a follower. I didn't know what to believe. Maybe the wire guy gave me wrong information to upset me. It worked. I was upset.

Frank's demise was evil, nothing short of it, just plain evil. I was having flashbacks of my youth, and I could see Frank as a youngster in the City, watching the neighborhood cops doing their job. He would approach them with his smile and his intense eyes and say, "Hi Police," hoping someday he could be like them. I had a tidal wave of realization and I knew why I had been trained in my youth in East St. Louis, Illinois not to join the crowd, not to conform, and to never trust cops.

I sat at my big time DEA desk and watched the little unimportant folks scurrying around downtown Clayton. This was the job every conspiracy loving cop desired. Classy office, classy cars, government expense money, jeans, T-shirts and chronograph watches. But I was feeling trapped by my circumstances. I needed an escape.

I started to reach for my desk phone, call my wife and tell her to gather up the kids, pack the camper and that I would be home in two hours for an escape to the beach for however long it would take for me to regain my sanity and put the violent death of a good cop somewhere back in my psyche; so far back that I wouldn't dwell on it.

But the scene had changed in my personal game of cops and crooks. My kids were now in school. My wife had taken a job. I was hardly ever home. I didn't blame her. I was too busy traveling for DEA. The Task Force was a flying squad of drug crusaders with blind dedication, and I had settled in with them. I was one of them. I had done the impossible. I had conformed. But I deserved a vacation. The thought upset me.

I had federal responsibilities, now. I had cases requiring federal court appearance. Federal grand juries, informants to hide and to dole out government cash to. I had search warrants to execute and filthy drug offenders to arrest. My appetite for drug conspiracies was like that of a heroin junky; always looking for a score.

I sat and compared the St. Louis system to the federal system. A cop isn't required to lie on a federal search warrant affidavit. You telephone the United States Attorney's office and tell one of the Assistants you need a search warrant. They make an appointment for you and you go there when it's your prescribed time. Kind of like going to a dentist to have your teeth cleaned.

You walk in and folks are friendly to you, not suspicious. You tell the assistant United States Attorney why you desire the search warrant, and he, or she, tells the secretary, and she types the address and description of the residence, and the alleged perpetrator's name. The computer does the rest. The affidavit and the warrant kicks out, and you and the assistant go to a federal magistrate's office and he issues the warrant.

I've never had to raise my right hand and swear to God that the information came from a reliable informant that I had used at least three times in the past. I wished Frank Reed had come to the task force with me. Things would have turned out better if he had been transferred with me. My pager was vibrating on my desk. I picked it up and looked at the number. It was an informant, one I had been giving federal cash to.

I knew he had conspiracy information for me and I was excited. I picked up the telephone receiver and dialed the number. This was my out, now. It was my beach and my solitude. Frank Reed moved back into the dark recesses of my mind.

I thought about Boob while the phone was ringing and his new job with the B'nai B'rith Society. He was an undercover operative. I pictured him preaching to some inbred Nazis, selling himself as a messenger of hate, prying and trying to gain insight on the allusive synagogue killer. He would report daily to David and Paul, and they would brainstorm his findings. He had made it out of Intel 210 with an impressive resume and a scabby head. He used his connections with the influential businessmen he had courted and who had courted him. He was now one of them, an influential guy.

Paul and David were still searching, praying for the right morsel of a clue gleaned by Boob to bring the murderer to justice. It was their obsession, their hobby and their calling in life, besides accumulating money.

Little did they know, Joseph Paul Franklin, mass murderer was incarcerated in the federal prison in Marion, Illinois, and had been for years. He would eventually confess to the synagogue sniping, but not to Boob or anyone in the St. Louis Metropolitan area. He confessed to some FBI agents.

It's like Boob so eloquently said:

"We're whores for the FBI. Everyone is."

Index

G

H

I

J

K

L

T

V

W